On Abstract and Historical Hypotheses and on Value Judgments in Economic Sciences

Luigi Einaudi (1874–1961) was a leading liberal economist, economic historian and political figure. This book provides the English-speaking world with a first critical edition of Einaudi's – hitherto unpublished – rewriting of one of his most unique and thoughtful essays.

The relevance of this essay is crucial from several perspectives: history and methodology of economic thought, role of economics and its relation to other disciplines and to social values, and role of economists in the public sphere, while also encompassing the discourse on man and the economist as a "whole man". The critical edition of *On Abstract and Historical Hypotheses and on Value Judgments in Economic Sciences* includes a comprehensive introduction and afterword. An extensive reappraisal of this newly discovered essay will help to cast light on Einaudi's uniqueness and originality within and beyond the Italian tradition in public finance, thereby also illuminating his attempt to provide an epistemological account of his long-lasting enquiry into the causes of good and bad polities.

This book is of great interest to those who study economic theory and philosophy, as well as history of economic thought, public economics and legal and political philosophy.

Luigi Einaudi (1874–1961) was a leading liberal economist, journalist, economic historian, one of the major representatives of the Italian tradition in public finance and political figure: Governor of the Bank of Italy, Minister for the Budget and President of the Italian Republic.

Paolo Silvestri is Research Fellow in Economics at the Department of Economics and Statistics "Cognetti de Martiis", University of Turin. He is also Habilitated Associate Professor both in Philosophy of Law and Political Philosophy.

Routledge Studies in the History of Economics

For a full list of titles in this series, please visit www.routledge.com/series/SE0341

180 **A Historical Political Economy of Capitalism**
After metaphysics
Andrea Micocci

181 **Comparisons in Economic Thought**
Economic interdependency reconsidered
Stavros A. Drakopoulos

182 **Four Central Theories of the Market Economy**
Conceptions, evolution and applications
Farhad Rassekh

183 **Ricardo and the History of Japanese Economic Thought**
A selection of Ricardo studies in Japan during the interwar period
Edited by Susumu Takenaga

184 **The Theory of the Firm**
An overview of the economic mainstream
Paul Walker

185 **On Abstract and Historical Hypotheses and on Value
Judgments in Economic Sciences**
Critical Edition, with an Introduction and Afterword
by Paolo Silvestri
Luigi Einaudi
Edited by Paolo Silvestri

186 **The Origins of Neoliberalism**
Insights from economics and philosophy
Giandomenica Becchio and Giovanni Leghissa

187 **The Political Economy of Latin American Independence**
Edited by Alexandre Mendes Cunha and Carlos Eduardo Suprinyak

On Abstract and Historical Hypotheses and on Value Judgments in Economic Sciences

Critical Edition, with an Introduction and Afterword by Paolo Silvestri

Luigi Einaudi
Edited by Paolo Silvestri

Routledge
Taylor & Francis Group

LONDON AND NEW YORK

First published 2017
by Routledge

2 Park Square, Milton Park, Abingdon, Oxfordshire OX14 4RN
52 Vanderbilt Avenue, New York, NY 10017

Routledge is an imprint of the Taylor & Francis Group, an informa business

First issued in paperback 2019

British Library Cataloguing in Publication Data
A catalogue record for this book is available from the British Library

Library of Congress Cataloging-in-Publication Data
Names: Einaudi, Luigi, 1874-1961, author. | Silvestri, Paolo, 1974- editor.
Title: On abstract and historical hypotheses and on value-judgments in
   economic sciences / Luigi Einaudi ; edited by Paolo Silvestri.
Description: Critical edition / with introduction and afterword by Paolo
   Silvestri | Abingdon, Oxon ; New York, NY : Routledge, 2017. |
   Includes bibliographical references.
Identifiers: LCCN 2016017555 | ISBN 9780415517904 (hardback) |
   ISBN 9781315637372 (ebook)
Subjects: LCSH: Economics. | Economics—History
Classification: LCC HB71 .E34 2017 | DDC 330.01—dc23
LC record available at https://lccn.loc.gov/2016017555

ISBN: 978-0-415-51790-4 (hbk)
ISBN: 978-0-367-86678-5 (pbk)

Typeset in Times New Roman
by Apex CoVantage, LLC

Contents

Detailed contents

Editorial foreword

The first edition of *Ipotesi astratte ed ipotesi storiche e dei giudizi di valore nelle scienze economiche* (*On Abstract and Historical Hypotheses and on Value Judgments in Economic Sciences*) was originally presented as a note to the "Royal Academy of Sciences of Turin", in the meeting held on 17 February 1943 and published in the same year (E. 1942–1943) (henceforth the "first edition").

The previously unpublished text presented here is what had been planned – at least in Einaudi's original intentions – as the second and profoundly modified edition of the same text. Depending on the context and/or when it is not necessary to distinguish between the two versions, the title *On Abstract and Historical Hypotheses and on Value Judgments in Economic Sciences* will be abbreviated as "the present essay".

I discovered the existence of this second unpublished version in the Archive of the Fondazione Luigi Einaudi of Turin as I was trying to clarify to myself the meaning that should be ascribed to the first edition of the essay (the interpretation of which I have always considered somewhat difficult) and, more generally, to the overall problem of the tormented and wavering nature of Einaudi's methodological reflection in the previous years.

When I encountered this text, I immediately realized I had come upon a work of exceedingly great importance. I strongly hope that the present critical edition will succeed in bringing to light a number of details that will help to clarify the reasons underlying this assessment.

The aim of this Editorial Foreword, however, is to provide the reader with some information of an archival, philological and editorial nature concerning this second version (those who wish to skip this foreword can proceed directly to the Preface). In particular, I intend to: 1) reconstruct briefly the chronology of the rewriting process of the first edition and give evidence on Einaudi's intention to republish it in a second expanded and modified edition, 2) make a few conjectures on the reasons why it never reached the stage of publication, 3) show the Abstract and Summary of the first edition in order to provide the reader with a means of orientation that will assist him or her in following the main path in the development of Einaudi's arguments, 4) highlight the major structural changes to the first edition, 5) provide the reader with introductory notes on the rewriting process and the debate between Einaudi and his interlocutors that led to the present essay, and

6) give an explicit account of the editorial decisions adopted in the publication of this second version.

1 Towards the second edition: On Einaudi's intention and the chronology of the rewriting

While the first edition of this essay arose in the wake of the debate between Einaudi and his pupil Fasiani, its rewriting was not only spurred by Einaudi's second thoughts on this debate and on the methodological reflection of the 1930s and the beginning of the 1940s, but it was also the result of an intense epistolary debate between Einaudi and several scholars and/or colleagues or pupils of his. Among them were Gioele Solari, Alessandro Passerin d'Entrèves, Giuseppe Bruguier Pacini and Antonio Giolitti.

That Einaudi clearly intended to publish a second edition emerges from the very process of rewriting the original essay as well as from the exchange of letters with his correspondents and from numerous other unequivocal types of evidence that I have discovered on various occasions subsequent to the finding of the second version. By virtue of the dates indicated in the aforementioned correspondence, the whole rewriting process can, in all likelihood, be ascribed to a period between July 1943 and 22 September of the same year. The latter cutoff date marks the moment Einaudi found out that the Nazi-Fascists were lying in wait for him near the University of Turin (Einaudi had been appointed Chancellor in August), whereupon he was compelled to prepare his flight to exile in Switzerland.

In July 1943, at the height of the discussion with Fasiani, and prompted – in primis – by comments and doubts from Solari concerning the first edition (Lett.: Solari to E., June 27, 1943), Einaudi prepared several typewritten pages addressed to his four correspondents in hopes of reviving the debate and receiving additional critical appraisals preparatory to a rewriting of the essay (for further discussion on the content of these pages, the debate with his correspondents and the rewriting process, see the text that follows).

The dating of the period in which Einaudi completed the definitive version of what he intended to be the second edition is far less certain. It is likely to have been sometime between August and September 22 of 1943. In a letter to d'Entrèves on 21 July, Einaudi explicitly states that he was 'intending to rework that note [i.e. the first edition presented to the Academy of Sciences] and turn it into something in its own right' (Lett.: E. to d'Entrèves, July 21, 1943). It seems from the letter that he was in somewhat of a hurry to complete it, and he urged d'Entrèves to give him critical comments and suggestions within August 7–8 (furthermore, it would seem from the contents of a letter by Giolitti that Einaudi had asked Giolitti himself to send some personal observations on the note within August 5 (Lett.: Giolitti to E., August 8, 1943)). Thus one may surmise that Einaudi wished to receive the comments before his departure for Gressoney (in the Vale of Aosta), where he was perhaps hoping to have a chance to finish his new version during a moment of relative peace and quiet. Einaudi may also have anticipated the imminent collapse of the fascist regime, which effectively took place on 25 July, and he probably assumed that September would be a very busy month. But he had no conception, at the time, of the degeneration of events that would follow as a result of the Nazi-Fascist invasion, and even less did he imagine his ensuing flight to Switzerland.

However, in the absence of further evidence, it cannot be ruled out with any certainty that the process of rewriting may actually have taken place after his return from exile, or even up to the day of his death. Naturally, the hypothesis of death as a sufficient reason to explain the failure to republish and/or the incompleteness of the editorial project that I discovered later (see below) would make all the questions raised in the rest of this foreword either superfluous or meaningless, as they are questions based on the hypothesis that the rewriting occurred between August and Einaudi's flight into exile.

Despite the fact that the second version contains modifications introduced directly in an offprint of the first edition and that the modified offprint was in all probability a final draft ready to be sent to the printer (as I will also show) not all doubts can be fully dispelled, because there are some annotations written in pencil on the second version that were made by an as yet unidentified hand: these annotations are not limited merely to suggesting formal corrections, but they also contain very short comments on the readability of the content or on its persuasive strength or weakness. Thus not only is there no absolute certainty about the date of the rewriting process, but it is equally difficult to ascertain when these annotations in pencil were made and whether Einaudi really intended to take them into account.

Furthermore, after the discovery of the second version, as I gradually extended my research in the Einaudi Archive, I little by little reached the conviction of the existence of a veritable editorial plan for a collection of Einaudian essays that was to include the reprinting of this second version. This collection, as I have only recently been able to ascertain and confirm, was intended to be one of the volumes of the *Opere complete di Luigi Einaudi* [*Complete Works of Luigi Einaudi*], the publication of which, under the editorship of the "Giulio Einaudi Editore" press run by his son, had begun in 1941 but was never completed. It emerges from the exchange of correspondence and jottings between father and son that Einaudi developed the idea of this work in 1942 (Lett.: E. to Giulio Einaudi, September 27, 1942), and a first draft of the index was drawn up in March 1943. Einaudi mentioned in those letters to his son that he intended to start work on this undertaking in May, i.e. once he returned to his home in San Giacomo (Dogliani, Cuneo), where he had the offprints of the articles he hoped to reformulate and include in the collection (Lett.: E. to Giulio Einaudi, March 1943). Moreover, Giulio himself, in a message he transmitted to his father via Giolitti – who at the time was working at the Giulio Einaudi Editore press – suggested the idea of republishing the revised and more extended version of the present essay (Lett.: Giolitti to E., July 10, 1943).

This notwithstanding, the definitive index of the volume drawn up by Einaudi has not yet been found, but I have been able to partially reconstruct it on the basis of various investigations. The evidence that has led me to formulate and then confirm the existence of the project for a volume of the *Complete Works* and the accompanying index is as follows:

a)   The insertion of a Roman numeral on the frontispiece of the offprint of each article intended to be included in the collection as an indication of its position within the collection itself;

b)   The Bibliographical Note in which Einaudi intended to put the last two (cut out) pages of the present essay (see also the following text). The editorial strategy of the insertion of the Bibliographical Note had already been used by Einaudi at the end of the first volume of his *Complete Works* (E. 1941e) to indicate the debates, the critical observations and the various correspondents involved and, more generally, the reasons that had spurred him to introduce changes in the subsequent editions of one or more of the essays republished in that collection. Unfortunately, there is no extant version of those comments that Einaudi planned to insert in the Bibliographical Note. It was designed to provide an explanation with regard to the variations introduced in his writings, but the volume of which the present essay was intended to form part of was not completed (see the following text). All I have found is a small sheet of paper where Einaudi jotted down and summarised in no more than a few lines the comments put forward by his correspondents;

c)   A reference added in the text of the present essay, with the wording 'cf. *supra*, essay . . .' (note 8, p. 91), clearly indicates – through use of the term "supra" – that this is a reference to an essay which, in the collection, was to precede this second edition. The part left blank refers, as can be seen from the context, to another review essay by Einaudi, 'Dell'uomo, fine o mezzo, e dei beni d'ozio' ['On man, an end or a means, and on leisure goods'] (E. 1942c), which had formed the object of a debate with Solari. Of this essay, as well, I later discovered another version, profoundly revised, with a view to a second edition. Here, too, the changes were written directly on the offprint. Unfortunately, it appears that the pages Einaudi intended to add (as can be inferred from the insertion symbols on the offprint itself) have gone missing (or, at least, have not yet been found). However, the fact that this is the only added note with a reference left blank could also be interpreted as a mere oversight, or as a sign that Einaudi did not succeed in completing the rewriting of this other essay (due to his flight into exile or for other unknown reasons);

d)   Another note added in the present essay (note 1, p. 48), which referred back to another fundamental essay by Einaudi: 'Le premesse del ragionamento economico e la realtà storica' [The Premises of Economic Reasoning and Historical Reality] (E. 1940c). I have since then discovered that this essay had likewise been extensively reworked, with a number of pages having been added;

e)   The latter two discoveries gave me a further impetus in the search for other possible essays reworked by Einaudi with a view to their reprinting in the collection. But, in the absence of the index of the contents of such a collection, I have had no alternative than to fumble, as it were, in the dark (of the Archive), guided only by my knowledge of Einaudi and by the attempt to find offprints with a Roman numeral on the frontispiece, corrections and modifications that point to editorial intervention and/or with the addition of notes cross-referencing other articles of the collection. At the current stage of my research, the index I have been able to reconstruct is the following (the articles I have not yet found are signalled by question marks):

I Le confessioni di un economista [The Confessions of an Economist] (E. 1917)

II [?]

III Il peccato originale e la teoria della classe eletta in Federico Le Play [Original Sin and the Theory of the Elect Class in Frédéric Le Play] (E. 1936a)

IV Tema per gli storici dell'economia. Dell'anacoretismo economico [Theme for Historians of Economics. On Economic Anachoritism] (E. 1937)

V Le premesse del ragionamento economico e la realtà storica [The Premises of Economic Reasoning and Historical Reality] (E. 1940c)

VI Ancora sulle premesse del ragionamento economico [More on the Premises of Economic Reasoning] (E. 1941a)

VII Intorno al contenuto dei concetti di liberismo, comunismo, interventismo e simili [Remarks on the Content of the Concepts of Free Trade, Communism, Interventionism and Similar Matters] (E. 1941b)

VIII Economia di concorrenza e capitalismo storico [Economy of Competition and Historical Capitalism] (E. 1942b)

IX Dell'uomo fine o mezzo, e dei beni d'ozio [On Man as End or Means, and on Leisure Goods] (E. 1942c)

X [?]

XI [?]

XII [?]

XIII Ipotesi astratte e ipotesi storiche e dei giudizi di valore nelle scienze economiche [On Abstract and Historical Hypotheses and on Value Judgments in Economic Sciences] (E. 1942–43)

What we do know, however, with a fair degree of certainty, as testified also by the exchange of correspondence with his son Giulio and the publishing house, is that right up to his death, Einaudi continued to work on the publication of his *Complete Works* and on the revision of the editorial plan pertaining to the volumes the *Complete Works* was to contain. The last draft that has come down to us with regard to this editorial plan dates from 1956. This draft does indeed mention the publication of roughly '3–5 volumes' of 'selected essays', one of which is almost certainly the earlier cited collection (Archivio Luigi Einaudi, busta 3, biografia, Giulio Einaudi Editore, 1956).

In any case, however, there remains open the problem of the meaning to be attributed to Einaudi's epistemological reflection after his return from exile. For example, if the final draft of the present essay was not drawn up during

August–September 1943 but at a later stage, then one might conjecture that in the present essay, Einaudi could have been spurred by reading Fasiani's further essays published some years later or posthumously (Fasiani 1949 [2007], 1951). In these essays Fasiani resumed the debate with his master and offered a response – albeit with only a few additions complementing the earlier debate – to the first edition by Einaudi and stated his intention of addressing this text in greater depth and in a separate work, it being 'too complex and too far-reaching' (Fasiani 1951: 8). In the end, however, death prevented him from doing so. If, on the other hand, Einaudi rewrote the essay at an advanced age or not long before his own death, this would change the meaning to be attributed to his subsequent but much shorter and sporadic reflections and/or methodological reflections (among them E. 1950c, 1962).

2 Conjectures on the reasons for the failure to publish the second version

Since it is likely that the question of the flight into exile interrupted the republication of this essay (in this connection, other unpublished essays by Einaudi have been found in the past, likewise written before his exile but not published) (see, for example, E. 1994) one may wonder why Einaudi did not proceed with republication upon his return to Italy. In this regard, I can only put forward a few conjectures, some of which may, of course, be mutually substantiating.

a) The death of Fasiani, which occurred in 1950: since the debate with Fasiani occupied the central portion of the essay, Einaudi may have felt that it would be improper to polemicise with a person who had passed away, who, among other things, was not only a pupil but also a distant relative of his. In fact, it was Einaudi who undertook to write his obituary (E. 1950b). To my knowledge, these were his last words on Fasiani. However, this conjecture does not appear to be decisive, especially since in the rewriting of the first edition, Einaudi had gradually attenuated the dispute, presenting it as an interpretation he himself had put upon Fasiani's thought; indeed, Fasiani went so far as to confess to him that he felt honoured to have been the object of such great attention and comments by his master.

b) Loss of the material: the offprint with the corrections and the additional typewritten pages had perhaps gone missing and/or the variations introduced in other essays had been mislaid (similarly to the aforementioned situation in par. 1, point c); all of these were intended to be included in the collection, and their loss may have prevented the republication of the entire volume.

c) Lack of time: upon his return to Italy, in December 1944, Einaudi had immediately taken on extremely challenging and time-consuming institutional commitments: Governor of the Bank of Italy (1945–47), Member of the National *Consulta* followed by Member of the Constituent Assembly (1945–47), Deputy President of the Council of Ministers and Budget Minister (1947), President of the Republic (1948–1955). Although after this period of public office Einaudi resumed intensive work on the publication of his *Complete Works*, one may hypothesise that he did not succeed in bringing to completion before his death (1961) both the introduction and the comments on the Bibliographical Note that were designed to provide the finishing touches for the volume in which the present essay was to be contained.

d) Financial difficulties of the Giulio Einaudi Press: if the present essay was indeed to become part of a collection of essays destined to be included in the edition of the *Complete Works* of Einaudi, it is worth repeating that no such edition was ever accomplished after his death. Perphaps that was partly on account of the financial difficulties affecting his son's publishing house.

3 The abstract and the summary of the first edition: The itinerary of Einaudi's arguments

It may be helpful for the reader to take a look at the Abstract and Summary of the first edition. However, given the considerable changes/modifications made in the present essay, it is well to note immediately that these outlines are of use simply as a means to follow the developmental path of Einaudi's arguments.

The previous Abstract stated the following:

The author studies the differences between abstract hypotheses and uniformities and empirical-historical uniformities in the field of economic science, distinguishing those that are valid *sub specie aeternitatis* but within the limits of the premises that have been established, from those which cannot be extended, except with great caution, beyond the time and place considered. Do the schemata of the different types of state proposed by economists for the study of financial phenomena belong to the category of abstract or historical tools of investigation? Logical incoherence of the concept of a state which, in pursuit of its own ends, focuses only on the individual or only the collective community. And finally, on the economist's decision to refrain from value judgments, which is legitimate if motivated by the scientific division of labor, but illogical in the perspective of the more general quest for truth.

The previous Summary of the sections was structured in the manner outlined here:

1 Abstract uniformities and historical uniformities. The method of successive approximations. Use of experiments is a hurdle in social science. Abstract uniformities are true *sub specie aeternitatis*.

2 Relations between abstract models and concrete reality. Economists – almost to a man – want to have their say in everyday disputes.

3 Close links between theorems and counsels. Difference between positing economic problems in the general equilibrium versus partial equilibrium framework. Theoretical identity between the problem of first approximation solved by Walras and Pareto in the general equilibrium framework and the

concrete problem of the price of wheat of a given quality at a given moment solved by the brokers of a great cereal market.

4   The solution that would be obtained by calculation, impossible to achieve due to lack of genuine data and the difficulty of fitting the data into equations, is replaced with the solution obtained intuitively by the operators.

5   The old economists, even the greatest among them, such as Cantillon and Ricardo, and not infrequently the recent theorists as well, such as Gossen and Walras, accompany abstract rules with counsels and projects. Monetary truths have almost always arisen from concrete counsels. The economist sometimes "discovers" the solutions to problems, or at other times translates the solutions already found by practitioners into hypothetical language.

6   Abstract laws fertile if capable of explaining concrete reality. Empirical laws valid to explain links that existed in a given place and in a given time interval. Value of empirical laws.

7   On the coincidence between abstract laws and concrete uniformities. On the so-called failure of economic science and on verification of its theorems in the case of war.

8   Tools of theoretical investigation and empirical testing of theoretical theorems. Theoretical-historical tools. Unproductiveness of the latter. Their inability to explain historical events.

9   De Viti's schemata of the monopolistic and cooperative state in public finance. His caution in the use of schemata.

10   On Fasiani's schemata applied to the study of the effects of taxes. *Note* on the necessary nature of the connection between general taxation defined in a given manner and the hypothesis of the monopolistic state.

11   On the definition of the "monopolistic" type of state and on the reasonableness of the hypothesis that illusions, in the form of a system, are well suited to it, whereas they may be absent in the other two types, the cooperative and modern state.

12   The correlation between fiscal illusions and monopolistic state is typical of the subtype of monopolistic state in which the dominant class, adopting a non-logical mode of behavior, exploits the dominated in such a manner as to prepare and bring about its own ruin. Need for careful revision of historical judgments on the finances of the states in the ancient regimes.

13   Analysis of the concepts of the cooperative and modern state.

14   If the dominators and the dominated are one and the same, the distinction between the cooperative and the modern state is an absurdity. Within the state there exist no individual citizens as distinct from the group, and the group does not exist as an entity in its own right distinct from the citizens.

15   The state can pursue ends that are typical of individuals singly considered; but such an approach amounts to a technical device to achieve ends that individuals could achieve by themselves or in free associations, even without the action of the state. The example of the colonies: individual aims can also be pursued by means of private companies; the aims of the state are those of the motherland.

16 In the modern state power cannot be exercised with exclusive concern for the interests of the public group considered as a unit. If this were the case, we would not be dealing with a "modern" state but rather with the deification of the state above the individual. – Lack of consistency of the concept of dualism between the individual and the state, and of a state that transcends the individual, being placed outside of and above individuals.

17 The real contrast is the dialectical opposition between state and non-state, i.e. between two entities that have always coexisted and which continue to exist side by side. This is one of the aspects of the deep-rooted contrast between the forces of good and the forces of evil.

18 The economist's abstention from passing value judgments, which is legitimate for reasons of the division of labor, cannot be sustained as a means of moving towards more general knowledge of truth. – The will of the state is the same as that of the scientist. – The alternative offered by Demosthenes: war against Philip of Macedonia or festivities and entertainment. Difference between the chemist and the economist.

19 The economist's attitude of indifference towards the reasons underlying choices is rooted in the study of price in the case of free competition. – The study of cases of monopoly, limited competition and such makes it crucial to go beyond the choice, and to seek to uncover the choices lying behind it, in order to gain a better understanding of the choice actually made and its manner of implementation. – Even the automatism of the hypothesis of full competition is in itself an artifice.

20 The convention according to which the pure economist, the applied economist, the politician, the scholar of law, etc. study different aspects of reality – a convention necessary for reasons pertaining to the scientific division of labor – is sometimes impossible to respect.

21 The right to insurrection, and the right to excommunicate, with regard to the limits on scientific investigation. – Study of the ruling class does not exclude study of the "elect class".

22 Schemata and reality. – Once the reality of situations changes, the schemata likewise change.

23 The proposition taken as a starting point by politicians concerning the exemption of a social minimum of existence is not a final proposition.

24 The appeal for a route leading from an ill-informed Pope to a better informed Pope.

25 The proposition taken as a starting point by the legislator is subject to judgment based on the ends pursued by human society.

26 Can economists decline all obligation to formulate value judgments?

27 There exist no artificial limits on scientific investigation. The ends and ideals of life play a crucial role in shaping men's decisions. It is impossible to study choices while pretending to be unaware of the ends from which they sprang. (E. 1942–1943).

4 The major structural changes

The changes Einaudi introduced are so profound and so far-reaching that they call for preliminary considerations both on form and content.

Einaudi struck out both the Abstract and the Summary, together with the original numbering of the sections in the text to which the Summary made reference. Thus the structure underwent a change, reducing it to the three parts of the present essay:

I   Abstract hypotheses and historical hypotheses
II   On some abstract hypotheses concerning the state and on their historical value
III   On value judgments in economic sciences

The reasons underlying these modifications do not appear to be a response merely to editorial and stylistic requirements designed to rectify such aspects as the non-uniform nature of the section titles (some too long or too short), or because Einaudi did not usually insert abstracts and summaries in his collections of essays.

Rather, issues regarding content also prompted the elimination of the Summary. To gain an idea of the extent of the changes made by Einaudi, suffice it to note that quite apart from the many formal language and punctuation corrections, and in addition to the fairly substantial handwritten insertions – not to mention the various parts of the text that are crossed out – Einaudi ended up also adding a total of 24 typewritten pages to the original 68 pages of the original offprint of the first edition. This resulted in a final text that had undergone profound change.

In this regard, the following observations should be borne in mind. The most extensive modifications and the greater part of the newly inserted pages concern the second and the third part, thus the old sections from nine onwards. In particular, sections 9, 10 and 11 have been almost entirely eliminated, rewritten and conflated into a single section, not only in order to eliminate the lengthy footnote – several pages long – referring to the debate with Fasiani, as the note was indeed certainly far too long and disproportionate in comparison to the main body of the text. It was deleted also because, one may surmise, Einaudi felt the need to dissociate himself from that discussion and the misunderstandings which had ensued and opted instead to add a note (note 1, p. 65) stating that this was "simply" his own interpretation of Fasiani's thought. Moreover, even if one disregards the nonetheless fairly long handwritten modifications, it can still be seen that many of the typewritten pages addressed the conclusions of sections 17, 22 and 23, not to mention the conclusions of the essay: of the old last section 27, Einaudi decided to retain the last two pages, shifting them, however, to a Bibliographical Note, and to completely rewrite the conclusions, with the addition of many pages and new sections, thus the last five sections (which, in the present essay, I have left without numbering).

5 Notes on the rewriting process: The debate with his correspondents

The rewriting process was mainly structured into three steps: it was spurred by some comments on the first edition made by Einaudi's correspondents; Einaudi then wrote several sheets, with his second thoughts and doubts, which were sent to his correspondents in order to receive further comments; after which he wrote the final draft of the present essay.

The actors in the epistolary debate were Gioele Solari, a philosopher of law and a friend and colleague of Einaudi's; Alessandro Passerin d'Entrèves, a historian, political and legal philosopher – a pupil of both Solari and Einaudi; Giuseppe Bruguier Pacini, interested in history and epistemology of economics; and Antonio Giolitti, at that time working with the publishing house Giulio Einaudi, which was directed by Einaudi's son.[1] Additionally, both Bruguier Pacini and Passerin d'Entrèves followed, commented on and reviewed some of Einaudi's previous epistemological reflections, among which was his re-reading of Robbins.

To rewrite the first edition, Einaudi prepared different sets of sheets that were transmitted so the recipients would have the opportunity of enhancing the debate and/or taking further criticisms into consideration.

The first set of pages, numbered and amounting to a total of 19, are divided into two sections entitled *Chiarimenti offerti al filosofo* [*Clarifications Offered to the Philosopher*] (pp. 1–9) and *Dubbi posti all'economista* [*Doubts Voiced to the Economist*] (pp. 10–19). They were sent without any particular differentiation to all four of the correspondents; however, it would appear that Solari also received another seven pages in response to a discussion already in progress between the two scholars. These additional pages were likewise divided into two sections: *Beni d'ozio, cioè antieconomici* [*Leisure goods, i.e. antieconomic goods*] (pp. 1–4) (destined for the revised version of a separate essay) and *Individuo, società, stato* [*Individual, Society, State*] (pp. 5–7).

Einaudi intended the thoughts embodied in these pages addressed to his correspondents to constitute, with few additional modifications, the core of the variations on the first edition, which he hoped to republish as the second edition. In particular, the pages *Individual, Society, State* (henceforth ISS) were rewritten and used to integrate and modify the final section (ex § 17) of the second part of the present essay (II. On Some Abstract Hypotheses Concerning the State and on Their Historical Value), while the pages *Clarifications Offered to the Philosopher* (henceforth COP) and *Doubts Voiced to the Economist* (henceforth DVE) were mainly destined to integrate the conclusions of the third part (III. On Value Judgments in Economic Sciences), in particular the first three of the last five sections following ex § 27 (as noted, its last two pages were cut out and destined to the Bibliographical Note).

In contrast, the last two sections of the present essay do not figure among the pages sent to his correspondents; rather, they seem to embody a reflection written independently by Einaudi to provide the whole of his essay with a fitting conclusion.

xx   *Editorial foreword*

I will restrict myself here to mentioning mainly the comments on the first edition that would appear to have played a significant role in leading Einaudi to write these pages, or to have second thoughts on certain issues and/or those that can shed some light, at least from a general perspective, on the reasons underlying the changes he introduced in the rewriting process.[2]

Some of the most significant epistemological objections came from Bruguier Pacini, who pointed out to Einaudi that the first 11 sections of the first edition displayed an 'uncertainty in the terminology concerning the use of "abstract", "concrete", "empirical", "historical" ', but also in the use of words such as "uniformity" and "law", "hypothesis" and "schema". (Lett.: Bruguier Pacini to E., August 2, 1943). Einaudi replaced the word "uniformity" with "law" and "concrete" with "empirical", although in some other cases, he did the opposite, and it may well have been Bruguier Pacini who prompted Einaudi to insert a note (note 4, p. 48) designed to distinguish "hypothesis" from "schema".

In effect, the uncertainties noticed by Bruguier Pacini betray one of the main difficulties that had led Einaudi to write and rewrite this essay, especially its second part: what is the epistemological nature of Fasiani's types of state? What distinguishes them from the types of state used by De Viti De Marco and, above all, from the "historical schemas" of good/bad polities established by Einaudi himself in his *Myths and Paradoxes of Justice in Taxation* (henceforth *MPJT*) and here further developed in terms of the dialectical opposition between "state" and "non-state"?

Among the correspondents involved in this debate, Solari was probably the one who gave a decisive thrust in prompting Einaudi to rethink some of the issues raised in the first edition. In this regard, three passages from a letter sent to Einaudi (after the publication of the first edition) are particularly significant.

In the first, Solari, paraphrasing Einaudi's reference to the 'Emperor's advocate' (p. 78), grasps one of the main concerns that had induced Einaudi to compose the first edition:

> I look very favorably on your criticism of the "Emperor's economists" who conceal their true being behind the screen of the *fait accompli*, elevating it to the status of a dogma of economic science. It saddens me to find Fasiani among these men, but the latter embodies a deplorable and immoral tendency of economic studies in the present period. And you are quite right to have unmasked them by setting your liberalism openly in opposition to them and establishing it openly as the foundation of your scientific activity.
>
> (Lett.: Solari to E., June 27, 1943)

The second passage occurs where Solari urges Einaudi to clarify his use of the concepts of individual, society, collectivity and state: what concerned Solari was that the terms "state" and "elite" as used by Einaudi could reintroduce – contrary to Einaudi's intentions – a concept of an 'ethical state' (Lett.: Solari to E., June 27, 1943). In this regard, Einaudi later answered in the ISS pages, subsequently reworked and included at the end of the last section (ex § 17) of the second part of the present essay.

The third comment – preceded by Solari's favourable response to Einaudi's long review essay on Röpke (E. 1942b), a 'philosopher economist', who, in Solari's view, reawakened Einaudi's interest in philosophy – seems fundamental. In fact, Einaudi went so far as to rewrite it in an impersonal manner (or cutting some sentences that contain an explicit reference to Solari, which here I have placed in square brackets) and placed it as an epigraph to the COP pages, which were sent to all the correspondents:

> recognizing that value judgements are indeed part of economics, the naturalistic character of economics is denied, and what is recognized is that economics belongs among the moral sciences, which are sciences that do not merely deal with facts that have come about or been performed arbitrarily: for economics is a science of facts that are not yet but *must be* set in relation with higher requirements of human nature. To say that it is a science of values and ends means that it is not justified simply through the application of the category of causality, as is the case with any natural science. Rather, it also implies the category of freedom, without which one cannot conceive of the world of duty. But who sets those ends that give orientation and value to economic investigation? The empirical or rational individual, or a reality that transcends such an individual? Where should one look for the truth criterion of the value or of the end? In the individual, in the collective community? It should by no means be presumed that the state can stand as a judge of the supreme values and ends. Here the investigation undergoes a shift from the scientific to the philosophical plane. [And you too, it seems to me, have reached the verge of this threshold.] Faith in an ideal can be justified only if it forms part of a general conception of life and reality. Economics, like all the sciences that deal with ends, cannot sidestep this imperative. Only an economist who conceives of economics within the limits of a descriptive and causal science (this is to say, naturalistic and mathematical) can sidestep this imperative. [But you go beyond these limits and proclaim a faith that is not only economic but also ethical and philosophical. And this is Croce's position].
>
> (E. 1942b)

By setting this passage by Solari as an epigraph in the COP (but without the phrases in square brackets), Einaudi was aiming to receive further comments on it from all his correspondents.

I will focus on the content and meaning of Einaudi's rewriting in more detail in the Introduction and Afterword.

6 Editorial decisions

The second version contains modifications introduced directly in an offprint of the first edition: these are handwritten changes in cases where alterations and/or insertions are relatively short, whereas longer changes/insertions are typed on additional and numbered pages. In both cases, the modifications and insertions Einaudi introduced to the text for the republication of his essay are marked clearly and precisely for the printer using the publishing symbols generally adopted in proof-reading.

The frontispiece of the offprint features acknowledgements and words of thanks to his four correspondents (Solari, Passerin d'Entreves, Bruguier Pacini, Giolitti) and an indication to 'reproduce the conclusions [of the first edition] in the Bibliographical Note'.

All the evidence I uncovered that pointed in the direction of confirmation for the earlier described index of a collection of essays came to light after I had already received Routledge's acceptance of my proposal for publication as well as during my thinking and writing process and/or while revising some partial translations of the present essay. All these discoveries occurred at diverse moments and led to considerable delays, second thoughts and continuous modifications and rewritings of what I (time and again) thought to be my last version. Above all, this stop-and-go process left me feeling somewhat skeptical with regard to my initial intention of republishing Einaudi's present essay with a purpose-designed Appendix that would highlight very precisely all the variations and departures from the first edition. Not only would the Appendix have become particularly tortuous and would have made difficult reading, but the undertaking would have called for a philological and annotated apparatus to allow detailed comparison both between the first edition and the present essay and between the present essay and the other rewritten essays composing the collection.

Readers willing to make a comparison between the first edition and the present essay will now find their work "simplified" by the recent publication, in English, of the first edition (E. 1942–43 [2014a]). However, a rigorous comparison is not a simple task. Firstly, because of the many changes and corrections introduced by Einaudi. Secondly, because the present translation of Einaudi's text is the result of a cooperative effort between the translator and myself, and reflects my understanding of its contents and meaning. In turn, my understanding has been mediated by Einaudi's second thoughts on his own first edition that helped me to clarify the meaning of various words and phrases, including words and phrases that have not undergone any change. In any case, to facilitate the task of comparison with the first edition, in the present essay the old numbering of the sections has been maintained and is now indicated in square brackets. In the end, I felt it was preferable to highlight and explain Einaudi's variations and additions to the first edition – above all, in cases where I regarded the variations as particularly significant and/or not easily understandable – through ad hoc reflections, even at the cost of making the Introduction and the Afterword longer and/or more laborious to read. Indisputably, however, all the recent discoveries of the other unpublished revised versions of essays that were due to be incorporated into the collection would call for a far more extensive interpretive and philological investigation in order to gain insight into Einaudi's overall design and into all the reconsiderations and second thoughts that streamed into his mind during that impassioned period of intellectual fervor.

In the end, the absence of several pages of the revised versions of other essays by Einaudi and the absence of the complete index of such a collection, together with the subsequent delays in delivery of the overall work due to my discovery of unpublished revised versions of other essays while I was already engaged on the main work and, above all, the uncertainty with regard to the time scale that would be required for further research in the Archive persuaded me to delay no longer and to respect (for once!) the target date for delivery to Routledge.

In short, whatever its evolutionary background, this essay is undoubtedly a *unicum* in Einaudi's scientific production, and it deserves to be published in its own right, regardless of any further episodes that may come to light in the future.

For *On Abstract and Historical Hypotheses and on Value Judgments in Economic Sciences*, the following editorial decisions were made.

All the modifications, corrections and insertions made by Einaudi have been faithfully reproduced. Only in rare cases, and only for reasons pertaining to the translation, does the punctuation sometimes differ from the original.

The Bibliographical Note, which contains the last two pages of the conclusions to the first edition, has been reproduced at the end of the present essay. Despite the absence of Einaudi's comments that were due to complete the aforesaid Bibliographical Note, I felt it was important to reproduce the previous conclusions in the form in which they were intended to be presented, given their importance and usefulness for a greater understanding of the conclusions rewritten in the present essay.

I have restricted myself to adding a few notes to Einaudi's text; such notes are indicated as "[Editor's note]", but only in cases where Einaudi seems to make either an implicit reference to a work of his or allusions to other texts he does not mention in a footnote. At times, I have also included a brief explanation of words or expressions that cannot easily be translated into English.

With regard to the many problems surrounding the difficult translation of Einaudi's text, I will restrict myself to the following comment. The Italian word *schema* used by Einaudi could have been translated with "model", according to current usage, given, also, that in this same text the Italian words *ipotesi* [hypothesis], *schema* or *modello* [model] are at times used as synonyms. However, the important terminological observation made by Einaudi in note 4 (p. 48) concerning the difference between *ipotesi* and *schema* led the tranlsator and me to render it with the Classical Greek term "schema" (pl.: "schemata"). To translate *modello*, on the other hand, we opted for the term "model" wherever Einaudi explicitly uses it.

Preface

1 Relevance and uniqueness of Einaudi's essay

Luigi Einaudi (1874–1961) was a leading liberal economist, journalist, economic historian, the most prominent figure of the economic "School of Turin", one of the major representatives of the Italian tradition in fiscal theory and public finance and a political figure: Governor of the Bank of Italy, Minister for the Budget and President of the Italian Republic.[3] Best known among scholars for his works on public finance, his long-lasting and profound methodological speculation is still today unknown. This book aims to provide the reader with a critical edition of an unpublished rewriting of one of Einaudi's most unique and thoughtful essays: *On Abstract and Historical Hypotheses and on Value Judgments in Economic Sciences*.

The relevance of this essay is crucial from (at least) three overlapping perspectives.

1) *History and methodology of economic thought*. The version of the essay presented in this volume is a hitherto unpublished "historical document" which, Einaudi intended, was to become the second edition of *On Abstract and Historical Hypotheses and on Value Judgments in Economic Sciences*. The methodological debate with Fasiani, which gave Einaudi the impetus to write the first edition, has also been considered as the methodological epilogue (Bellanca 1993, Fossati 2014b) of the Italian tradition in public finance. Nevertheless, Einaudi's essay fell into a strange and inexplicable oblivion. It regained the attention it deserved following its inclusion in an anthological collection (E. 1973) published ahead of the commemorations of the centenary of Einaudi's birth. It then gradually became recognized as his most important methodological investigation, though with very different and even opposing interpretations.[4]

An extensive reappraisal of this unpublished version will help to reconsider and cast new light on Einaudi's position in the Italian tradition of public finance. Such a tradition is best known for its interdisciplinary approach and catallactical orientation for having brought the political process within the analytical scope of economics and public finance and for its influence on Buchanan and the public choice approach.[5] On the other hand, it is not so well known with regard to the intense and long-lasting methodological debate among its scholars.[6] This unpublished essay, therefore, represents an opportunity to reassess Einaudi's uniqueness and originality within and beyond this tradition.

2) *Role of economics and the role of economists. Relation of economics to other disciplines and to social values.* The present essay is a profound rewriting of the first edition – a rewriting which, as such, testifies to Einaudi's awareness of the importance as well as the great complexity and difficulty of the problems he was endeavoring to solve. For such problems extended far beyond methodological questions to the point of calling into question the role of economics and the role of economists, as well as the relation of economics to other disciplines and to social values. From this perspective, it is no coincidence that Einaudi had sought to prompt interdisciplinary debate not only with economists and epistemologues but also with legal and political philosophers: Gioele Solari, Alessandro Passerin d'Entrèves, Giuseppe Bruguier Pacini and Antonio Giolitti.

Although this essay is not Einaudi's last methodological work, it may not be an exaggeration to describe it as his "personal *summa*" not only by virtue of the breadth of its enquiry and the intricate web of themes addressed but also for more precise reasons: a) it was a final effort to clarify and address, in greater depth, the positions Einaudi had put forward in the book he most greatly cherished, *MPJT* (E. 1938b), particularly in the last two chapters added to the 1940 edition; in turn, these chapters were partly the fruit of discussions with his pupil Fasiani (Fossati, Silvestri 2012), which ultimately led him to give a more explicit rendering of his vision of liberalism and good government; b) it was conceived as a "final" reworking of the methodological reflections he had developed in the 1930s during the fascist era, which he had partly intended as a defense of economic science, where a decisive role was also played by a re-reading of Robbins and, above all, by the long debate with Croce on the relation between *liberism and liberalism*, which prompted him to undertake a more profound study of the interplay between economic science and philosophy, also with due attention to the comments and critiques by his interlocutors; and c) because it has an almost autobiographical character, at times assuming the features of "the confessions of an economist". For all these reasons, this essay can indeed be considered a unique work, not easily classifiable in the context of Einaudi's scientific production and, as noted, not easily reducible to a mere methodological work.

The polemic with his pupil Fasiani that sparked the first edition of this essay, as also the lively exchange of ideas observable in the correspondence with the aforementioned scholars and the subsequent rewriting offered the contingent occasion for Einaudi to dwell in greater depth on questions that had long troubled him, above all, since the 1930s. The issues analyzed here by Einaudi lie at the core of his reflection on the nature and scope of economic sciences and the role played by economists in the public sphere – first and foremost, by Einaudi himself as an economist-columnist – with particular emphasis on the interaction between economists and the ruling class. Written at the end of a prolonged speculation during which Einaudi addressed a wide range of issues and engaged in far-reaching debates with critics, scholars and pupils, this work represents Einaudi's most comprehensive effort to tackle, overcome and rethink, in a unitary framework, issues and dichotomies on which he had meditated for many years: theory and history, induction and deduction, theorems and counsels, theory and practice, theoretical and normative language, facts and values, *is* and *ought, homo oeconomicus* and *homo politicus*, reason and passions, knowing and wanting, science and faith, true and good, liberism and liberalism, means and ends, abstraction and reality, economics and philosophy and – last but not least – the preaching of economic science as a science for "good government".

3) *An anthropological perspective, or discourse on the human.* Although every term of each of the aforementioned dichotomies would deserve a monographic study in its own right, it is symptomatic that Einaudi often tended to treat such dichotomies within the question of the alleged distinction between the economist *qua* economist and the "whole man". This was one of the main issues at the origin of the rewriting process and on which Einaudi reflected till his spiritual testament, *Politicians and Economists* (E. 1962).

These three perspectives lead us to a preliminary assessment of the uniqueness of this essay and the meaning of methodological reflection for Einaudi.

The assessment of this essay as an *unicum* in Einaudi's scientific production is based on three major considerations: a) although methodological reflections can be found scattered throughout his works, Einaudi was not, in the strict sense, a methodologist or a philosopher of economic science, at least in the sense we can attribute to such terms today;[7] b) never before, and never again after this essay, did Einaudi attempt such a far-reaching revision of his (not only) methodological speculation; and c) never to such an extent, and never again thereafter, did Einaudi touch on questions of such profound impact from a philosophical, legal, political and economic perspective to the point that the present essay is also the only essay in which Einaudi tried to formulate an epistemological account and justification of his long-lasting enquiry into the causes of good/bad societies and good/bad governments and prosperous and decadent societies, here renamed "state" and "non-state".

Einaudi was well aware that the various methodological debates and reconsiderations of the late 1930s had led him into a philosophical sphere which was challenging and complex, in many ways new to him, and he felt less confident of his ground.

> I have always been afraid of making statements that seem preposterous from a logical point of view, or of revealing my ignorance of things that are common knowledge to philosophers. I am obliged to address problems in the way they would be dealt with by a person who develops his own arguments, self-taught and listening in to things he would like to get to know.
>
> (Lett.: E. to Passerin d'Entrèves, May 7, 1940)

Such were the words Einaudi wrote, candidly or perhaps with an understatement, in a letter to d'Entrèves, whom he asked for advice and criticism on both the two final chapters added to the second edition of *MPJT* – which are crucial for an understanding of the present essay – and the section of *Doubts and Queries* that he began to include, starting from the same year, as an appendix to his *Principii di scienza della finanza* [Principles of Public Finance] (1940b [1945]): this was a sort of careful study plan for students who were preparing for their examinations, which, however, should also be read as a complement to the present essay. Years later, such words were also recalled by d'Entrèves as an 'admirable lesson of humility and modesty' (Passerin d'Entrèves 1971: 453).

What is certain is that during those years of intense thought and reworking of his ideas that led him to write the present essay, methodological reflection had become the line of enquiry he cherished 'most dearly', and those *Doubts and Queries* had almost turned into his own doubts and queries. As he wrote in the *Notes to the Reader* that appeared with the reprinting of the fourth edition of *Principii di scienza della finanza* (1948), Einaudi explained the importance and the spirit (now no longer didactic) that underlay the questions raised in the *Doubts and Queries*:

> I have not lost – or so I hope – my curiosity in new ideas and the desire to modify my old ideas by listening to the fresh voices of so many young scholars; what I lack is the time needed for meditation and re-elaboration, the latter necessarily being slow and laborious. I have grown strongly attached to this book, particularly the bibliographical part and the 'Doubts and Queries' section: indeed, this is the one I have come to hold most dear, as happens to those who, as age approaches, become more and more convinced that wisdom consists in awareness of the too many things that escape our knowledge. It is my hope that this work will, even now, prove to be of some advantage to young people seeking to discover which problems have been deemed worthy of study by an elderly man who, for close to half a century, has been at pains never to forget that he always needs to clarify his own ideas to himself before expounding them to others.
>
> (E. 1948)

In Einaudi's approach, methodological reflection was never an end in itself. Rather, if an explanation is sought for its elevation to the status of the aspect of his reflection he cherished 'most dearly', then the answer is to be found in his awareness that it had become a vital aspect of his *identity* as an economist, teacher, opinion maker and liberal thinker. Hence the need to 'clarify his own ideas to himself before expounding them to others'. It is no coincidence that his reflection was always prompted by debates that compelled him, on numerous occasions, to search for or redefine the *boundaries* and the premises of economic science and, accordingly, to spell out his own role as an economist in the public sphere, where he acted as the repository of this knowledge, in the name of which he spoke. Without a clear understanding of this crucial theme, it is difficult not only to understand Einaudi's doubts on the issue of value judgments and his effort to keep together the economist *qua* economist and the (economist as a) whole man, but also to gain a clear idea of the meaning of this essay and its position in overall Einaudian reflection and scientific production.

A clue to the inner torment that prompted the methodological reflection of those years can be perceived in the article *Confessioni di un Economista* [Confessions of an Economists] (E. 1917). It can be described as a review essay on the work by William Smart, *Second Thought of an Economist* (1916), which Einaudi had significantly interpreted as *Confessioni* and decided to republish it as the opening essay of the volume of his *Complete Works* of which the present essay represented the conclusion (see the Editorial Foreword). This was very clearly a re-reading and reinterpretation of himself, since the essay in question had been written many years prior to the methodological reflection of the 1930s and '40s. Here Einaudi is seemingly talking about Smart, but implicitly he is speaking about himself.

> These pages of Smart's are highly personal and very revealing [. . .]; they implicitly allow us a glimpse into a confession of his scientific doubts, into his effort to look beyond the hedge of the garden reserved to the economist, so as to see what is happening in the vast world and how economic problems are linked to moral and religious problems, and to the very question of the ends for which life is worth living.
>
> (E. 1917)

Another clue to the inner torment that led to the present essay can be found in the statement, or rather a different kind of confession, contained in this same essay:

> There exists no plausible reason for setting the boundaries of any scientific territory according to one line rather than another, there may be someone whose curiosity is aroused by a different range of phenomena. Thus an inquiring mind little swayed by any urge to take up a position in this or that particular column of the table of scientific classifications may quite legitimately study the links between ends and choices, if for no other reason than to investigate whether by consecrating himself to a particular science he might not be performing a sacrifice to an idol devoid of soul.
>
> (p. 85)

As a humanist-economist, and perhaps one of the last humanist-economists with a legal education and background, Einaudi had always 'proudly claimed' economics as a moral science or a 'humanistic discipline' (E. 1959: IX), as he repeated till the end of his life. The judgement he gave on Adam Smith's three souls – '*moralist, historian and economist*', the three souls which addressed the same problem, though from different perspectives and/or in different moments (E. 1938a) – can rightly be addressed to Einaudi himself (Forte, Marchionatti 2012: 620). To put it another way: if for Adam Smith political economy was the 'science of a statesman or legislator' (Smith 1776 [1976]: 428), for Einaudi, the "economic sciences" – evoked in the title of the present essay: mainly political economy and the "*Scienza*" *delle finanze* – were the sciences of good/bad society and good/bad government.

For these reasons, Einaudi's "methodological" speculation cannot be separated from his liberalism, just as his liberalism cannot be separated from his enquiry into the causes of good and bad polities.[8] With such an enquiry Einaudi, as humanist-economist and "whole man", went well 'beyond the hedge of the garden reserved to the economist'.

2 Structure of this critical edition

The present critical edition is formed of three parts: the Introduction, Einaudi's essay, followed by his (incomplete) Bibliographical Note, and the Afterword. Although, naturally, no introduction or afterword can ever substitute a direct reading of Einaudi's text, both the Introduction and the Afterword aim to provide readers with some possible suggestions for an interpretation or access to the text by highlighting the main problems, the reflections and discussions that led Einaudi, firstly, to compose the first edition and then to decide to rewrite it as it is in the present essay. In particular, the Introduction is mainly focused on the thought process that led Einaudi to the present essay, while the Afterword seeks to offer an in-depth appraisal of some of the passages that are characterized by greater complexity and/or which were rewritten in various ways by Einaudi – namely those belonging to part II and III of the present essay.

The main purpose of both the Introduction and Afterword is to provide the reader with a meaningful account of Einaudi's essay, but also to make it comprehensible to an international public and to all those who may be unacquainted with his thought.[9] However, Einaudi's essay could reserve a few surprises even for those already acquainted with his thought and/or with the Italian tradition in public finance and for those interested in philosophy of economics, law and politics.

This notwithstanding, my work makes no claim to give an exhaustive account of the complexity of the problems Einaudi treated, nor to treat them systematically or give a step-by-step commentary on the way his arguments are set out. Rather, and this should be emphasized, it seeks merely to highlight some of the passages that readers could find somewhat complex, if not genuinely obscure because of the many implicit references to Einaudi's earlier reflections that are scattered throughout the essay, or because of his allusive style,[10] or because of the dubitative way through which he presented the rewriting of the conclusions.

The Introduction, 'The Defense of Economic Science and the Issue of Value Judgments', aims primarily at understanding how Einaudi's position evolved from the 1930s to the beginning of the 1940s and how the debate with Fasiani had an impact on Einaudi's second thoughts regarding the position he had held in those years. The Introduction is organized as follows. After a brief overview of some of the main concerns and thoughts that led Einaudi to the present essay, which can be traced back to his position (and conception) of economist in the public sphere (par. 1), I will try to contextualize the entire evolution of his thought within two significant limits: the most remote (par. 1.1) and the nearest (par. 4.2) antecedent of the present essay. In turn, the starting point of the debate with Fasiani will be contextualized within the methodological reflections of the 1930s, with specific reference to the methodological discourse in defense of the economics Einaudi had adopted during those years (par. 2), where his re-reading of Robbins (par. 2.1) is particularly important. The debate with Fasiani, from *Myths and Paradoxes of Justice in Taxation* to the present essay, is then analyzed (par. 3). I will first provide the reader with an overview of this debate, with specific reference to the demarcation issue (par. 3.1), and then I will analytically subdivide its main issues as follows: the demarcation between counsels and theorems, theoretical and normative language and the issue of their reciprocal translatability (par. 3.2); the distinction between science and history and the supposed detached or dispassionate knowledge of the economist (par. 3.3); and the epistemological nature of the types of state used by Fasiani as compared to the "historical" schemata of good/ bad polities used by Einaudi (par. 3.4). In the last paragraph, I will then analyze the most significant steps and turning points of the 1940s (par. 4). Among these, I will take into account Einaudi's reflection on the historicity of economics and the "passionate economist" (par. 4.1); the nearest antecedent of the present essay, which contains Einaudi's explicit confession of his second thoughts as to the issue of value judgments (par. 4.2); and, last but not least, the epistemological aspects of the debate with Croce on the relation between liberalism and liberism, as well as the debate between Einaudi and his interlocutors, in order to cast light on the rewriting of the conclusions of the present essay, thus on Einaudi's intention to focus on the distinction between philosophy and economics (par. 4.3).

The Afterword, 'Freedom and Taxation between Good and Bad Polity and the Economist-Whole-Man', aims to provide the reader with a perspective designed to illuminate the meaning of the complex rewriting and passages of part II and III of the present essay. It is organized as follows. After a brief overview of the *telos* and argumentative strategy adopted by Einaudi in his reflection on the *schemata* of the state developed in part II, and led by his search for a liberal good polity (par. 1), I will mainly focus on Einaudi's way of engaging with the Italian tradition in public finance. I will start from the reflections developed in *MPJT* that led to the present essay, focusing on his attempt to go beyond the so-called economic approach to public finance and taxation (par. 1.1). I will then try to cast light on Einaudi's concern about Fasiani's hypotheses of state, with specific reference to the relation between theory, interpretation and communication of historical reality (par. 1.2). I will then focus on the fundamental anthropological background of the 'dialectical contrast between the state and the non-state'. This anthropological background, in turn, sheds light on Einaudi's attempt to consider the relation between the individual and the collective community in dual and non-dualistic terms (par. 1.3). The subsequent paragraph is a brief excursus on Einaudi's preface to the 1959 edition of *MPJT*, which can shed a retrospective light both on the second and third part of the present essay, since it is an admirable reinterpretation and synthesis of some of the ideas that prompted his enquiry into the causes of good and bad polities (par. 2). The last paragraph is mainly focused on part III of the present essay and the rewriting of the conclusions, where the issue of value judgments is further developed by Einaudi through a reflection on the distinction between philosophy and economics (par. 3). Starting from Einaudi's general claim of the conventional nature of the division among disciplines, I will try to distinguish his arguments and doubts analytically into two main topics: the issue of value judgments, which I will further subdivide into the issue of taking a stand and the difficulty of separating the study of means from the understanding of ends (par. 3.1), and Einaudi's attempt to clarify both the distinction between economics and philosophy, and the alleged separation between the economist *qua* scientist and the whole man (par. 3.2).

Notes

1 More specifically, Gioele Solari, a philosopher of law, was a friend and colleague of Einaudi's at the Faculty of Law in Turin who, like Einaudi, had completed his training at the "Laboratorio di Economia politica" headed by Salvatore Cognetti de Martiis (see E. 1949c and Solari 2006). Both Einaudi and Solari were the leading academic figures whose guidance and teaching shaped many members of the intellectual elite of Turin and Italy. Alessandro Passerin d'Entrèves, a political and legal philosopher, wrote his dissertation under the guidance of Solari and was helped by Einaudi in his academic career both in Italy and abroad (with a grant from the Rockefeller Foundation); he eventually went to Oxford. He paid a last homage to Einaudi in the concluding chapter of one of his most successful books (Passerin d'Entrèves 1962). Giuseppe Bruguier Pacini, a pupil of Giuseppe Toniolo, was interested in history and the epistemology of economics, and he was also a junior assistant of Einaudi's at the Bocconi University as well as one of Einaudi's most insightful reviewers. Influenced by Italian idealism and Benedetto Croce's historicism and engaged in an attempt to revise the epistemological "conclusion" of the *Methodenstreit*, Pacini was also the Italian translator and editor of some of the most important economic and epistemological works of the period: those of Menger, Schumpeter and Myrdal. Also, Pacini depicted one of the best portraits of Luigi Einaudi as 'moralist' (Bruguier Pacini 1950). Antonio Giolitti, grandson of the statesman Giovanni Giolitti and an important Italian politician, was at that time working with the publishing house directed by Giulio Einaudi; he was also the translator of the first Italian edition of Max Weber's *Science as a Vocation* and *Politics as a Vocation* and the Italian translator of Cantillon and Röpke.

2 A word of warning is called for to alert readers to a crucial difficulty in the attempt to understand how Einaudi reworked the various points that arose during this exchange of ideas and how he incorporated them into the present essay. Namely, we do not have a textual testimony of Einaudi's detailed comments on the debate, which he would surely have included in the Bibliographical Note he planned to set at the end of the volume in which the present essay was to be included. Such comments would most likely have been devoted to explaining the profound changes and additions introduced in the conclusions of the present essay, especially given the fact that Einaudi decided to keep track of the conclusions eliminated from the first edition by quoting them precisely in this Bibliographical Note.

The only document that has come down to us is a small sheet of paper on which Einaudi jotted down a few sentences summarizing the comments made by his correspondents. Even though Einaudi's short annotations do not list all of the modifications he introduced during the rewriting process – for instance, the fundamental terminological changes introduced in the first part, mainly spurred by Bruguier Pacini – one may surmise that his jottings were meant to serve as an outline for further comments on the discussion, which he planned to include in the Bibliographical Note. It is likely that such comments would have focused on the most important changes – that is to say, those introduced in the second part and in the conclusions.

3 The most comprehensive biography of Einaudi is that by Faucci (1986), but see also the more recent biography by Farese (2012). On the economic School of Turin, see the essays collected in Marchionatti, Becchio (2003–2004). For a general introduction to Einaudi's economic, political and legal thought see: Einaudi, Faucci, Marchionatti (2006), Forte, Marchionatti (2009), Silvestri (2012a). Among the many monographic works see: Forte (1982, 2009), Giordano (2006), Silvestri (2008a), Tomatis (2011).

For a recent overall reappraisal of Einaudi's thought, see the essays collected in Giglio-bianco (2010), Heritier, Silvestri (2012a) and Marchionatti, Soddu (2010).

4 Among them see Barucci (1974), Forte (2009: 137–142), Forte, Marchionatti (2012: 593–595), Fusco (2009), Portinaro (1979), Romeo (1974), Silvestri (2008a: 87–122, 2010a), Fossati (2015).

5 See Buchanan (1960), Kayaalp (1985, 1989, 2004), Musgrave, Peacock (1958b), Backhaus, Wagner (2005a, 2005b), Fausto (2003), the essays in Fausto, De Bonis (2003), Medema (2005), Wagner (2003).

6 See Bellanca (1993).

7 The current philosophy of economics is usually subdivided into 1) action theory, 2) ethics (or normative social and political philosophy) and 3) philosophy of science (Hausman 2013), or (to consider a slightly different division) 1) political economy as political philosophy, 2) the methodology and epistemology of economics, 3) social ontology and the ontology of economics (Davis, Marciano, Runde 2004). On "new directions" in philosophy of economics, see Binder, Heilmann, Vromen (2015) and Ross, Kincaid (2009). Although all three of these dimensions are present in Einaudi's "philosophy of economics", especially in the present essay, his "philosophy" as well as his language and style are much closer to "continental" philosophy than "analytic".

8 It may be that Buchanan's conclusive argument on the Italian tradition in public finance – 'no reforming spirit has guided the Italians. This has made their arguments seem sterile and devoid of normative content. The normative elements which are present are usually clouded over, perhaps unintentionally, with pseudo-scientific pronouncements' (Buchanan 1960: 72) – has not helped develop an appropriate evaluation of Einaudi's methodological reflection, which Buchanan was probably not familiar with. In actual fact, in the present essay, Einaudi's claims exactly the contrary of Buchanan's dismissive statement. Quite curiously, Einaudi's conclusions are very similar to what Buchanan has recently argued – in contrast to the lesson of "political realism" (Buchanan, Musgrave 1999: 19) that he claimed to have learned from the Italian tradition – on the "*normativity of vision*", apropos of his liberal credo, which he expressed in terms of *the soul of classical liberalism*: 'I suggest invoking the soul of classical liberalism, an aesthetic-ethical-ideological potential attractor, one that stands independent of ordinary science, both below the latter's rigor and above its antiseptic neutrality' (Buchanan 2000 [2005]: 55). Through his epistemological reflections, Einaudi increasingly felt and feared that the science to which he had devoted his life was becoming an 'idol devoid of soul'. Buchanan's 'vision' seems to be similar to the kind of "vision" Einaudi rediscovered, in the later period of his life, in Ambrogio Lorenzetti's celebrated frescoes on *good government*, which he pointed out to Italians, as President of the Italian Republic (E. 1954). In Buchanan's words, Lorenzetti's frescoes are 'an aesthetic-ethical-ideological potential attractor' in which Einaudi had "seen", in a condensed and allusive form, the invisible foundations (civic virtues, social bond, social capital, trust) of his liberal good polity (Silvestri 2012b).

9 Until not long ago, relatively few of Einaudi's essays were available in an English translation, and only the recent edition of *Selected Essays* in three volumes (E. 2006, 2014a, 2014b) has begun to bridge this cognitive gap.

10 The essay was originally read in its first version at the Royal Academy of Science of Turin (where Einaudi as well as Fasiani were members) and probably presented away from the prying eyes of fascism, especially in the light of the far-from-implicit charges against 'the Emperor's advocate' (p. 78). It would seem, anyway, that Einaudi's essay was addressed to a select public that could be assumed to have familiarity with his scientific production.

Acknowledgements

As this work draws to its close, I am aware that I owe many, too many, debts. Yet they are indeed those kinds of debts with regard to which it can be said, anthropologically speaking, that one is delighted to have contracted.

I will limit myself here to expressing gratitude to those who in the past few years have most greatly contributed to the success of this work with their support and/ or with debate and criticisms that never failed to be constructive: Paolo Heritier, for many, by now innumerable, reasons; Luigi Roberto Einaudi, towards whom I can no longer find the words to express my infinite gratitude and to whom I owe special thanks for releasing the rights to this work of Einaudi's; Roberto Marchionatti for the many years during which I have been able to enjoy stimulating discussion on the thought of Einaudi and for countless other reasons; Francesco Forte for always being a source of suggestions and valuable advice on Einaudi but also on Fasiani; Fiorenzo Mornati for helping me to clarify some of my doubts concerning the thought of Pareto. I am particularly grateful to A.F. for reading and commenting on parts of the very first draft and the final version of this work; Nicolò Bellanca for helping me to clarify some methodological aspects of the Italian tradition in public finance; the Fondazione Luigi Einaudi for authorizing me to work on this text by Einaudi; Paolo Soddu, who is in charge of cultural affairs at the Fondazione Einaudi, for having had faith, since the very beginning, in the significance of this Einaudian essay; Guido Mones, who is in charge of the Archive of the Fondazione Luigi Einaudi of Turin, for his constant assistance and always being helpful and willing; and the San Giacomo Charitable Foundation and the Fondazione Cassa di Risparmio di Cuneo for contributing to the translation costs.

Small portions of the research and/or working papers directly or indirectly related to the development of this work have been presented and discussed in various institutions and moments, universities, research centers, conferences and seminars, as well as during visiting periods abroad, including the Research Center on History and Methodology of Economics, Department of Economics and Statistics "Cognetti de Martiis" (University of Torino); the Centre Walras-Pareto d'études interdisciplinaires de la pensée économique et politique (University of Lausanne); the Cornell Institute for European Studies, the Mario Einaudi Center and the Cornell Law School (Cornell University); and the yearly Conferences of the Italian Association for the History of Political Economy (STOREP).

This work was brought to completion during my research stay as external Senior Fellow at Freiburg Institute for Advanced Studies (FRIAS), University of Freiburg, Germany, and then at the London School of Economics, Department of Government (UK) thanks to the grant World Wide Style II from the University of Torino, which I thank for its financial support. In this regard, I would like to remember and thank the representatives of these institutions and/or academic hosts for having invited me and all those who have given me the opportunity to share part of my research with them: Roberto Marchionatti, Roberto Baranzini, Christopher Way, Annelise Riles and Hirokazu Miyazaki, Viktor Vanberg, Lars Feld, Bernd Kortmann, Günther Schulze, Lea Ypi and Chandran Kukathas. A heartfelt thanks goes to all the participants and discussants from whom I have always received insightful comments and constructive critiques.

A word of thanks also to Rachel Barritt Costa for performing the difficult task of translating Einaudi's text and reviewing parts of my Introduction and Afterword with her ceaseless endeavor to transmit to the English-speaking world the infinite nuances and subtleties of Einaudi's "voice" and language and for exercising forbearance, in a constant and patient dialogue, with my punctilious revisions.

Finally, a truly special expression of thanks to Routledge (and to the two anonymous and generous reviewers) for accepting the proposal for publication; to the editor, Emily Kindleysides; and the editorial assistant, Laura Johnson, for following the various stages of the publication process with constant attention, infinite patience and humane comprehension.

I would strongly have wished that this could be considered as the *definitive edition* of *On Abstract and Historical Hypotheses and on Value Judgments in Economic Sciences*. If, by a stroke of luck, I were to chance upon the overall design of the collection of Einaudian essays and the other revised versions Einaudi intended to incorporate in the collection together with the present essay, I express the sincere hope that Routledge would decide to publish all of them in a *second and definitive edition*. "Definitive", unless, that is, history happened to introduce yet another twist in this chain of events and reserve for me new compelling surprises.

I wish to dedicate my work to my father and mother from whom I have learned that 'faith, hope and love' resist till the end, and survive to the end. And to Elena, from whom I have learned that 'the greatest of these is love' and to whom I owe the greatest debt of all.

Paolo Silvestri

Abbreviations

§ [number]	=	the old numbering of sections (1–27) used by Einaudi in the first edition and maintained in the present essay to facilitate generic references to parts/sections of the text.
Afterword	=	Afterword to the present volume: P. Silvestri, 'Freedom and Taxation between Good and Bad Polity and the Economist-Whole-Man'.
COP	=	*Chiarimenti offerti al filosofo* [*Clarifications Offered to the Philosopher*]. Sheets sent by Einaudi to his correspondents during the rewriting process (in Archivio Luigi Einaudi of the Fondazione Luigi Einaudi of Turin).
DVE	=	*Dubbi posti all'economista* [*Doubts Voiced to the Economist*]. Sheets sent by Einaudi to his correspondents during the rewriting process (in Archivio Luigi Einaudi of the Fondazione Luigi Einaudi of Turin).
E.	=	Einaudi.
first edition	=	First edition of *On Abstract and Historical Hypotheses and on Value Judgments in Economic Sciences* (E. 1942–1943).
Introduction	=	Introduction to the present volume: P. Silvestri, 'The Defense of Economic Science and the Issue of Value Judgments'.
ISS	=	*Individuo, società, stato* [*Individual, Society, State*]. Sheets sent by Einaudi to Gioele Solari during the rewriting process (in Archivio Luigi Einaudi of the Fondazione Luigi Einaudi of Turin).
lett.	=	letter. Unless otherwise stated, all the letters of Einaudi's correspondence cited in the text are taken from the Archivio Luigi Einaudi of the Fondazione Luigi Einaudi of Turin and will be quoted with the following format: Lett.: [from] "Surname" to "Surname", date of the letter.
MPJT	=	*Myths and Paradoxes of Justice in Taxation*. The first edition of *MPJT* is E. 1938, the second modified and expanded edition is E. 1940a, and the third, with a new preface, is E. 1959. Unless otherwise stated, the reference edition is E. 1940a.
p./pp.	=	page/pages of the present essay cited in the Introduction and Afterword.

par. [number] = reference to a paragraph of the Introduction or Afterword to the present volume.

present essay = Second and unpublished edition of *On Abstract and Historical Hypotheses and on Value Judgments in Economic Sciences* published here.

Introduction

The defense of economic science and the issue of value judgments

Paolo Silvestri

1 The economist in the public sphere: Between governors, governed and lay public

The first section of the present essay has the character of a generic introduction and bears witness to Einaudi's combination of the inductive and deductive methods,[1] but the part that in many ways best illuminates Einaudi's intentions and his endeavour to build up his arguments and keep together the diverse issues that led to this essay is the second section. Since I will focus on these issues a number of times in the following pages, it is worth reading the full section:

> if economic science consisted only in considering abstract problems and demonstrating similarly abstract laws, it would hardly benefit from even that minimal following among the lay public it does still enjoy, and it would not exert the least influence on human affairs, not even that infinitesimal trace which it can indeed boast. Following and influence are due to the connections scholars and the lay public believe to exist between abstract schemata and concrete reality, or which are held to link problems and first approximation theorems with the problems and the associated urgent solutions in the daily life of human society. Physicists, chemists and astronomers can, if they so desire, spend their entire life without the slightest concern for the concrete applications others will draw from the theorems they, as scientists, have discovered. Not so for the economist. No economist has ever stayed rigidly closed up in the ivory tower of first principles, first approximation theorems. Pantaleoni and Pareto, to mention but two of the celebrated economists of the past generation, were combative fighters in the debate centering on the everyday problems of their time just as much as they were great theoreticians. The attitude they adopted in facing the battles of real life repeatedly molded their manner of addressing theoretical problems. To be sure, they took immense care to distinguish a *theorem* from *counsels*; they endeavored to avoid any contamination between the one and the other; sometimes both men – especially one of the two (Pareto) – spoke scornfully and ironically of *literary* economists who mistook science for politics, giving counsels to princes instead of declaring uniformities. Yet by dint of fine distinctions and

clarifications, they never ceased to reproach, criticize, contemptuously belittle – and only very seldom did they deign to praise – governors and the governed, pointing out which path was best avoided and which was the right one to take. It is a fact that in economic sciences, there exists a field of theorems, properly speaking, and a field of counsels: but these two fields are not separate and independent of each other. Economists who do have something to say, even though sometimes delighting in contemptuously belittling the other and perhaps better part of themselves, cultivate the land for the purpose of knowledge and dig the land over for the purpose of acting upon reality; the imitators, the servile pen-pushers, incapable of perceiving the links between the two aspects of the whole person, construct insipid theory and supply the counsels they know will find favor with the powerful.

(p. 38)

It can be noted that some of the questions of greatest concern to Einaudi are here clearly set out within these few lines. Even though not all of the issues mentioned here were developed in the first edition, during the rewriting he tried to recall and develop some of them in a new conclusion. Such questions summarize and reformulate some of the main issues that Einaudi had addressed in previous years, most of them prompted by the discussion with Fasiani. The issues touched upon include the critique of Pareto, whom Einaudi chided for belittling '*literary* economists', a critique which, in turn, sparked the discussion with Fasiani; the relationship between theorems and counsels; the revisitation or, rather, the "use" of Pareto (and Pantaleoni), whom Einaudi esteemed as 'combative fighters' in the public sphere, against Pareto himself and, at the same time, against Fasiani's Paretian notion of science and the impersonal detachment of the scientist; the relevance of passions and sentiments as 'the other and perhaps better part' of the (economist as a) 'whole person'; the critique of the (economist's) servile pen-pushers; and, above all, the 'following' and 'influence' exerted by economics and economists, or the significance, credibility and legitimacy of economic science and the economist as a *clerc* or intellectual in the public sphere addressing his comments to the lay public and occupying a peculiar and always difficult position between 'governors' and 'governed'.

Einaudi embodied the role of the economist-columnist in an era when communicating through newspaper feature articles could be just as important (if not more so) as taking the stand in parliament. In his innermost mind, this role was no less than a genuine and twofold vocation: the 'priestly ministry of science' and the 'priestly ministry of journalism' (Lett.: E. to Croci, November 28, 1925).[2]

As an economist-journalist, through thousands of articles (E. 1959–65, 2000), Einaudi testified to his faith in the English liberal tradition which held that, from the time of Hume onwards, government is based on opinion and a liberal government on the possibility of criticism. This is indeed eloquently demonstrated by the pseudonym Junius that Einaudi adopted in his own *Lettere politiche di Junius* (E. 1920c), which highlights his explicit reference to the tradition of a press that felt free to criticize those who held power (Silvestri 2008a: 125–132).

As far as the Italian context was concerned, Einaudi felt that his allegiance was to the tradition inaugurated by Ferrara, which attributed to the economist a mission as an educator of public opinion: 'Economists as a class figured from the very start as a qualified component of the post-unity ruling class, an indispensable link in the chain between governors and the governed, between the state and civil society' (Faucci 1982: 19).[3]

Einaudi's nineteenth-century conception of the press and, in general, of the public sphere as a place of mediation between civil society and the state, between governors and the governed and also a place where criticism of the power of the Establishment can be voiced, is crucial for an understand of various passages in the present essay, which more or less explicitly presuppose the political function of critical debate in the public sphere (Silvestri 2008a: 139–144, 2012a: 74–88) and the idea that it may be possible to 'enlighten' the 'public opinion' (p. 80, 86) through the knowledge and tools of economic science (Silvestri 2010a).

Suffice it for the moment to point out that one of the greatest efforts made by Einaudi in this essay is to explain if, how and to what extent the economist *qua* economist can legitimately exercise a role of *criticism* vis-à-vis power *but* without stepping beyond the confines of science and if, by doing so, he has, nevertheless, made a value judgment. The "but" is fundamental here because the accusation of a non-scientific mode of conducting his activity had already been levelled against him by none other than Fasiani.

Before examining the discussion with Fasiani in greater detail, both in this Introduction (par. 3) and in the Afterword, it is worth contextualizing its starting point within the methodological reflections of the 1930s. In effect, the discussion with Fasiani had spurred Einaudi to reflect critically on the methodological discourse in defense of economics he had adopted during those years (par. 2) and to have second thoughts on the issue of value judgments from the beginning of the 1940s (par. 4) up to the present essay. In turn, in order to better grasp the entire evolution of Einaudi's thought, it is helpful to contextualize it within two significant limits: the most remote (par. 1.1) and the nearest (par. 4.2) antecedents of the present essay.

1.1 The most remote antecedent of the present essay

Einaudi's preface to his book *La finanza della guerra e delle opere pubbliche* [The Finance of War and of Public Works] (1914) can be considered as the most remote antecedent of the present essay, which is significant at least to grasp Einaudi's conception of the role and responsibility of the economist in the public sphere, the reasons behind his concern for economists' language and his awareness of the ambiguous uses of the rhetoric of "science".

Einaudi presents his book as a sort of exercise in criticism of the governing class and in unmasking its mistakes or the 'illusions' that have been built up to conceal the truth: this is the 'practical end' that prompted him to write. He classifies those forming part of the governing class as either reactive or a-reactive, according to whether they are lovers or enemies of parliamentary control and of ensuring that public debate is within the public domain. In this regard, Einaudi criticizes the sociological approaches to public finance claiming a neutrality stance against any ends pursued by politicians (Forte 2009: 75):

> among writers on economics and finance, a ludicrous mania has come into vogue, whereby they regard as 'scientific' only those investigations that are least suited to practical applications [. . .]. It would seem quite legitimate to propose that the throng of writers who delight in pure science, reputing that it should limit itself to clarifying the conditions or causes on account of which governors embrace now the economically advantageous, now the harmful, solutions to the problems they find themselves facing, should be asked also to address the issue of the effectiveness or ineffectiveness of the various solutions that can be put forward to deal with financial problems.
>
> (E. 1914: III)

According to Einaudi this type of scientific activity provided 'just the right excuse for unrepentant rulers, giving them an opportunity to show that their misdeeds and the villainous wrongdoings they perpetrated in public affairs were historically inevitable' in such a manner that their mistake was 'eminently excusable' and 'the inevitable outcome of fate'. Hence Einaudi's warning:

> by merely taking never-ending note of the facts and the relations holding among them, behaving in the fashion, as it were, of aloof bonzes [we may end up] in a band of mercenary lackeys of the powerful; [. . .] allow me to recall that the finest traditions of economic science and its most glorious achievements, both theoretical and practical, date back to the era when economists were fairly unconcerned with trying to explain the genesis of the facts, nor did they consider them all as equally and exclusively "interesting" objects of study. Rather, they classified the facts according to whether the results springing therefrom were useful or detrimental to the generality or the majority of the people or whether, on the contrary, they were useful to a limited number and detrimental to the greater part of the community.
>
> (E. 1914: VIII)

The impassiveness of modern science has the effect of smoothing the path for governments to engage in harmful action, whereas the passional nature of ancient science prompted people to react against the harm produced by bad laws. Now, consider the following premises: first, it is absolutely certain that both the modern and the ancient modes fall within the realm of scientific activity, and second, if reasoning is opened up to the multitudes and becomes a cause of sentiment and action, it is likely to succeed in modifying the behavior of men, whether governed or governing, and thus to become a fact in its own right, capable of acting upon other facts. Since this is so, allow me to voice the hope that after the protracted dominion of what has been dubbed as "genetic", "historical", "impartial" science the mood will swing back in favor of "critical" and "spirited" investigations, prompted by a passion for truth and hatred for error. Such investigations will serve as a valuable tool in the hands of men who are active in the political and economic life of the country and seek to combat those among their fellow men who live in error and abhor the truth.

(E. 1914: IX)

A signal of the relevance of this preface, written in 1914, is to be found in the date of its republication: Einaudi started to republish it in the already mentioned section of *Doubts and Queries* that he began to include as an appendix to his *Principii di scienza della finanza* [Principles of Public Finance] (E. 1940b [1945]). As we will see later (par. 4), the beginning of the 1940s coincides with a turning point in Einaudi's methodological reflection and, in some respects, a return to the position he expressed in this preface.

If this preface, as I said, testifies to Einaudi's conception of the role and responsibility of economists in the public sphere and his concern for economists' language, as well as his awareness of the ambiguous uses of the rhetoric of "science", it can also be of help in understanding the kind of rhetoric of "science" used by Einaudi in defense of economics during the 1930s.

2 The methodological position of the 1930s: In defense of economic science[4]

A good way to understand the position held by Einaudi during the 1930s is to start from the methodological discourse he developed in the first edition of *MPJT* (E. 1938b), which, in turn, is also relevant to understand the debate with Fasiani.

In Fasiani's view, *MPJT* (E. 1938b) marked a substantial epistemological change in the point of view previously held by his one-time master (Fossati, Silvestri 2012): it represented a departure from a purely positive and value-free conception of economic science, in which Fasiani believed he had been trained and which he had embraced as a profession of faith, towards a more decidedly normative position, which Fasiani felt he could no longer recognize as coinciding with his own position. Rather, he believed he was now separated from Einaudi by 'a distance that terrifies me': indeed, Fasiani now felt that the distance was so great as to undermine his own 'scientific self' (Lett.: Fasiani to E., June 1938, in Fossati, Silvestri 2012: 72). Fasiani is referring to Einaudi's critique of Pareto, perceived by Fasiani as a sort of personal attack. As a reaction, Fasiani criticized *MPJT* (E. 1938b) for being flawed by a profound contradiction: that is to say, although it started out from a critique of the "doctrinaires" and "planners" who were always ready to offer counsels to whoever happened to be in power, in the conclusions, Einaudi had started out on a quest to find the ideal conditions of good government and an ideal form of taxation conceived as taxation of the average income. Thus it is important here to try to understand whether and why Einaudi had effectively embraced a value-free conception of economic science, as Fasiani believed.

MPJT can be seen, from as early as the introduction, as a tirade 'against the doctrinaires', set against the background of the problem – or rather, of Einaudi's concern, which had become increasingly felt under fascism – about the '*Trahison des clercs*',[5] or of the intellectual who bows to the powers-that-be and offers his 'projects' to serve the 'political conditions or needs of the moment' (E. 1959: 3–9), i.e. who ends up, intentionally or unintentionally, subscribing to the doings of the regime.

Einaudi's thoughts were further complicated by the fact that in his position as the most influential economic scientist, he had found himself constrained to defend economic science not only against the attacks launched by the corporativist economists, who invoked a revitalisation of economic science to bring it in line with the doctrine of corporatism[6] but also against the various attempts to make the construction of economic science dependent on some ideology or to subordinate it to some other form of knowledge, such as law, morals or politics, thereby depriving it of any autonomy of its own.

Several debates and essays are emblematic of the atmosphere of those years: for instance the debate with the sociologist Michels, *On the Manner of Writing the History of the Economic Dogma* (E. 1932a, E. 1932b, Michels 1932);[7] or the essay *Morale et économique* (E. 1936c) in which Einaudi takes up the positions expressed in the celebrated *Essay on the Nature and Significance of Economic Science* by Robbins (1932) (par. 2.1) in order to criticize the views put forward by the philosopher of law Giorgio Del Vecchio, who proposed subordinating economic science to law and to morals. Equally emblematic is the debate with Croce on the relation between liberism and liberalism (par. 4.3). In particular, at the beginning of the debate, Einaudi had formulated a 'technical' conception of economic science as a means of disengaging it from any ideology, whether liberist or communist, while at the same time endeavouring to safeguard the value of liberism at least in the form of 'practical rule' or a rule of a prudential nature (E. 1928a), as in fact he had already suggested when arguing against Keynes's *The End of Laissez-Faire* (E. 1926a, Keynes 1926).[8]

In any case, Einaudi's arguments concerning the autonomy or scientific nature of economic science concealed the question of the intellectual's independence from the ruling powers; in other words, it was not so much an issue of neutrality of economics as, rather, an issue of *neutrality of the economist*. Therefore, during that period, the difficulties and dilemma Einaudi found himself facing were as follows.

On the one hand, he sought to preserve for economics an advisory or critical-propositive function, while nevertheless avoiding the risk that such a function could lay itself open to the charge of following the political convenience of the moment, or that the economist could be reduced to the position of a (bad) counsellor of the prince.

On the other hand, it was necessary to build a defensive wall around economic science and insist on its "scientific" nature, with the latter implying in a minimal sense an alleged neutrality or "indifference" of the economist, ends-means instrumental reasoning and the possibility of a technical critique of values, but without taking up any specific position vis-à-vis the political aims in question. In effect, Einaudi seemed to fear that if economic science were to lose its label as a "science" it would lose all defensive barriers and would fall into the hands of charlatans or doctrinaires who were always ready to offer counsels to whoever happened to be in power.

To better understand how Einaudi's position evolved from the 1930s to the beginning of the 1940s and how the debate with Fasiani had an impact on Einaudi's second thoughts, leading him to confess, in the present essay, that the alleged indifference or neutrality was nothing but a mere rhetorical strategy he had adopted in defense of economics, it is necessary to dwell on one of the most significant moments of this defense.

2.1 The re-reading of Robbins: Instrumental reasoning and significance of economic science

In *Morale et économique* (E. 1936c), nettled as he was by the arguments of the philosopher of law Giorgio Del Vecchio (1935), who was eager to subordinate economic science to law and morals, Einaudi drew on a re-reading of Robbins's famous essay *Essay on the Nature and Significance of Economic Science* (Robbins 1932).

Taking his cue from the line of reasoning put forward by Robbins, Einaudi adopted a twofold approach: on the one hand, he reflected on the *nature* of economic science, while on the other he strongly claimed its *significance* or importance. However, the fact of basing his discourse on both aspects implied a subtle reorientation of the hypothesis of means-ends rationality, from a positive to a normative plane. Thus while establishing a clear-cut separation between economic science – founded on the hypothesis of means-ends rationality – and other branches of knowledge (ethics, politics, law and so forth), he also pointed to a possible reunification between ethics and economics: his line of reasoning thus broadens out to encompass (and is also directed to) the political sphere and society. In this context, he expressed the hope that the hypothesis of means-ends rationality, which is the core of economic science, would contribute to the education of the ruling class and of society.

In other words, on the one hand, Einaudi refers to means-ends rationality in the sense of a *pure form* of human behavior – that is to say, coherent and intentional – which the economist analyzes simply as a *fact*, i.e. the fact of the choice, precisely because science is *Wertfrei*. On the other hand, however, Einaudi appealed to the "logic" and the value of means-ends rationality which can contribute to the creation of an 'ethically more perfect society' (E. 1936c: 311).[9] In this acceptation, rationality is taken as a sort of Weberian *ethic of responsibility* that consists in an ethic of the limit or of the sense of reality; accordingly, ideals or ends need to be commensurate with the scarce means capable of pursuing them.

As noted years later by Del Vecchio, in Einaudi, the rationality hypothesis ultimately coincides with the virtue of 'prudence' (Del Vecchio 1935 [1954]: 58), or of the *bonus pater familias*. Effectively, Einaudi regarded this virtue as the virtue *par excellence* of the middle class and, at the same time, as the criterion that should regulate the actions of the good governor. In this sense, to the extent to which economic science teaches an informed awareness of ends and means, it thereby also teaches how to deal with scarcity and thus with the sense of the limit. It is with this concept in mind that Einaudi was wont to say he was composing *Preachings* (E. 1920a) and that what he preached was the value of knowing economic science, which was elsewhere also expressed with the motto and warning addressed first and foremost to the ruling class and the world of politics as *Conoscere per deliberare* [*Knowing for Decision Making*] (E. 1956). And, finally, it was with this concept in mind that Einaudi ascribed to economic science the status and value of *counsels*, both *cognitive* and *normative* at the same time, with normative taken not as a command or precept but, precisely, as a counsel that is illuminated by the knowledge of economics. As he stated, many years later, in *I consigli del buon senso* [Common Sense Counsels] – written as the introduction to the Italian edition of the work by Wicksteed (1910), *The Common Sense of Political Economy Including a Study of the Human Basis of Economic Law* –

> [Wicksteed wrote] the treatise on good government of revenue and expenditure, in the present and the past, of each of us, according to the advice an ordinary man gleans from common sense [. . .]. In private life man is well advised to study the elegant and cautionary ramifications of the theory of choice, so as to avoid the inevitable sanction of ruin, failure, poverty and desperation for himself and his offspring. But what is advisable above all is for man in the sphere of public life to make those rules into flesh of his own flesh, because the sanctions resulting from mistaken choices in public life lamentably do not fall on whoever was responsible for the mistakes, but on the innocent.
>
> (E. 1961: 11–12)

Einaudi never forsook his claim of the value of (economic) science for political action and society. He would return specifically to this point later in the conclusions added to the present essay, but in a different context in which his reflections broaden out to extend from economic science to the value of science and reason in general and to the relation between science and philosophy (with an implicitly polemical stance towards Croce: par. 4.3):

> learning how to use the power of reasoning, to contemplate the external world with open and discerning eyes, to replace mere intuition and wonderment with critical reasoning, and to move towards an attitude whereby impulsive – i.e. irrational – behavior gives way to a different behavioral mode in which human action is preceded by conscious specification of it aims: does not all this constitute the true value of science?
>
> (p. 90)

The essay *Morale et économique* elicited a number of comments, in particular from Bruguier Pacini (1936), Passerin d'Entrèves (1937) and Croce, and it cannot be ruled out that such comments may have lain at the root of the second thoughts

Einaudi voiced in subsequent years. Among such second thoughts, a prominent role is awarded to the critique by Pacini, who had already expressed doubts concerning the position of indifference and neutrality Einaudi had espoused in the essay in question:

> in Einaudi the sense of concrete reality is far too vivid to stifle the echoes of the thousands of voices of his day. [. . .] Here he is no arid theoretician closeted within the perimeter of his theorems [. . .]: rather, he is engrossed in thought, a man steeped in awareness of the great drama of humankind [and of the evils of the latter, a man for whom] it becomes the subject of his most profound, intense, human empathy.
>
> (Bruguier Pacini 1936: 708)

At the same time, Einaudi had also received praise from Croce for his 'critical attitude' towards Del Vecchio, a 'terribly unsophisticated brain, who is therefore incapable of realizing that the *science of economics is science and not philosophy*' (Croce, Einaudi 1988: 87 (italics mine)). As we will see, Einaudi ended up calling into question the dualism between economic science and philosophy: an issue that led him to rewrite the conclusions of the present essay (Afterword, par. 3.2).

Here it is worth noting that in this process of rewriting, when Einaudi once more pondered on the question of value judgments, he ended up revealing the reasons behind his defense of economic science and, implicitly, the rhetorical or discursive strategy of the position of indifference and neutrality held during the 1930s:

> this indifference, which is the essence of the scientist's garb, is the most fundamental – indeed I would say the one and only – defense available to economists in their attempt to impede charlatans and lackeys from bursting into their field. [. . .] What tool is available to economists to defend themselves – and thus all other men as well – against charlatans and lackeys? Precisely that of adopting a position of indifference vis-à-vis the ends.
>
> (p. 86)

With regard to the claim that the economist studies the pure fact of choice, without making any evaluation as to the ends pursued in human action, it might be worth noting that never before had Einaudi's position ended up resembling Pareto's position so closely as in this essay on Robbins. And perhaps it is not by chance that, years later, Fasiani pointed to Einaudi's essay on Robbins as his reference model of "neutrality" of science (Fasiani 1951: 9, footnote). Perhaps this was the only aspect of Einaudian discourse through which Fasiani could recognise his master (and himself), even though mainly (if not exclusively) interpreted through a Paretian lens (Fasiani 1951: 7, footnote). Indeed, it is likely that Fasiani never understood that Einaudi was using Robbins's methodological discourse in defense of economics. In this regard, we cannot exclude that the aforementioned quote by Einaudi on 'indifference' (the 'scientist's garb') was also a sort of confession addressed to Fasiani who believed that in *MPJT* his master had really "changed" his methodological position.

Moreover, Einaudi ended by claiming that it is not always possible to put ends and values into brackets if one wants to fully grasp the meaning of human action, the societal order and all the implications and consequences of policy making (par. 4.2 and Afterword, par. 3.1).

3 The debate with Fasiani (1938–1943): From *Myths and paradoxes of justice in taxation* to the present essay

The simplest (albeit not the only) way of interpreting the present essay is to consider it an epistemological explanation and a further development of *MPJT* and, accordingly, a continuation and subsequent conclusion of the debate with Fasiani, sparked shortly after the publication of the first edition of *MPJT* (E. 1938b), which Fasiani had criticized for adopting 'an anti-scientific mode of proceeding' (p. 66). It was a critique that Einaudi perceived as a sort of excommunication.

Einaudi's exchange of ideas with Fasiani is of such profound importance that it can justifiably be considered as the methodological "epilogue" (Bellanca 1993, Fossati 2014b) of the Italian tradition in public finance, yet it has received little attention, save for a few exceptions (Da Empoli 2010: 97–98; Forte 2009: 77–80; Fossati 2011, 2012, 2014a, 2014b; Fossati, Silvestri 2012), despite the fact the Einaudi devoted great effort to the interpretation and critical appraisal of Fasiani's works.[10] Indeed, in terms of the intensity of the debate and the number of writings devoted to Fasiani, his critical engagement with the latter was second only to his debates with a select number of thinkers who were his contemporaries, including Keynes, Croce and Griziotti. Furthermore, among these thinkers, only Fasiani severely criticized the methodological approach adopted by Einaudi in *MPJT*, which, up to the very end, he considered one of his most successful (and perhaps best loved) books.

The controversy with Fasiani gave rise to an array of intricate and, sometimes, overlapping issues. In order to help the reader better understand how Einaudi's thought evolved up to the rewriting of the present essay, I will first provide an overview of the Einaudi–Fasiani debate, with specific reference to the demarcation issue (par. 3.1). Then I will analytically subdivide its main issues as follows: the demarcation between counsels and theorems, normative and theoretical language, and the issue of their reciprocal translatability (par. 3.2), the distinction between science and history and the supposed detached or dispassionate knowledge of the economist (par. 3.3), the epistemological nature of the types of state used by Fasiani as compared to the 'historical' schemata of good/bad polities used by Einaudi (par. 3.4) (to which I will dedicate a broader consideration in the Afterword).

3.1 An overview: The demarcation issue

To understand the main issues of the debate with Fasiani that led Einaudi to write the present essay, it is worth recalling the epistemological background, mainly Paretian,[11] in the name of which Fasiani (see, above all, Fasiani 1949 [2007])[12] elaborated his major methodological critiques of Einaudi – namely, the great positivistic demarcation between *science* and *non-science*. In this perspective, "science" was not only 'the search for laws and uniformities' (Fasiani 1951: 5), but also the reign of reason, logic-experimental, positive, neutrality, measurable, objective and factual, while non-science was the reign of metaphysics, ethics, politics, normative economics, counsels, precepts, value judgments, passions, sentiments, beliefs, faiths, projects and "practical" aims, i.e. political and/or ethical aims, all the way to the irrational. In turn, this conception of science, largely derived from the analogy between economic science and natural sciences, implied the identification of the economist with 'physicists', 'chemists' or 'astronomers' (Fasiani 1951: 6).

Here it is important to recall this demarcation issue for several reasons.

First of all, because of Einaudi's debate with Fasiani, his reflections at the beginning of the 1940s, the paragraphs of the first part dedicated to normative and theoretical language and almost the entire third part of both the first edition and the present essay can be understood as an attempt to critically assess, clarify and disambiguate some of the terms of the aforementioned dichotomy and to rescue some of the terms of the non-science side of the dichotomy from the negativity to which they were condemned. In this regard, one of the most significant accomplishments of Einaudi's reflections was to show that the demarcation line between the two sides of the dichotomy was all but a clear-cut line (see Afterword, par. 3).

Although the Einaudi–Fasiani debate took place long before the post-Popperian debates aimed at introducing a solid demarcation criterion in economics[13] and the positive-normative distinction implied in the Einaudi–Fasiani debate seems to be much closer to the traditional distinction between economics and ethics than to logical positivism,[14] it is in my view important to stress that one of Einaudi's main concerns was the rhetorical or even dogmatic use of science and the resulting logic of *excommunication* for anything that is labelled as non-science (see Bobbio 1973: 6, Silvestri 2016). Einaudi's awareness, in this regard, cannot be overlooked since it is also connected to his awareness of the issue of language of science. For example, one cannot overlook Einaudi's remark in his review of Fasiani's *Principii*, according to which the *Scienza delle finanze* 'took the name of "science" only to give a name to the chair created in the Faculty of law in Italy' (E. 1942a: 36). In my view, this statement was addressed to Fasiani not only because Fasiani believed that he was really building up a science, while Einaudi believed that in public economics 'there is something that rebels against the scientific construction', but also because, in the name of a certain conception of science, Fasiani excommunicated Einaudi's research in *MPJT*.

Second, Einaudi had criticized the Pareto–Fasiani conception of science and the economists ever since his review of Fasiani's *Principii* by adopting the rhetorical strategy of "using" Pareto, the 'combative fighters' in the public sphere, against Pareto himself and, at the same time, against Fasiani's Paretian notion of science and the impersonal detachment of the scientist (par. 3.3). Einaudi repeated this critique from the very beginning of the present essay (p. 38). With considerable simplification, it could be said that the distance separating Einaudi from Pareto (and Fasiani) is equal to that which, over time, separated Pareto from himself: the Pareto of the *Cours*, from the Pareto of the *Manual*. The Pareto whom Einaudi admired was almost always exclusively the first. As has been effectively summarized,

> in the *Cours* the political passions and liberal battles of Pareto are clearly present, the pure analysis of the world is mixed with political concern for the Italian situation. In the *Cours*, Pareto writes not only for his fellow scholars, but also for the media, for the policy maker, maybe with the hope of converting them to the correct use of reason. In the *Manual* all of this is abandoned, with the feeling of repentance for a sin of youth. The economist, biologist-like, deals with human beings as if they were ants, mushrooms, or grass, taking the place of the engaged scientist. From the pure theory all sentiments are taken away; all metaphysics is expelled from science.
>
> (Bruni, Montesano 2009: 2)

The distance between Einaudi and Pareto replicates the distance between Einaudi and Fasiani, as Fasiani himself well understood: 'You [Einaudi] *feel* you speak of things concerning men, while I reason about them as if they were ants or bees' (Lett.: Fasiani to E., June 1938, in Fossati, Silvestri 2012: 72).

Moreover, Einaudi's insistence (particularly developed in the third part of the present essay) on addressing the demarcation issue between science and non-science, with specific reference to his attempt to legitimate the study of the ends of human choices within the dominion of economic science, may be understood, in my view, if one considers the already mentioned Fasianian critique of Einaudi in the name of Pareto's epistemology. Pareto, through the discovery of the pure and 'naked fact of choice' (Pareto 1900 [1953]), re-founded economics, distinguishing the economic field from the social (non-economical) field through the distinction between logical actions (means-end rationality) and non-logical actions, which were in the domain, respectively, of economics and sociology (Pareto 1916 [1964]).[15] In Pareto's epistemology, there is a structural analogy between the positivistic demarcation science/non-science and logical/non-logical categories (Albert 2004). In this regard, by attacking the alleged detachment or indifference of the economist towards the ends of choices, Einaudi was also trying to defend his own enquiry into the causes of good and bad polities – an enquiry where the values and motifs implied by human choices played a fundamental role in understanding good and bad societies, state and non-state (see Afterword).

Last but not least, the shift of emphasis impressed by Einaudi on the rewriting of the conclusions, with reference to his intention to address the demarcation between science and philosophy (see par. 4.3, and Afterword, par. 3.2) can be interpreted as a further exploration and variation on the issue of demarcation.

In a nutshell, and to resort (with a bit of a stretch) to a useful distinction introduced by Mongin, we may assert that Fasiani's position was that of "strong neutrality" – thus "normative economics is illegitimate" – while Einaudi's position was much closer to a "weak non-neutrality" position – thus "economics cannot be entirely neutral", and value judgments cannot always be disentangled from facts and from the overall judgment regarding a situation analyzed by the econo-mist" (Mongin 2006, but see also Baujard 2013).

As to the evolution of Einaudi's thought, that can be traced by examining the debate with Fasiani, by drawing up an extremely simplified overview of such a debate – which, nevertheless, can be helpful to grasp the meaning of the title of the present essay – it can be reduced to two main moments.

At the beginning, it was Fasiani who criticized Einaudi's *MPJT* (1938b). In par-ticular, he pointed out the contradiction between Einaudi's initial admonishment, addressed to economists, in which he favoured a scientific and neutral stance against political interests and discouraged giving counsels to the powerful (read-ing between the lines: to the fascist regime) and his concluding search for good government. This was a quest which, in Fasiani's view, went well beyond the bor-ders of science, thus describing not what *is* but what *ought* to be (Lett.: Fasiani to E., April 1938, in Fossati, Silvestri 2012: 59; Lett.: Fasiani to E., June 19, 1938).

Later, the publication of Fasiani's *Principles* (1941), represented a definitive turning point in Einaudi's reflection: he had become clearly aware that the scien-tific and neutral stance of the economist and his claim of referring only to facts may not only conceal his value-ladenness but, above all, could end up by legitimating the powerful. This was Einaudi's attitude towards the types of state introduced by Fasiani, defined as the 'modern state' – that in which 'power is exercised with due concern for the interests of the public group, considered as a unit' (Fasiani 1941, I: 42) – and towards Fasiani's claim to take the ends of the ruling class as a mere *'fact*, a *given'* (Fasiani 1941, II: 59–60, here p. 75). In Einaudi's view, such a type of state runs the risk – by representing 'that which is', thus the organicism of the corporative and nationalist fascist state[16] – of playing into the hands of the regime, if not indeed of legitimating it. By the same token, the attitude of consid-ering the ends of the ruling class as a mere fact or given, without any possibility of criticizing them (at least through a technical critique of values), risks turning the economist into the '*emperor's advocate*' (p. 78).

One might almost say that over time, this exchange of views became, as it were, a pretext for Einaudi by enabling him to state his views more explicitly and to reformulate his ideas more clearly (and thereby, first and foremost, to clarify the issues in his own mind). In particular, it allowed a specific focus on his epistemo-logical reflection and his related defense of economic science during the fascist era. At the same time it enabled him to outline his own position in the Italian tra-dition of public finance and the epistemological meaning of his enquiry into the causes of good and bad polities.

This shift of emphasis is more noticeable above all else in the rewriting process that led to the present essay: both in the added note (note 1, p. 65) at the beginning of the second part (*On Some Abstract Hypotheses Concerning the State and on Their Historical Value*), where Einaudi specifies that his observations reflect his own personal interpretation of the types of state portrayed by Fasiani (and by De Viti De Marco), and also in the elimination of sizeable portions of the text which, in the first edition of this second part (§ 9, 10, 11), were explicitly devoted to the earlier debate with Fasiani.

Furthermore, the publication of Fasiani's *Principii* (1941) had already prompted Einaudi to seek to give a clearer account of the epistemological nature of the political-economic and 'historical schemas' of good/bad polities he had used in the two final chapters added to the second edition of *MPJT* and to explain how his position differed from that found in Fasiani's schemas of a state.

In this regard, it is important to recall that these two final chapters, significantly titled 'The Supreme Taxation Paradox' (i.e. the problem of taxation as "coercion") and 'Historical Schemas and Ideal Schemas', are fundamental for an understanding of the present essay. As has recently been discovered (Fossati, Silvestri 2012), the methodological (though not exclusively methodological) reflections put forward by Einaudi in the conclusions of *MPJT* were themselves also an outcome of the debate with Fasiani. They can effectively be seen as an attempt to rework Fasiani's critique of the first edition of *MPJT* (E. 1938b), while, however, setting such critiques within the broader framework of the more long-standing legal-political and philosophical speculation on the theory of the elite and liberal good government and good society, which was further developed in the second and third part of the first edition as well as in the present essay (see Afterword).

Last but not least, it is worth recalling the other shift of emphasis, mainly spurred by Einaudi's interlocutors, that might have led him to give less importance to the debate with Fasiani and, at the same time, to enlarge his reflection: namely the demarcation, established by Croce after the unfruitful epistemological debate with Pareto, between philosophy and science (and economic science in particular), which had deeply marked the epistemology of social sciences in Italy and interrupted the communication routes between philosophers and economists.

3.2 Counsels and theorems: Normative and theoretical language and their reciprocal translatability

Fasiani confessed he was particularly hurt by the arguments Einaudi adduced in *MPJT* (E. 1938b) in defense of 'literary economists' and against Pareto's 'self-importance' – where Einaudi implicitly refers to the hot debate on the *Paretaio* (Jannacone 1912, Sensini 1912).[17] Years later, this debate would be recalled by Einaudi himself for the 'anti-historical tone with which [Pareto] treated great economists' rather badly, and for Pareto's 'intolerance' and dogmatism against anyone who did not think like him (E. 1928b [1933]: 101–102, n.).[18]

Fasiani felt that his "scientific self" was under attack. As a counter-reaction, he criticized Einaudi, signalling that his master had now set off on the path of "projects" and "counsels" that were not science.

According to Einaudi,

> it all began, unfortunately, with Pareto, a consummate scientist, when he adopted a supercilious attitude to the so-called literary economists, contending that they were giving an imperfect vernacular rendering of theorems which others, among whom Walras and Pareto himself, later expounded afresh in a more rigorous and perfected form, or else that by adopting a discursive form

they were using normative rather than theoretical terminology. While admiring those who, standing dispassionately on one side and almost aloof from the world, have the ability to preserve rigorous or theoretical terminology from the beginning to the end of their essays or books, I myself cannot share the facile scornfulness displayed by certain figures among their ranks towards poor fellows – some bearing names such as Galiani or Smith or Ricardo or Ferrara! – who were not schooled in mathematics or who, passionately concerned with the things of this world, acting as men among men, moved seamlessly from purely theoretical to normative language and gave counsels, provided men with guidelines for good behavior and outlined programs of action. Down with self-importance and haughtiness! What is important is not the dress in which a truth is attired, but the truth itself.

(E. 1938b: 256–257)

In this regard Fasiani complained to Einaudi of the

offenses you have inflicted on the Paretian position, which is also mine. I am exceedingly aggrieved, because if the theoretical form in question is abandoned, consoling oneself with the persuasion that the preceptistic form can be translated into that form, then the path of logic is inexorably doomed to lose its way.

(Lett.: Fasiani to E., June 24, 1938)

The issue was taken up again by Einaudi both at the beginning of the present essay (§ 2) – where his critique of Pareto's critique of literary economists is reformulated in anthropological terms as to the relation between language and passions, or the 'other and perhaps better part' of the whole man – and in § 5, in an attempt to better clearify the relation between counsels and theorems, normative language and theoretical or hypothetical language ("if X then Y"). Their relation is usually examined by Einaudi in two complementary ways: a) chrono-logical-genetic – namely, economic science was originally expressed in the form of counsels, subsequently transformed or "enrobed" in scientific, theoretical or hypothetical garb – and b) logical-linguistic – namely, normative and theoretical propositions are mutually translatable (which is a claim that Einaudi shared with the philosopher Giovanni Vailati[19]). As noted earlier, it was this second claim that became the main target of Fasiani's critique.

In Einaudi's view, recognising the possibility of such a translation fulfilled at least two functions: a) as a warning addressed to whoever claimed to have discovered something new, in that such pretensions often turned out to be little more than a reformulation, using a different language, of thoughts already expressed by other thinkers, and b) a pedagogic function that involved learning how to distinguish one language from another to 'inculcate the need to define concepts very clearly, to clarify the premises of an argument, to avoid mistaking action for a historical or sociological explanation of action, and the analysis of its causes for its effects' (E. 1940b [1945]: 532).

This notwithstanding, one sometimes has the impression that Einaudi tended to use the translatability of normative propositions into theoretical propositions for defensive purposes. Anticipating the charge of having written in a preceptive and therefore non-scientific form, Einaudi's typical reply was that it would suffice to translate his "counsels" into the form "if X, then Y" to guarantee their "scientific-ity" (see also E. 1949a: XVI).

However, Einaudi seems to realise that there is a limit to translatability, for he does not go so far as to maintain 'that the ancient and modern *precepts* can always be so easily translated into theoretical principles' (p. 43). Nevertheless, he does not specify the *when* and *why* of the impossibility of translating (we will see that Fasiani, focusing on the same point, attempts to be more precise by invoking none other than Pareto himself).

One might thus surmise that Einaudi's interest focused on a different aspect pertaining to the limits of translatabilty: when the 'translation is impossible' and it has been 'demonstrated that the proposition has no scientific meaning in the field of economic science', this need not mean that such a proposition is a *non-sense*: quite the opposite, it will have 'meaning from some other point of view, e.g. polit-ical, juridical or social' (Einaudi 1940b [1945]: 532). This testifies to Einaudi's awareness that all the social sciences are established by a language, which in turn establishes a "point of view" of the world. Such a realization explains why Ein-audi warned against the "excommunications" uttered by "schools" of thought – as often happened between the approaches of the different "schools" of the Italian tradition of public finance – or by whoever claims to have a privileged vantage point over the world; accordingly, his admonishments warned against

> [discussions] on the political, economic, sociological and juridical character of financial investigations if the comments are designed to inflict an amusing excommunication on those who take pleasure in studying a problem from a perspective distinct from that laid down by the heads of the so-called political, economic, sociological and juridical schools in the field of financial studies.
>
> (Einaudi [1940b] 1948: 533)

Later, after the publication of the first edition of the present essay, Fasiani resumed the debate with Einaudi, taking up a position in defense of Pareto. Fasiani was particularly keen to point out to his master that Pareto was perfectly 'aware of the possibility of translating a proposition starting "*one must*" into another propo-sition starting "*if one wishes*"' and he added,

> to seriously think that Pareto or any other ever dreamt to deny all this, or believed they had invented everything, after carrying out a series of such translations is to tilt against the largest windmills I have ever come across.
>
> (Fasiani 1949 [2007]: 282)

To clarify the point, Fasiani brought up again Pareto's arguments:

> political economy tells us that bad money drives out good money. This prop-osition is of a scientific kind, and it is only up to science to check if it is true or

false. But if one said that the State must not issue bad money, one would have a proposition that would have nothing to do with science. [Nevertheless, this proposition] could be elliptical, and in this case it would become scientific, if the ellipsis were to be aptly eliminated. For example, if one wishes to obtain maximum utility for the society, and if what is meant by that maximum utility were defined through facts, then the proposition would become susceptible of experimental verification and would therefore be scientific.

(Pareto 1906, §§ 39–40, quoted from Fasiani 1949 [2007]: 281)

On this particular issue, the differences between Fasiani and Einaudi seemed almost to fade, although neither the one nor the other delved more deeply into the crux of a problem that sprang from this very same Paretian argument – namely, who decides whether a given proposition is "elliptical"? This decision always pre-supposes a certain dose of *interpretation*, if not indeed of discretionary decision-making power on the part of whoever performs the translation.

Moreover, Einaudi's main concern as to the issue of counsels and the polemic on literary economists seems to hide two problems: how is the "good" counsel distinguished from the "bad" counsel? What is the foundation of the excommuni-cation of passionate language from the realm of science? In Einaudi's reflection, these two questions seem to be connected in the following way: the bad counsels are those having 'the aim of achieving advantages for themselves or for a social class or professional group or of currying favor with the powerful or the common crowds' (p. 42), but such an aim may be pursued and *masked* precisely by those who claim a purification of the language and a dispassionate stance of scientific neutrality or indifference. It is also in this sense that, in my view, one may inter-pret the sentence concluding § 2 as an implicit warning to Fasiani: '[those who are] incapable of perceiving the links between the two aspects of the whole per-son, construct insipid theory and supply the counsels they know will find favor with the powerful' (p. 38).

Finally, as we have seen (par. 2.1), Einaudi constantly ascribed to economic science the possibility of providing counsels on the basis of its cognitive strength. There is no doubt, however, that Einaudi's language is full of *pathos* (Della Valle 2010)[20] and that, in this regard, by trying to save the language of counsels, he was also trying to defend himself and at the same time trying to save passions, which had been condemned to a sort of epistemological and anthropological clandestin-ity by Pareto and Fasiani in the name of a presumed and unjustified superiority of science and reason.

What is worth noting, however, is that Fasiani did not embark on a critical examination of the polemical issue of literary economists, which, however, was the question that seemed to be of greater interest to Einaudi, as would appear to emerge from his last letter written to Fasiani after reading the essay by the latter on Pareto. In Einaudi's vision, the crucial question was to gain insight into the reasons behind Pareto's 'scorn' (Lett.: E. to Fasiani, June 25, 1949)[21] for the liter-ary economists, given that his expostulations sounded surprisingly like excom-munications. And as we have seen, Einaudi regarded these excommunications as unjustifiable, both from an epistemological perspective – the plurality of points of view – and, above all, from an anthropological perspective – the whole man.

3.3 Science and history and the (alleged) detachment of the scholar

Einaudi has often been remembered for his sense of history and the concrete, as well as for his continuous attempts to fertilize a fruitful exchange between history and theory in economics. In Schumpeter's words, at a time when Italian economics 'was second to none', Einaudi was a representative of the 'historical or empirical work, which in Italy made a seminal contribution to general economics and did not enter [. . .] into conflict with theory' (Schumpeter 1954: 855).[22] Moreover, by writing many works on economic history, 'Einaudi was probably [among Italian twentieth-century economists] the one most open and receptive to the themes of history' (Romeo 1974: 93). In effect, in his approach to applied economics, Einaudi considered history the "great ally" of economic theory (Forte, Marchionatti 2012: 599–608).

All these meanings and uses of history are touched upon in various ways by Einaudi in the present essay. Yet at the same time, another Einaudian meaning of history can be found here. It concerns the selective and reconstructive gaze of the historian, in addition to history as the reign of the individual. Both these interpretations are used by Einaudi against scientific-sociological approaches to history, economics or public finance, as also against any naïve conception of *facts* taken as "that which is":

> history does not lend itself to being reduced to schemata and uniform types. [. . .] History is made up of individual facts, single events, not of types. To be sure, the historian must have an idea, a guiding thread that prompts him to choose the individual facts he deems to be most important amongst the innumerable facts and trivia that are devoid of any real importance or any importance at all.
>
> (p. 48)

This quote, drawn from § 8 of the present essay (but see also E. 1936d: 155), refers implicitly to Einaudi's previous critique of the ambiguous or undecided nature of Fasiani's type of state: between history and theory (see Afterword, par. 1.2), which was formulated by Einaudi in the review devoted to Fasiani's *Principii*.

Einaudi's review bore the telling title *Scienza e storia, o dello stacco dello studioso dalla cosa studiata* [Science and History, or on the Scholar's Detachment from the Question Studied] (E. 1942a), which also reflects the turning point in Einaudi's reflections of the 1940s (par. 4). For the moment, we will restrict the discussion to what appear to be Einaudi's two main critical observations, which were distinct yet linked. Fasiani professed a dispassionate and a value-free conception of the economic scientist, yet he 1) did not consistently adhere to this conception, betraying that he too, like every human being, had passions and ideals and 2) failed to realize that it was precisely these 'sentiments' that guided his research and, *in primis*, the configuration and choice of the types of state on which he founded his subsequent hypothetical-deductive arguments pertaining to the effects of taxation. Fasiani, Einaudi felt, was pursuing the aim of

> standing back dispassionately – almost as if he were living in a world beyond the human dimension – from the passions, sentiment and ideals that so dramatically affect the motions and emotions of men. The same proposals have been put forward by others; and one's mind immediately goes to the great theorist [Pareto] who sought to build, on this same basis, a "General sociology",[23] of which the present [Fasiani's] "Financial sociology" is presumed to be a chapter. But where in Vilfredo Pareto one discerns, under the detachment of the pure scientist, the ardent and passional spirit of a man who [had fought] the liberist fight, [or opposed] the predominance of the divisive and disruptive forces that threatened [. . .] Europe [. . .], in Fasiani one finds no trace whatsoever of political or moral passion.
>
> (E. 1942a: 32)

This notwithstanding, Einaudi pointed out that a number of Fasiani's references

> to the troubles of the present time [. . .] or to political ideals ("The nation state represents the final and most vivid expression of the evolution of European civilization", Fasiani 1941: I, 55) would seem to suggest that Fasiani is a man among men and suffers and cherishes hopes like all other men, [. . .] [as also shown by the] dedication to the two brothers "who fell for Italy" [. . .] [Therefore the] detachment imposed upon him by the scientific imperative must have cost him, like any other man strongly swayed by sentiment, a far from trifling effort.
>
> (ivi: 32–33)

Perhaps Einaudi was seeking to 'unmask' – as also noticed later by Solari (see Editorial Foreword) – what seemed to him to be his pupil's 'political' passion for the 'nation state' or fascist corporatism,[24] or at the very least to bring him face-to-face with the responsibility for the choice of an ideal type that would represent such a state as a starting schema of his arguments. And it should be recalled that a few years earlier, Fasiani had confessed to Einaudi his 'grave disagreement' with De Viti and his criticism of the "cooperative state" advocated by the latter, which Fasiani saw as a representation of the liberal state – a form he regarded as dead and gone forever (whereas Einaudi believed it should be rebuilt on new foundations):

> even if he does not say so forthrightly, De Viti sets out his argument as if the liberal organization were the final stage of social evolution: whereas for it is *one* stage, *one* historical moment, and a *short* moment, which will not

be repeated. Therefore, scientifically speaking, his is a theory (of rudimental approximation) of that which was, and it is of little use in explaining that which is.

(Lett.: Fasiani to E., December 18, 1937)

Thus Einaudi's review of Fasiani's book, although written in the style of the benevolent master who chides his pupil and gives him suggestions for future developments of his work, seems to contain – reading between the lines – a much sterner and more severe admonishment: the type defined as the "modern state" introduced by Fasiani – described as the state in which 'power is exercised with due concern for the interests of the public group, considered as a unit' (Fasiani 1941: I, 42) – by representing the organicism of the corporative and nationalist fascist state as "that which is" runs the risk of legitimating such a regime.

Otherwise stated, the following would seem to have been Einaudi's real concern: the aim, as pursued by Fasiani, of making public finance into a "scientific theory", taken here in the sense of neutral or value-free, in order to "explain *that which is*", in the fascist era cannot but mean "explaining" or describing the one and only *present* reality – namely, fascism. But for Einaudi, explaining, representing, talking about and giving visibility to the fascist state through a theory of the types of state was quite a different matter from opting not to speak of it at all, or speaking of alternative political-social types, as he did in *MPJT*. Words, Einaudi believed, especially if uttered in the public sphere, carry a weight of their own and are always potentially capable of producing communicative, normative or performative effects (see also Afterword, par. 1.2).

Accordingly, in drawing up a commentary on Fasiani's types of state in a note of the first edition of the present essay, Einaudi appears to have endeavored to be even more explicit (albeit still within the limits of what could be said against fascism[25]). Einaudi wrote that he intended to 'abstain' from the 'equivocal' use of those 'adjectives' and 'synonyms' utilized by Fasiani to characterize the types of state. For Einaudi, the "liberal" state was not the same thing as the "cooperative" state, because the former had 'a far broader and more complex content than the adjective *cooperative*', and the latter a content more appropriate (from the point of view of public finance) for indicating the 'economic' aspect of the state. Analogously, the "modern" state was by no means the same as "nationalist" or "corporative", since the latter was 'limited to a phenomenon within our own country', while the nation states, contrary to the claim put forward by Fasiani, appeared to be something from the past that was dying out 'in comparison to modern tendencies towards the great ultranational political groupings'. Therefore, only in reference to these new political entities should one speak of "modern" states (Einaudi 1942–1943 [2014a]: 302, note 7). Here Einaudi not only refers to his prophetic reflection on the European federation as the only solution to the crisis of the dogma of sovereignty, meant as the legal-political foundation of nation states (1943b),[26] but also to the fact, as he wrote in another essay, that Fasiani's characteristics of the state (partly derived from Seligman 1926) seem to uncritically introduce the 'dogma' of state sovereignty into public economics, thus assuming such a dogma as a mere given (E. 1942e).

In actual fact, Fasiani, building on the Paretian conceptual framework, had also given two more concise and technical definitions of the two types of state: '*cooperative* being that in which the governing class aspires to a maximum of utility *for* society, and *modern* that in which those in power aspire to a maximum of utility *of* society' (E. 1942–43 [2014]: 303n.). Furthermore, at a later date, after Einaudi pointed out the aforementioned terminological "ambiguities", Fasiani would subsequently proceed to eliminate them in the second edition of his *Principii* (Fasiani 1951: 53, note 12), which was rewritten after fascism had fallen. Here "modern state" would be replaced by "tutorial state", in which he placed greater emphasis on the two technical concepts of maximum of utility *for* society and *of* society. However, the third volume of *Principii* in which Fasiani was planning to deal with the characteristics of the "modern" state in greater detail would never be composed, on account of his untimely death.

However, quite apart from the technical concepts of maximum of utility *for* society and *of* society, the aspects that most greatly interested (and worried) Einaudi, as we have seen, involved the role (and the responsibility) of the economist in the public sphere when an economist seeks to "describe" the behavior of the ruling class and summarize it in a type of state.

3.4 Abstract versus historical schemata of state

It is also worth highlighting here three further points of Einaudi's review of Fasiani's book, which, in many respects, prefigure the arguments developed in the second part both of the first edition and of the present essay.

First, the critique of Fasiani's types of state for their historical-theoretical ambiguity – thus their undecided nature between the historical and the abstract – and second, their internal contradiction or a "flaw" of self-confutation:

> they are historical because they endeavour to give a synopsis of a set of uniformities capable of being repeated at different times and in different countries. They are theoretical precisely because they do not intend to refer to a given time and place; on the contrary, they rule out that there has ever been created during the course of history a state which fully conforms to the "type". Yet they wish to portray what a state would be like if its essential characteristics were taken to the limit. The difficulties of the investigation are extremely severe. I do not know, apart from the definition and a brief contrast with the cooperative type, what Fasiani's "modern" state is supposed to consist of, and therefore nothing can be said about it at all. But the two types of the monopolistic and the cooperative state have within themselves, in my view, the fatal flaw of their own denial. The former seems to me to live for the purpose of destroying itself, while the second for the purpose of dissolving into the single individuals that compose it.
> (Einaudi 1942a: 35–36)

Third, but not least in importance, Einaudi also seized the opportunity to high-light the difference between such schemata and his own "financial typology of states" that he had developed in the final chapter, 'Historical Schemata and Ideal Schemata', added to the second edition of *MPJT*.

> [In my] financial typology of states [I described the types] of the Greek tyrant, the Periclean city, Bourbon finance, Cavourrian finance and that of Wicksell, otherwise known as that of compromise and accession. But what I drew up were schemata that conformed to a given historical situation in a given coun-try, and only the last one intended to depict the tendency of the states that Le Play termed "prosperous".
>
> (Einaudi 1942a: 35)

In *MPJT*, Einaudi had started out on a search for ideal types of state and of finance, but in order to avoid the charge of utopianism, he coupled them with his-torical experiences which, albeit exceptional, had genuinely existed.

Fasiani had raised the objection that precisely because such types referred to unique historical experiences and special political conditions, they could not be treated in terms of scientific generalizations. That typology 'is none other than a way to cast in fine suasive literary garb all the teachings Einaudi wants to impose' (Lett.: Fasiani to E., June 12, 1942).

This critique obliged Einaudi to provide a better epistemological account of his historical enquiry into the causes of good and bad polity, later reformulated in terms of the dialectical contrast between state and non-state, based on a historical-anthropological foundation. To this aspect he devoted almost the entire second part of the present essay. I will return to this in greater detail in the Afterword.

4 The turning point of the 1940s: The issue of value judgments

In order to understand the entire evolution of Einaudi's thought that led to the present essay, it is now necessary to analyze the most significant steps and turning points of the 1940s. Among them, I will take into account Einaudi's reflection on the historicity of economics and the "passionate economist"; the nearest anteced-ent of the present essay, which contains Einaudi's explicit confession of his sec-ond thoughts as to the issue of value judgments; the epistemological aspects of the debate with Croce on the relation between liberalism and liberism, which is also important for understanding the rewriting of the conclusions of the present essay.

4.1 Historicity of economics and the "passionate economist"

In Einaudi's reflection, the awareness that the economist cannot always put in brackets the issue of values represented a true turning point. This became clear in Einaudi's mind when Cabiati published an article that reopened the so-called Socialist Calculation Debate (Cabiati 1940),[27] which years earlier had seen the participation of a number of protagonists, including Barone, Mises and Hayek (Hayek 1935). Cabiati, adopting the Barone–Pareto line, had insisted that the logical and mathematical demonstration of the possibility of a collectivist economy was in no way flawed. In this regard, Einaudi stated his position in the essay *Le premesse del ragionamento economico e la realtà storica* [The Premises of Economic Reasoning and the Historical Reality] (E. 1940c). The essay marked the beginning of a profound rethinking of his earlier epistemological reflection and put forward two main arguments.

First, he called for renewed attention to the "historicity" nature of economic science and of the economist, contending that the very premises or the first postulates of economic science arose in specific historical contexts and therefore could not be transferred into other contexts (such as communist Russia) without the risk of making a travesty of such premises or postulates. But this, in turn, implied abandoning the presumed universality of economic science and the corresponding conception of the neutral observer.

In this regard, Einaudi went as far as to maintain – in strong agreement with Röpke's perspective (*Die Gesellschaftskrisis der Gegenwart* [*The Social Crisis of our Time*]) (1942) – that the claim to construct an argument *sub specie aeternitatis* is a fiction devised by economists, who, however, tend to lose track of its fictive character, so that the premises of value on which the very argument is based are sidelined and relegated to a position within brackets (Einaudi, 1942b: 51–52).

Secondly, he maintained that even if the quantitative tools and the logic of economic science were to succeed in demonstrating the possibility of collectivism, other far more serious problems would still be disregarded – namely, authoritarianism and the 'denial of all freedoms' that a communist system of such a kind would need in order to be able to function. This is why, Einaudi went on, 'economic science cannot restrict itself [to mere calculation of the means] but rather, is irresistibly obliged to question itself about the problem of the ends' (E. 1940c: 199).

Finally, a significant indication of the epistemological revision Einaudi was undertaking during those years can be found in his insistence on the *genetic* moment of theories. Turning his attention in this direction, Einaudi had gradually moved towards a more favourable reappraisal of a) the historical-social context from which the premises of theories or reasoning were drawn – the *ifs* of a hypothetico-deductive reasoning (p. 72) and b) the subjective point of view of the scholar in the very act of "feeling" the problem: as Einaudi wrote, following a work by Passerin d'Entrèves (1939), who in turn was guided by the Crocean historicism and his notion of 'historical judgment', there is always something 'spiritual' or axiological in the very act of the scholar who captures the problem (E. 1939).

This also led Einaudi to a more open opposition against the devaluation of the *passional, faith, beliefs* and *"Weltanschauung"*, which were considered as if they were non-science, irrational or simply meaningless. Emblematic of the reflections of those years is the essay *Sismondi economista appassionato* [*Sismondi, Passionate Economist*] (E. 1941c). Here Einaudi talks about Sismondi, but he is also talking about himself: 'his gaze was directed above all towards concrete reality, which he experienced passionately. His analysis of the concrete was passional; he was very sensitive to human suffering'. Here passion becomes, as it were, the 'limit' 'of application of abstract truths', but also their *possibility condition*: that which had allowed Sismondi to 'see that "a" problem existed' (ivi: 127–134) – the very problem which, through its solution, gives rise to theories.

As Einaudi wrote, in the pages added to § 22 in which part of these earlier reflections were implicitly recalled, even the most theoretical or abstract economist (as Fasiani claimed to be) were 'drawn to economic science by their feeling of *human* involvement in the problems they found themselves addressing' (p. 73).

Einaudi's insistence on the economist's *Weltanschauung* – which, in some respects, may be paralleled to Shumpeter's (1949) reflection on 'Ideology' or pre-analytical assumptions – did not imply that the ensuing analysis made by the economist is to be considered entirely normative or vitiated by value judgments, since the economist can always reach a logical conclusion through a 'deduction of well-placed and well-defined premises' (E. 1941d: 176).

4.2 The nearest antecedent of the present essay

The nearest antecedent of the present essay, a short preface written for a book by Bresciani Turroni (E. 1942g), is extremely significant – and in certain respects, even more significant than its most remote antecedent (par. 1.1) – since it encapsulates some of the major problems, thoughts and second thoughts that troubled Einaudi in the previous years and that he further developed and reformulated in the first edition and in the rewriting of the present essay. As Einaudi confessed,

> I myself also long believed that the economist's task did not consist in setting governments a number of ends to pursue, but rather in offering a reminder, like the slave sitting on the victor's chariot, that the Tarpeian Rock is close to the Capitol: in other words, whatever happen to be the ends pursued by those wielding power in the political process, the means adopted must be adequate and appropriate. Today I have misgivings and I may end up concluding that an economist cannot divorce his duty to criticize the means from his duty to declare the ends, and that a study of the ends forms parts of the science fully on a par with a study of the means, to which economists presently limit themselves. But I have to acknowledge that seeking to ascertain whether the means are adequate to achieve the ends and whether the means are logically consistent with one another is far more arduous and certainly no less morally elevated than addressing the other question, namely an inquiry into the dignity and acceptability of the ends. However the greatest advancements in the difficult construction of that science of reconciling limited existing means with multiple and unlimited ends that has become known by name of economic science have not been achieved by thinkers who were genuinely indifferent. The latter are always ready to advise on matters concerning the government's desire to pursue a particular end or a whole host of possibly

contrasting ends, and they have no qualms about bolstering politicians' proposals with the aid of specious or biased arguments of proposals based on
stealth. Only economists who are profoundly conscious of the good or evil
inherent in certain ends have succeeded in giving a full scientific demonstration
of the adequacy or inadequacy of the means chosen in pursuit of a given end.

(E. 1942g [2014]: 195–196)

The intricacy and the implicit difficulties of this passage – closely linked to
Einaudi's 'misgivings', which, in turn, were mainly sparked by the debate with
Fasiani and his second thoughts from the beginning of 1940s – may be clarified by
analytically distinguishing (at least) two major issues encapsulated in the key sentence 'an economist cannot divorce his duty to criticize the means from his duty
to declare the ends, and that a study of the ends forms parts of the science fully on
a par with a study of the means, to which economists presently limit themselves':

a)   the difficulty of separating rigorously the study of the means and the 'study
     of the ends', which is an issue mainly referring to an economist's work and to
     his analysis of society in general;
b)   the economist's 'duty to declare the ends', which is an issue mainly referring
     to the relationship between the economist and the ruling class. Thus when the
     ends are established by the ruling class, the economist feels that his own ends
     are in contrast with those of the ruling class.

The first problem derives from Einaudi's enquiry into the causes of good and
bad, prosperous and decadent polities and governments – an enquiry that was significantly developed in *MPJT* and epistemologically justified in the present essay,
introducing the dialectical contrast between state and non-state. As Hayek commented, underling that his position had become similar to that of Einaudi, with
specific reference to the 'false belief that science has nothing to do with values':

the existing factual order of society exists only because people accept certain
values. With regard to such a social system, we cannot even make statements
about the effects of particular events without assuming that certain norms are
being generally obeyed. From such premises containing values it is perfectly
possible to derive conclusions about the compatibility, or incompatibility, of
the various values presupposed in an argument.

(Hayek 1970 [2014]: 355)[28]

The second problem, on the other hand, seems to hide (at least) three sub-
issues: a) the responsibility of the intellectual-economist towards civil society in
terms of speaking the truth to power and, depending on the circumstances, even
'his duty to declare the ends'; b) the 'morality' of ends-means reasoning as an
instrument of criticism, at least in the sense of technical critique of the ends pursued (or imposed) by governments; and c) the issue of the alleged 'indifference' or
neutrality of the economist and the ambiguous use of ends-means reasoning, since

it can always become an instrument in the hands of the self-proclaimed indifferent to legitimize any end pursued by governments.

These sub-issues betray the great deontological dilemma that was pressing and worrisome, especially under fascism, and which, perhaps, Einaudi could not state explicitly, precisely because of fascism: should the economist remain *super partes* or take sides – should he remain in the 'ivory tower' or enter the 'tumultuous arena of passions' (E. 1950c)? It was not so much an issue of to be or not to be engaged in the public sphere, because Einaudi, as an economist-journalist, was always engaged. However, he believed that the economist would betray his duty if and only if he were to go to the public square pursuing or fostering a political passion or ideology or if he were to claim a moral position without declaring it explicitly.

Einaudi's growing awareness of the problem of ends and value, which weighed on his mind increasingly from the 1940s onwards, i.e. after the second draft of the *MPJT*, thus merged with his growing awareness that the very claim of the neutrality *of* science itself was none other than a *discourse* (by the scholar) *on* science and that such a claim could serve to mask what was effectively an enslavement of the economist and economic science to the demands of any power whatsoever. Thus for Einaudi, the problem of aims and values became the problem of finding a way to formalize not only in what sense but also within what limits it is legitimate for the economist to take up a position with regard to the ruling powers, and this also implied a return to the position that he had stated in the earlier mentioned preface of the 1914 text and republished in the 1940 text – namely, the recognition that not all aims can be pursued equally.

4.3   The debate with Croce: Liberism and liberalism, economics and philosophy

As we have seen (par. 2.1), Croce's praise addressed to Einaudi for his endorsement of Robbins's epistemology was formulated in the name of the distinction between philosophy and economics. This praise came precisely at a moment of his debate with Einaudi, on the relation between liberism and liberalism (Croce, Einaudi 1957), in which the technical and neutral conception of economic science embraced by Einaudi had relegated economics to a subordinate position vis-à-vis philosophy.

With reference to the distinction between philosophy and economics, it is also worth noting that when Einaudi began the debate with Croce (E. 1928a), he opened the discussion precisely by recalling the split that had come about between Croce and Pareto (Croce 1900 [1953], 1901 [1953], Pareto 1900 [1953], 1901 [1953]) on the question of the epistemological status of the premises or the initial hypotheses of economic arguments. Einaudi seemed to want to avoid reopening that wound, which Croce himself had subsequently remarked with the distinction between "philosophy of the economic" and "economic science", philosophy and science, pure concept and pseudo-concept (or fictional concepts), reality-history and abstraction. The debate with Pareto ended with Croce's injunction against economists: 'save yourselves the trouble of philosophizing. Calculate and don't bother to think!' (1909 [1945]: 263). Those remarks are conventionally held, in Italy, to mark the breakdown of the "communication routes" between philosophy on the one hand and economics and social sciences on the other, as Einaudi also recalled years later (E. 1950a). After the Croce–Pareto debate, only Einaudi was "bold" enough to re-open the dialogue with the philosopher, and, spurred by Croce himself, Einaudi was constrained to dwell once more on the problem of the premises of economic arguments and of their relationship with historical reality.

The Croce–Einaudi debate (Croce, Einaudi 1957), in extremely concise terms, and with specific reference exclusively to epistemological questions, can be summarized as follows.[29] At first, Einaudi took up a *neutral* position towards liberism, as he was concerned (as indeed were many economists after Marx) about unfettering economic science from the charge of liberist ideology or from the accusation of deriving its theorems from an ideology. Subsequently, Einaudi endorsed a 'technical' (E. 1928a) conception of economic science, leaving the realm of ends in the hands of the philosophers (Croce), moralists or politicians.

However, at the same time, Einaudi also had to *defend* liberism – plastically represented by the competition model – against an excessive cheapening of its value, as claimed by Croce. In Einaudi's perspective, liberism, as free competition and free trade, presupposed a series of values, in primis *freedom*, of which economic freedom was an aspect, but such values also included private property, freedom of contract, freedom of initiative, freedom of choice and social wellbeing and eventually led to a model of society composed of small producers and consumers, where power is fairly fragmented. Hence the nexus between liberism and liberalism, in Einaudi's world view. Defending liberism meant setting aside all reserve and admitting its axiological character. But if liberism is indeed channelled and rendered visible by the competition model, this also implies the admission that the competition model, and the economic science as well as the economist who takes such a model as a *premise*, presupposes values.

It is also in this regard that Einaudi, with an implicit reference to his liberal values – the liberal values that drove his enquiry into the causes of state and non-state, good polity and bad polity (held in his *MPJT* and then further explained in the second and third part of the present essay) – thought that it was time to 'publicly' declare his own liberal reasons:

> he [the economist] decides in favor of one or the other decision [of the ruling class] for some reason he considers to be valid, and the reason that is valid for him – which he has to make public – is [. . .], as stated by many, and in the opinion of this writer, the imperative of the moral and therefore also material elevation of man.
>
> (p. 66)

In the conclusions of the first edition, such a claim was further developed and explained in an attempt to sum up both his critical observations on Fasiani and his reflections of the 1940s:

> dispassionateness and objectivity do not exist in human affairs. An economist who knows what kind of rules govern a liberal or communist or plutocratic-protectionist economic society cannot have failed to make his choice, in

accordance with his ideal of life, and it is his duty to declare the reasons underlying such a choice. Whoever, as is the case of this writer, abhors the communist or plutocratic-protectionist ideal cannot refrain from declaring himself to be a champion of the liberal ideal; and this vision of life cannot but exert a major influence on his treatment of economic problems.

(p. 92)

In the rewriting process Einaudi decided to cut out these conclusions and put them in the Bibliographical Note. Though the reasons for such a cut are not entirely clear (since the further comments that Einaudi should have added to the Bibliographical Note are missing; see Editorial Foreword), it is very likely that Einaudi had second thoughts spurred by the comments of his interlocutors.

First of all, Solari, who, after reading Einaudi's essay on Röpke, praised Einaudi's 'shift from the scientific to the philosophical plane' and noticed an analogy between Einaudi's liberal vision and Croce's liberalism, thus relaunching the issue of value judgments within the distinction between natural sciences and moral sciences. The comment by Solari was later placed by Einaudi as an epigraph in the COP addressed to all his correspondents (see Editorial Foreword, par. 5).

Though in a different epistemological context, Bruguier Pacini likewise remarked on the Crocean background of Einaudi's reflection (partly mediated by Passerin d'Entrèves) concerning history and *Weltanschauung* (Bruguier Pacini 1943: 23).

In turn, while Solari praised Einaudi for his reawakened interest in philosophy via Röpke's thought, Einaudi received an opposite evaluation by Giolitti as to the issue of value judgments. As we have seen (par. 4.1), in the essay on Röpke, Einaudi claimed that economists too often forget to render explicit the value judgments that are implicit in the premises of their reasoning. Giolitti objected that economists 'do not have to formulate value judgments on the premises of their enquiry', since they make 'science and not philosophy' (Giolitti 1943), which implicitly called into question the Crocean distinction between science and philosophy and, respectively, between abstraction and history-reality. Einaudi replied that the refusal to make value judgments is based on a not very clear 'distinction' that would require a 'more precise formulation' (Lett.: E. to Giolitti, 1943).

As seen in the Editorial Foreword (par. 5), by setting Solari's comment as an epigraph in the COP, Einaudi was probably aiming to receive further comments on it from all his correspondents. However, only d'Entrèves expressed some doubts on the contrast between moral sciences and natural sciences, but without further clarifications (Lett.: d'Entrèves to E., August 1943).

This notwithstanding, the question that seems to have been uppermost in Einaudi's mind was not so much the distinction between natural sciences and moral sciences, nor the Kantian background of Solari's distinction between the 'category of causality' and the 'catgory of freedom' (Editorial Foreword, par. 5). Although there is no doubt that Einaudi, as a liberal economist, had always assumed freedom as the category through which to understand interactions among human beings and the dynamics of society. Similarly, there can be no doubt that Einaudi had always conceived economics as a moral science, or a 'humanistic discipline', as he 'proudly claimed' till the end of his life (E. 1959: IX).

Rather, in this context, Einaudi was concerned with the distinction between philosophy and (economic) science together with the related (and problematic) distinction between the philosopher and the economist *qua* scientist, as well as the identities and differences that his correspondents had established between himself and Croce.

With all these comments, thoughts and second thoughts in mind, Einaudi undertook the rewriting of the conclusions of his most challenging methodological essay.

Notes

1 In consonance with the line that starts from Mill and extends through Marshall and Pareto (Forte, Marchionatti 2012: 590).
2 These were the words with which he expressed his farewell to the *Corriere della Sera* (the most widely read daily newspaper at that time) when, after twenty-five years of 'battles fought in these columns', as part of an untiring endeavor to 'apply to facts and economic problems the canons of interpretation imposed by science' with a production of thousands of articles, he decided to resign in order to remain faithful to his friend and editor-in-chief Albertini, who had been expelled by the fascist authorities. Einaudi experienced his resignation as a veritable amputation, to the point that 'the strain of the priestly ministry of science, shorn of the accompaniment of journalism, was an unbearably heavy burden' (Lett.: E. to Croci, November 28, 1925).
3 In this context, a further comment is called for. In comparing the numerous works by Ferrara, Pareto and Einaudi, Faucci has argued that on the question of trust in the persuasive virtue of the economist, '[Ferrara is situated, ideally] in an intermediate position between them [. . .]. Pareto is totally skeptical with regard to this power; Einaudi is unwavering in his conviction. In Pareto's *Lettres d'Italie* (1887–1901) [Letters from Italy] and *Cronache Italiane* [Italian Chronicles] one perceives a progressive intellectual scorn for the world of "practical men" and, at best, a naturalist curiosity in the "non-logical" character of their actions. In contrast, Einaudi's *Cronache Economiche e Politiche di un trentennio* (1893–1925) [Economic and Political Chronicles of a Thirty-Year Period (E. 1959–65)] reveals the constant belief that the message will not fall on deaf ears. [One may therefore surmise that for the Turinese economist] unlike for Pareto, *homo politicus* – if appropriately enlightened – pursues objectives that are not in contradiction with those of *homo oeconomicus*' (Faucci 1982: 28–29).
4 Some parts of this paragraph are drawn by Fossati, Silvestri (2012: 35–40).
5 Here Einaudi is implicitly quoting Benda (1927). The issue of the *trahison des clercs*, which is at the heart of Einaudi's concerns of those years, has never ceased to be present. See Gellner (1990), Kimball (2009), Walzer (1988).
6 On corporativist economics, see Cavalieri (1994).
7 On the Einaudian conception of dogma derived from the legal-dogmatics, see Silvestri (2016).
8 On the Einaudi–Keynes debate see Marchionatti (2000b).
9 Robbins' conception of economics in terms of *Wertfreiheit* or value-free science is very well known, but there is the tendency to overlook his concluding preachings on the "significance" of economics, where the notion of rationality takes on a different and normative meaning. As he writes (and Einaudi echoes his words) in the concluding thought of his essay, '[Economic science] relies upon no assumption that individuals act rationally. But it does depend for its practical *raison d'etre* upon the assumption

that it is desirable that they should do so. It does assume that, within the bounds of necessity, it is desirable to choose ends which can be achieved harmoniously. And thus in the last analysis Economics does depend, if not for its existence, at least for its significance, on an ultimate valuation – the affirmation that rationality and ability to choose with knowledge is desirable. If irrationality, if the surrender to the blind force of external stimuli and uncoordinated impulse at every moment is a good to be preferred above all others, then it is true that the *raison d'etre* of Economics disappears [. . .]. For all those who still affirm more positive values, that branch of knowledge which, above all others, is the symbol and safeguard of rationality in social arrangements, must, in the anxious days which are to come, by very reason of this menace to that for which it stands, possess a peculiar and a heightened significance' (Robbins 1932: 141). On Robbins's methodological position, the literature is huge. For a recent reappraisal, see at least the essays collected in Castro Caldas, Neves (2012), Cowell, Witzum (2009), Groenewegen (1996), Masini (2009) and Scarantino (2009).

10 From a historiographic point of view, the epilogue of the Italian tradition of public finance could be made to coincide either with the second edition of Fasiani's *Principii di scienza delle Finanze* (Fasiani 1951) (see Fossati 2011) – published posthumously – where echoes of the debate and references to the interaction with Einaudi can still be found (see *infra*), or with the present essay by Einaudi, by means of which, one might feel, Einaudi appeared to have been seeking to have the "last word".

The debate between Einaudi and Fasiani (epistolary and public) was protracted and complex and addressed many issues, not only methodological. The only existing wide-ranging reconstruction of this debate is that by Fossati (2014a, 2014b) and Fossati and Silvestri (2012), which also includes the publication of the epistolary debate between Einaudi and Fasiani. From a purely chronological point of view, and to the extent to which insight can be gained from the correspondence that has come down to us and from his published writings, the most significant divergences were manifested in the following order. The first signs of discord came to the fore at the point when Fasiani began to introduce into public finance the Paretian conceptual framework, with particular reference to the 'derivations' (Lett.: Fasiani to E., Dec. 9, 1935); there followed a further difference of opinion on De Viti's theory and his concept of the cooperative state (Lett.: Fasiani to E., Dec. 18, 1937).

But the first significant rift between the two began to emerge following the publication of the first edition of *MPJT* by Einaudi (1938b). Fasiani sidestepped the task of writing a full-blown review of the text, restricting himself instead to a private critical commentary of forty or so pages, which in the end he decided not to send to Einaudi. Through a mutual friend, Einaudi then learned of the existence of these critical pages, and Fasiani was obliged to confess the reasons underlying his failure to write an official review and/or to send his written observations: 'since they might have struck you as lacking in respect and even spiteful' (Lett.: Fasiani to E., June 19, 1938). (For a detailed account of this debate, with specific reference to the extreme relevance of these letters for the rewritings of the last two added chapters of *MPJT*, see Fossati, Silvestri 2012.) The reasons behind the two scholars' disagreement, in particular with regard to the idea of science and the distinction between science and precepts, were explained later by Fasiani in another letter (Lett.: Fasiani to E., June 24, 1938).

The second significant rift began after the publication of Fasiani's *Principii* (1941), followed by Einaudi's book review (1942a); the ensuing intense debate took shape as a collection of lengthy letters cast in the form of "memoirs" and counter-memoirs not designed for publication (Lett.: E. to Fasiani, June 21, 1942; Fasiani to E., June 12, 1942; Fasiani to E., July 21, 1942), but the debate later became public with a long series of articles, replies and critical annotations produced by both sides in which the contestants once again wrangled over crucial issues such as the characteristics of the public group, the concept of public wants, the idea of the state as a production factor and the theory of tax-exempt savings. (see Einaudi 1942d, 1942e, 1942f,

1943a) Fasiani (1942, 1943a, 1943b). As far as the first edition of *Ipotesi astratte* was concerned, Fasiani devoted further attention to this work both in his essay on Pareto (Fasiani 1949) and also in the second edition of his *Principii* (Fasiani 1951, published posthumously), thus setting the aim of taking the subject up again at a later date in a 'separate study' (ivi: 7–8, note 6). The reference to the first edition of *Ipotesi astratte* may suggest that Fasiani was unaware of Einaudi's intention of working on a second edition. In any case, it was the death of Fasiani, in 1950, that put an end forever to this fertile dialogue.

11 On Pareto's early development of pure economics see Baranzini, Bridel (1997), Marchionatti, Mornati (2007). On Pareto's experimental method, see Marchionatti (2000a) and Marchionatti, Gambino (1997). On the epistemological background of Pareto's *Manuele*, see Mornati (2006).

12 See Fossati (2013).

13 On this see, at least, Blaug (1980), Boland (1989), Caldwell (1982), Hausman (1988) and the essays in de Marchi (1988, 1992).

14 Perhaps one of the best attempts to analytically disambiguate the confusion among the many terms of the dichotomy positive/normative is that by Machlup (1969). See also Blaug (1998). For a recent critical reappraisal see Davis (2014) and van der Laar, Peil (2009). Though most of the essays on the positive-normative distinction start from the analysis of the influence of the logical positivism, and/or from the is/ought or fact/value dichotomy (see, recently, Walsh (2009)), it is important to stress here that Einaudi's position seems to be closer to the traditional distinction between ethics and economics. For this see Yuengert (2000). As to the positive-normative distinction developed in British history of economic thought and from the Mill–Keynes methodological tradition see, respectively Colander, Su (2015) and Weston (2009).

15 On Pareto's sociology see Bobbio (1964), Busino (2000).

16 This admonishment from Einaudi to Fasiani, perceptible between the lines, was detected by Faucci (1986) and Fossati (2011: 106–107).

17 The hot debate on literary economists reached its apex in the so-called *Paretaio* episode. The issue arose from the polemics between Pantaleoni and Sensini (a pupil of Pareto's); the dispute then became fiercer with the publication of Sensini's book *La teoria della rendita* [The Theory of Rent] (1912), where the author played on the polemical opposition between "literary economists" and "mathematical economists", arguing that Pantaleoni understood nothing of mathematics. The clash came to a head with the article by Jannacone (1912) bearing the title *Il paretaio*, which was published in the journal of which Einaudi was the editor-in-chief: it was an article that accused Pareto's followers, Sensini in particular, of aping, slavishly imitating or even plagiarizing their master. Pareto himself was then obliged to mediate between his pupil, Sensini, and his friend Pantaleoni. On this debate, see Magnani (2005), McLure (2007: 107–113), Mornati (2004).

18 On Pareto's dogmatic use of science see: Pareto (1917) and Bobbio (1973) and Silvestri's (2016) interpretations of this writing by Pareto.

19 It has been noticed (Baffigi 2010) that Einaudi may have taken over the argument on translatability from Vailati (1898, 1906). In effect, Einaudi shared with Vailati more than one strand of interest in the problem of the language of science, and Einaudi himself had specifically commented on Vailati's expertise in translating from one scientific language to another (E. 1930); see also Einaudi (1971). On the identities and differences between Pareto, Vailati and Einaudi see Bruni (2003–2004).

20 It may well be true, as Passerin d'Entrèves (1971: 453) noticed years later that Einaudi's reflection on language is a 'striking anticipation' of the post–Second World War attempts to solve methodological problems through a philosophy of language. Nevertheless, and from a historical point of view, the tradition of "counsels" defended by Einaudi belonged to the natural law tradition, where *counsels* and *precepts* were not opposed to each other but regarded as complementary (Bobbio 2012, Heritier

2012b: 137–147). Moreover, although he delighted in presenting himself under an anti-rhetorical guise, he was a master of rhetoric, switching skillfully between 'classicism and pathos' (Della Valle 2010). In this regard, it is worth noting that Einaudi considered the 'elegance of reasoning' as one of the most distinguished characteristics of Italian economists (E. 1950a [1955]: 16–17, 25). It is only so-called modernism (McCloskey 1985) that has relegated the rhetoric to the reign of non-sense. In this perspective, Einaudi's awareness as to the economist's language and discourse is not far from the contemporary rediscovery of the rhetoric of economics; see, at least, Backhouse, Dudley-Evans, Henderson (1993), McCloskey (1985), Samuels (1990).

21 I found this letter in the Archive of Banca d'Italia.

22 On Schumpeter's judgment and the relevance of Einaudi within the Turin School of Economics see Marchionatti, Cassata, Becchio, Mornati (2013) and Romano (1973: XXV).

23 Both to the first and the second edition of Pareto's *Treatise*, Einaudi devoted no more than a very short newspaper article. On account of his conception of history as made up of individual facts and single events, Einaudi never approved of the sociological drift of Pareto and his 'method of classification into type and sub-type', as he explained years later, echoing Croce, and casting doubt on the empirical character of the sociological approach adopted by Pareto, who passed off as 'facts' a number of ideas that were actually interpretations derived, among other things, from 'newspaper cuttings' (E. 1950a [1955]: 9, 13–14).

24 According to Fossati (2015), Fasiani 'labelled the tutorial state as "modern", "nationalistic", or even "corporative" in homage to the regime, because, although not committed in politics, like many, he had faith then in Fascism, which he identified with the Fatherland'. With regard to Fasiani's contributions to corporatist economics, I will limit myself to the following brief observations. In the essay entitled *Contributo alla teoria dell'"uomo corporativo"* [Contribution to the Theory of the "Corporative Man"], Fasiani had analyzed the hypothesis of the *homo corporativus* as a further approximation to the hypothesis of the *homo oeconomicus*. The *homo corporativus* is a man 'who behaves according to the fundamental principles of the Labor Charter and who, unlike the former (homo oeconomicus), should also be endowed with the sentiment of the higher interest of the collective community to which he belongs' (Fasiani 1932: 326). In 1937, after analyzing the policies against the crisis, Fasiani argued that the solutions linked to the liberal state were outdated, whereas he felt it was feasible to adopt an approach that was 'totalitarian, continuous, directed towards all points of the system, with the intent of harmonizing its movements' (Fasiani 1937: 96). The totalitarian solution is subdivided into the 'Fascist corporative solution' and the 'communist solution'; the former is declared to be preferable inasmuch as it eschews a plan integrally arranged by a central organ in favor of a 'plan' springing from individual initiative, which the central organ controls and molds, coordinating its various parts' (ivi: 104). It is perhaps significant that although Einaudi often made mention of his pupil's essays (for instance, by citing them in his *Principii di Scienza delle Finanze* [Principles of Public Finance] or writing reviews of these texts), he consistently maintained a rigorous silence on the subject of these two essays.

25 As hypothesized by Francesco Forte, the first edition was not published in *Rivista di storia economica* of which Einaudi was the editor-in-chief, but came out instead in the *Atti dell'accademia delle Scienze*, precisely because the regime did not keep as close of an eye on this publication (Forte 2009: 57).

26 See also Einaudi (1918 [1920], 1944b [2006], 1945a [2001]). On Einaudi's reflection on the European federation see D'Auria (2012), Forte (2009: 303–342), Masini (2012), Morelli (1990), Oddenino, Silvestri (2011), Quadrio Curzio, Rotondi (2005).

27 On this debate see Fiori (2007).

28 To quote Hayek (1970 [2014]: 355) extensively, 'the *true* statement that, from our understanding of causal connections between facts alone, we can derive no conclusions about the validity of values, has been extended into the false belief that science

has nothing to do with values. This attitude should change immediately: scientific analysis shows that the existing factual order of society exists only because people accept certain values. With regard to such a social system, we cannot even make statements about the effects of particular events without assuming that certain norms are being generally obeyed. From such premises containing values it is perfectly possible to derive conclusions about the compatibility, or incompatibility, of the various values presupposed in an argument. It is therefore incorrect if, from the postulate that science ought to be free of values, the conclusion is drawn that within a given system problems of value cannot be rationally decided. When we have to deal with an ongoing process for the ordering of society, in which most of the governing values are unquestioned, there will often be only one certain answer to particular questions that is compatible with the rest of the system'.

29 On the Croce–Einaudi debate, see Faucci (1989), Forte (2009: 193–221), Silvestri (2007, 2010b, 2012c: 201–272, 2016).

On abstract and historical hypotheses and on value judgments in economic sciences

Luigi Einaudi

I Abstract hypotheses and historical hypotheses

[1.] The laws investigated by economic science are of two kinds: one is abstract, the other historical. The quest for an abstract law is preceded by *if*. Let us suppose that at a given time and place the hypothesis of full competition is fulfilled and that under this hypothesis the state levies a personal tax on citizens' net income; further, if we suppose that the society in question is static, i.e. that no new savings are accumulated within this society and the population and its tastes undergo no variation, and if we also suppose, etc., etc., then the consequences deriving from the tax thus construed are such and such. Subsequently, the hypothesized circumstances are made to vary, one by one, or additional circumstances are added to those already posited. With each variation in the data pertaining to the problem, suitable deductions are then made by adducing the appropriate arguments. For ease of investigation, the problem is first set out according to the simplest hypothesis, bringing to bear only the minimum number of data; then complications are gradually brought in by introducing new, more complicated and more numerous hypotheses. This logical procedure has long been known as the method of successive approximations. It has the advantage of drawing theoretical schemata little by little closer to reality, but without ever reaching a true contemplation of it. The extreme schemata of perfect competition and perfect monopoly, the intermediate conceptions of imperfect competition and imperfect monopoly as well as their innumerable subspecies are not claimed by scholars to be a genuine portrayal or a photograph of reality; rather, they are rough outlines intended to depict reality at first with barely drafted strokes and then with somewhat firmer brushwork, without it ever being possible to take into account the whole range of circumstances that shape its composition at a given time and place. Yet even though the results of the abstract line of reasoning cannot be checked by setting up a purpose-designed experiment under the desired conditions, as is the normal procedure in the physical and chemical sciences, it is still the case that if the premises are clearly enunciated and the argument is developed rigorously, then the theorems constructed by economists are true, within the limits of the premises stated. They are *abstract* laws, which tell us what would necessarily happen whenever *all and only* the premises stated by the thinker were to hold in actual reality.

There is no need, in order to ensure that a theorem resulting from a demonstration is true, for the premises, the problem, the argument and the theorem to be set in a specific historical, political or moral place and time. The theorem is true *sub specie aeternitatis*: it is a truth whose conformity to events that genuinely occurred need not be demonstrated, precisely because the investigator never set himself such an aim.

***

[2.] However, if economic science consisted only in considering abstract problems and demonstrating similarly abstract laws, it would hardly benefit from even that minimal following among the lay public it does still enjoy, and it would not exert the least influence on human affairs, not even that infinitesimal trace which it can indeed boast. Following and influence are due to the connections scholars and the lay public believe to exist between abstract schemata and concrete reality, or which are held to link problems and first approximation theorems with the problems and the associated urgent solutions in the daily life of human society. Physicists, chemists and astronomers can, if they so desire, spend their entire life without the slightest concern for the concrete applications others will draw from the theorems they, as scientists, have discovered. Not so for the economist. No economist has ever stayed rigidly closed up in the ivory tower of first principles, first approximation theorems. Pantaleoni and Pareto, to mention but two of the celebrated economists of the past generation, were combative fighters in the debate centering on the everyday problems of their time just as much as they were great theoreticians. The attitude they adopted in facing the battles of real life repeatedly molded their manner of addressing theoretical problems. To be sure, they took immense care to distinguish a *theorem* from *counsels*; they endeavored to avoid any contamination between the one and the other; sometimes both men – especially one of the two (Pareto) – spoke scornfully and ironically of *literary* economists who mistook science for politics, giving counsels to princes instead of declaring uniformities. Yet by dint of fine distinctions and clarifications, they never ceased to reproach, criticize, contemptuously belittle – and only very seldom did they deign to praise – governors and the governed, pointing out which path was best avoided and which was the right one to take. It is a fact that in economic sciences there exists a field of theorems, properly speaking, and a field of counsels: but these two fields are not separate and independent of each other. Economists who do have something to say, even though sometimes delighting in contemptuously belittling the other and perhaps better part of themselves, cultivate the land for the purpose of knowledge and dig the land over for the purpose of acting upon reality; the imitators, the servile pen-pushers, incapable of perceiving the links between the two aspects of the whole person, construct insipid theory and supply the counsels they know will find favor with the powerful.

***

[3.] In actual fact, there is an extremely close link between theorems and counsels. When Walras and Pareto constructed the theory of general equilibrium, they based their arguments on an array of premises: no more than a small handful of premises, yet these were at the same time a substantial array of presuppositions. A small handful, in the sense that Walras and Pareto worked on certain simplified assumptions: perfect competition or perfect monopoly, unlimited reproducibility of production factors or limitation of this or that factor, free market or closed market and the like. A substantial array, because they did not suppose that when one of the premises of the problem changes, all the other premises remain unaltered. Quite the opposite: they supposed that when there is a variation in one of the data of the problem, all the other data change accordingly, at the same time. Thus in their vision, on account of the movement and during the movement of one of the dots in the economic firmament, all the other dots likewise shift, influenced by and, in turn, acting on the motion of the first dot. In this manner, they achieved the most general and certainly most fertile breakthrough of modern economic science: what reigns supreme on the market is the law of interdependence, with the result that the price of a given good cannot be altered without this entailing a change, slight or great, in the price of all other goods, whether close or distant, present or future. But what a long-drawn-out stretch of path had to be covered before it became possible to take a step forwards from this principle, or from the one which holds that the price of a consumption good is, on a given market, the price that makes the quantity demanded equal to the supply and which, at the same time, achieves equality between demand and supply of producers' durable goods and of production services, and between the savings and capital required for production of the consumption goods. And what a long-drawn-out stretch of path had to be covered before a step forwards could be taken from extremely general theorems to the formulation of theorems closer to living man. For it is only this latter type of theorem that is of any interest to living man, whose concern is to try to understand why the price of a bushel of wheat, at some given time and place and under the particular market conditions in question, is 25 and not 30, 240 and not 300 liras! Such a long winding path that no-one has even ventured to set out along it at all! Marshall, in despair, embarked on the route of partial equilibria, i.e. the study of price laws under the hypothesis that not all the premises of the problem change simultaneously but, *coeteris paribus*, that change occurs in only one premise at a time or in only a small handful: otherwise stated, that change affects only the number of premises whose variations can be grasped and followed and combined together by the limited human mind.[1] By proceeding along this route, which is, after all – with due respect for the theory of general equilibrium – the path followed by all theoretical economists, notable progress has indeed been made. But, as a result of the above-mentioned limitation of the human mind, it has so far been impossible – and is likely to be for the foreseeable future – to complicate the problem and multiply the data or the underlying premises so as to take into account even just a small number of the countless data that would have to be considered in order to solve the concrete problem on a case-by-case basis. Advancing along the road of successive approximations, sooner or later there comes a point when one has to come to a halt. Only very rarely do economists move beyond a second or third stage in approximating to reality. To reach the final arrival point, just imagine the number of steps leading down from the high peaks of the contemplators of first truths! If the likes of Walras and Pareto could descend from that lofty summit whence their gaze takes in and dominates the horizons and sees the price laws in the different types of market, and could move further and further down to the bottom of a concrete market, for instance right down to the bottom of the deafening ear-splitting pit of the Chicago cereal market, its air filled with raucous cries and wild gesticulations, then they would solve a scientific problem of precisely the same nature as the problems they solved earlier when they set the correct equations of their first approximations. Were the likes of Walras and Pareto to possess the necessary panoramic vision, they would silently set to work in that place where at this very moment the heaving crowds jostle and butt one another, and they would posit the thousands of equations required by the thousands of unknowns to be determined. And just imagine how many unknowns there would be amid the myriad data, all of them needing to be known! Do we know or can we guess – in other words can we determine by setting the appropriate equations at lightning speed – the answers to questions concerning the extent of the area, fertility, position, etc., of the lands that were or will be destined to wheat growing in Dakota, Iowa, Indiana, Alberta, Calabria, Lombardy, Sicily, Russia, Australia, Argentina and India, etc., the number and productivity of workers who will be assigned to wheat cropping, the quantity of savings necessary to produce the tools and agricultural machines, the means and costs of river, land, sea and air transport, the tastes and incomes of wheat consumers scattered over the different countries of the world, and at the same time the types of land, production factors and consumption patterns relating to all the products that may be competitors or replacements of wheat? Laid out before them, visible as equations, those sovereign intellects would have the entire picture of the economic and social world photographed at that very instant, and the photograph would be a thumbnail vision of that world, offering a preview of its future evolution and, at the same time, an overview of all the repercussions its evolution exerts on action in the present world. If that calculation could be carried out and if at that instant the price calculated were 1 dollar and 17 cents per bushel of wheat of the given variety and quality, then that price would have the value of a necessary inference of a scientific law: *necessary* because it would be the inevitable logical consequence of all the appropriate premises clearly posited by a rational argument.

***

[4.] In actual fact, such calculations are beyond the potential of the reasoning human mind. Instead of the likes of Walras and Pareto, what we see in the Chicago wheat pit – and, with regard to other economic goods, in the other stock markets where the prices of the main goods or notes publicly traded every day are or were determined – is the pandemonium of thousands or hundreds of frenzied individuals vociferating and hollering and elbowing their way to the front, who, lo and behold, amid the hullabaloo and hurly-burly, at that very same instant reach the very same result of 1 dollar and 17 cents per bushel of wheat of the given variety and quality. How do they get to this result? Basically, the process is the same as would have been seen by the likes of Walras and Pareto, had they happened to be there. The cereal speculators of the Chicago wheat pit formulate the data of the problem in a set of equations, in just the same manner: land currently or later to be under wheat cultivation in competition with land destined to other crops; productivity of the land in question and in particular of marginal land; production factor costs; transportation costs; adverse seasonal weather or conditions favorable to wheat growing; on-going or forthcoming harvests in the various countries of the world; left-over stockpiles; consumer tastes and incomes; transfer of wheat from the elevators to the flour mills and from the latter to the bakeries; customs duties and a ban on importation in consumer countries; competition from rice and rye and potato; competition and bargaining by individual traders, agricultural cooperatives or flour-mill trusts; railroad and lake shipping company monopolies, etc., etc. All these data on the problem and innumerable others as well are taken into consideration by the brokers in the Chicago pit who deal with the buying and selling of present and future wheat supplies on the basis of news reports, cablegrams to journalists, special information transmitted over the phone as brokers race from the phone booths back to the pit, and so forth. And every phone call is a message that makes it possible to insert a definite or approximate item of information as a replacement of an unknown in the system of equations the brokers are feverishly and frantically trying to solve at that very moment. And from the kaleidoscope of often conflicting and uncertain scraps of information, out jumps that very price at that very moment: 1 dollar and 17 cents per bushel. If this is, at that very moment, the price that renders the quantity demanded equal to that supplied, then as far as I can see, the process that led up to that price formation is in no way different from the scientific procedure by which the pure economist solved his problem of first approximation on the basis of no more than a few explicitly and clearly posited premises. There is no difference at all between the abstract laws of first approximation posited by the theoretician in the quiet seclusion of his study and the empirical laws posited by the brokers in the uproar of the stock market. Both modes of operating are laws: the former are said to be abstract because they are true within the limits of the handful of premises posited; the latter are said to be empirical because they are true given the working of all the existing premises, whether known or unknown; the former are said to be true *sub specie aeternitatis* because, and as long as, the theoretician does not alter the premises of the problem; the latter are true only for a fleeting instant in the sense that once the moment has passed, the data of the problem inexorably change in a flash; the former can be expounded and demonstrated in academic papers and in scientific treatises, because it is perfectly possible to devise most elegant and sometimes remarkable arguments to account for the interactions and reactions of no more than a few well-defined forces; the latter are not written down in any book because they are the fruit of momentary impressions, miraculous intuitions: they embody that quasi-magical flow which creates seers, prophets, captains, heads of state and which also creates the great operators who dictate the price laws on the economic goods markets, until the day comes when even the brokers meet their Waterloo. Caesar and Napoleon wrote memoirs, but the great brokers know neither how to write nor to deliver grand speeches. It would be beneficial if some economist were to become their secretary and, like a latter-day Boswell, were to transcribe any secret disclosures the stock market Johnsons deigned to whisper in their ears. But the minor economists, to whom such a post would be assigned, prefer to look down their noses at *practitioners* and shower the contempt of the *pure* on those who would portray the intuitions of the men who make or register the real prices on actual markets. If, miraculously, someone were willing to listen, this would probably lead to a distortion of the report by transcribing it into pure economic language, forgetting that what distinguishes reality from the schema is the manner of expression and overlooking that the language of the schema has become technical, i.e. specifically designed to take into account only the premises and arguments that form part of the schema itself. Its language is completely unsuited to account for the multiplicity of data unknown to the first and second and third approximations, which the broker working on the stock market really does take into account, either because he was born into this *trade* or has lived in the milieu for years or because, thanks to a peculiar sixth sense, his conjectures and guess-work are underpinned by miraculous intuition.

***

[5.] Due to the temperament and disposition of those who state them, the decidedly scientific laws derived by practitioners from the equations solved with the aid of intuition rather than by calculation almost always end up taking the form of *counsels* and *projects*, if and when they are written down. And it was in the form of counsels that such laws were incorporated into the body of science by the old economists. Only extremely rarely does one find the admirable case of great practitioners, such as Cantillon and Ricardo, who had the wisdom to use a manner of expression based on the statement purely of laws when they composed their theoretical works. But even these great scholars not infrequently added counsels or a project to the statement of theoretical principles. Were they, in so doing, straying beyond the bounds of science? Were Walras and Gossen engaging in non-scientific activity when they proposed some of their monetary or land tax reforms? I would make a distinction between form and content. Today, we are repeatedly advised to heed the precept which holds that the duty of science is to dictate laws and not to fabricate projects. Now, while these words of wisdom command respect if uttered by the likes of Cairnes and Pareto, a degree of impatience is understandable if the admonition comes from those whose manner of expounding the problems is manifestly prompted not by the quest for truth, but by some practical aim. Note that by practical aim I do not mean the above-mentioned approximation of reality, but rather the aim of achieving advantages for themselves or for a social class or professional group or of currying favor with the powerful or the common crowds. However, if it is merely a question of the manner of writing, I would say that a greater measure of indulgence is warranted, whether the guilty economists are ancient or modern. For what is crucial is certainly not the form in which the arguments are cast, but rather their content. Almost all the truths discovered in the monetary field of yesterday and today were occasioned by projects and counsels. Did not the monetary falsifications of the Middle Ages, the lowerings and raisings of imaginary money[2] as compared to real money in the seventeenth and eighteenth centuries, the spells of forced circulation in the first quarter of the nineteenth century, the bimetallic systems between 1850 and 1880, the monetary devaluations and revaluations of the period from 1914 to 1940 provide the occasion for great theoretical works on money? Did not countless of the ideas that left a lasting mark in monetary theory originate from polemics and counter-projects? I by no means wish to belittle the merit of theoretical economists who followed in their wake and translated the *precepts* of the discoverers into scientific language, but I certainly feel it is very bad taste to disparage the discoverers and extol the theoreticians. The effort involved in translating a proposition expressed in the terms of a precept

> do not mint a gold coin which, in comparison to a silver coin of the same weight and titre, is valued as 15½ to 1, when in common trade a kilogram of gold is exchanged for 16 kilograms of silver, because the country will be left completely without gold coins, to the great inconvenience of the public

into the identical proposition of a scientific or hypothetical type

> if, when 1 kilogram of gold is exchanged in common trade for 16 kilograms of silver, a gold coin and a silver coin are minted with the proportionate weight and equal titre, but the silver coin legally has a redemption value equal to one fifteenth and a half part of the gold coin, then the money (silver) that is relatively debased in the commercial relation as compared to the legal relation will be left as the only one in circulation

is actually a trifling effort and, I would say, of a trifling order, once one has learned the modest skills required. I am not saying that the ancient and modern *precepts* can always be so easily translated into theoretical principles, but I contend that even today it is by no means rare to find that economists' attention to a given problem is awakened by the solution which was in actual fact devised in a given time and place, and that the first treatments take the form of projects of other and different solutions. Thus it may happen, albeit somewhat more rarely, that during debate focusing on development of such projects, and on the attendant effects of a solution that has already been accepted and on the different effects likely to arise from the proposed new solution, ideas are put forward which are in essence purely scientific arguments and theorems. If that is the case, then any economist of a later generation who undertakes to give a rendering of the preceptive terminology in the guise of a hypothesis-based version would certainly perform a useful task, but the didactic usefulness of the exercise would in no way authorize him to look the gift horse in the mouth after milking its lifeblood. By the same token, such an exercise, however useful, would hardly mitigate one's sense of frustration at the distasteful sight of the presumption of those who, purely by accomplishing that modest enterprise of rendering the vivid tongue of combatants into the dull conventional language of also-rans, consider themselves the inventors of the theorem they have merely cloaked in the usual terminology of academic hacks. What an abyss lies between these translators – and their often pompous over-blown style – and the scientists who without pomp and circumstance proffer the truth that they are genuinely the first to have discovered and submit it to scholarly evaluation!

***

[6.] Whereas the laws discussed here so far are frankly *abstract*, and therefore necessarily regulate relations among circumstances, premises or facts that are defined, numbered and weighed in the manner the investigator saw fit to adopt, the character of the inferences that can be deduced from hypotheses formulated on the basis of historical schemata appears to be different. In economics, I define the hypothesis of pure monopoly as that of the private entrepreneur who is the one and only producer-supplier of a given good on a given market at a given time, without any limitation or potential competitors (or substitute goods) or even legis-lative constraints, and I thus deduce that the market price will be that determined by the Cournot point of the maximum net profit. On the other hand, this does not mean I am claiming that there exists or has ever existed or will ever actually exist in the real world a pure monopolist and that the price can therefore be genuinely established precisely at the Cournot point. My proposition is purely hypothetical, and the price law that I deduce therefrom is a purely *abstract* law. If, perchance, the hypothesis should happen to become true in any historical period and place, then the price law would *necessarily* be the afore-stated law. In actual fact, it is not necessarily the case that price is truly regulated at any time or place by that particular law or by the others that are formulated in the – equally abstract – hypotheses of full competition or bilateral monopoly and so forth. The hypotheses and the consequent abstract laws are only types from which some indications can be drawn as to price trends and price uniformities in concrete reality, which is complex and changeable.

Let us say that the hypotheses or premises or schemata or types are fertile when a comparison between the abstract laws and the empirically observed uniformities reveals a fairly good resemblance between the abstract law and concrete trend. But one can also proceed in the inverse direction, by starting out from precise observation of the trends discernible in certain given series of empirical facts and using the results to derive statements of laws – not abstract and not necessary – concerning relations that truly did exist, e.g. in some given place or period of time, for a given good or array of goods, between quantity produced and quantity con-sumed and the corresponding prices. The realization that the demand and supply elasticity of a given good at place x over the stretch of time from a to b obeyed a certain law may provide the stimulus to investigate whether that law is also appli-cable in its entirety or in part to other goods or places or times that bear a resem-blance to the previous cases. Statisticians and econometricians are past masters in such investigations, and their reluctance to extend and generalize uniformities observed at a given time and place is a touchstone of their scientific awareness. For only with extreme caution and with the aid of highly delicate expedients can a man's observation encompass all or at least the main data that made the demand and supply elasticity at that moment and time what it was and not something else. Who can tell what influence was exerted in the determination and discovery of an empirical uniformity by the height of nominal and real incomes, the number and tastes of consumers, the competition of other present and future goods, etc., etc.? All it needs is for just one of these factors to change and – behold – the empirical uniformity that held in a given place or time turns out to be different from that which can now be genuinely observed. This notwithstanding, the efforts made in ascertaining empirical or *de facto* uniformities, which cannot be extrapolated beyond the time, place or good to which they refer, are certainly highly commendable; indeed, they will become even more praiseworthy as investigations are gradually extended further and further over time and space, with the aid of ever more sophisticated methods which will make it increasingly possible to ascertain the weight and variations of each one of the factors whose influence contributed to determining the solution that effectively came about. And the investigations will be even more greatly enhanced as the investigators gradually succeed in imagining schemata or types which, while remaining empirical, become progressively more suited to depicting the behavior of given economic phenomena over prolonged periods of time and extensive tracts of land. The development of empirical schemata or types of this kind will in turn offer theoreticians an opportunity to exercise their imagination in devising simplified abstract premises schemata or types that show a good or fairly good fit with the pattern of the empirical data, from which new illuminating theorems can be derived. Quite apart from the modern mastery of the method, the recommendation to make use of both deductive and inductive manners of proceeding, abstract reasoning as well as its empirical verification, has always been praised, and that great abstract logician, Jevons, drew much of the fame he still enjoys from his masterful ability to switch from abstraction to observation, and then to build on the latter as a means of developing new and fertile abstractions.

***

[7.] Remarkably, the laws formulated by theoretical economists as a first approximation frequently coincide with the concrete behavior of the commonest economic facts, even in new and extraordinary circumstances. The dismissive comment foolishly voiced by laymen during and after the last war and proclaimed again today, "the war, the post-war period and the new war bear witness to the failure of economic science",[3] can be neatly inverted as follows: "the war, the post-war period and the new war have given a crystal-clear demonstration of the exactness – and figuratively speaking, the inexorable nature – of the laws posited by classical economists". Indeed, never before have the consequences they foresaw been more clearly borne out: in vain did they caution against the abundant printing of paper money, the introduction of ceiling prices without requisitioning and without coupons, or of coupons established for incongruous quantities compared to prices. And never has social unrest been so enormously magnified by impoverishment and the accumulation of massive fortunes, reproducing a situation described in earlier times by the classics, who, however, portrayed it in more muted tones since the underlying causes were less grave. Thus what was viewed by the layman as the failure of economic science was, on the contrary, its greatest triumph, and it was only the extravagant expectations of laymen that were doomed to failure: unacquainted with anything that was written in the economists' books, they imagined that economists were little short of necromancers, endowed with the power to prevent error from giving birth to the damage that is error's intrinsic nature. They pictured economists as persons who would forestall the risk that laws fabricated with total disregard for the interdependence among all actions and that economic forces may produce startlingly different effects compared to the beneficial results confidently forecast by the so-called experts, i.e. by people whose distinctive feature is their total ignorance of whatever lies beyond the bounds of their limited province. In short, it was only the illogical line of reasoning pursued by industrialists and by owners of large agricultural estates and merchants that was doomed to failure. Highly proficient though the members of such classes may be in relying on their intuition to formulate theorems and particular corollaries – which actually turn out to be identical to the general propositions expounded by theoretical economists in the form of pure theory – they tend to cultivate their particular interests and disclaim the validity of these very same theorems just as soon as the focus of attention shifts from their own field to the general sphere. In other words, they begin to feel that economists ought to forget about theorems and corollaries, and instead should champion other ideas better suited to the private interests of the aforesaid classes. But since this is out of the question, the laymen contemptuously revile science as useless and, by the same token, revile scientists themselves almost as if they were enemies of the homeland.

***

[8.] The fruitfulness of using deduction and induction simultaneously and in alternation within the field of economic science – or, otherwise stated, the abstract hypothesis used in conjunction with empirical observation of actual trends – has prompted the deployment of expedients and instruments (which the English aptly call "tools") different from those adopted in traditional methods. I will refrain from dwelling here in depth on the tools recently invented or proposed or adopted by some modern economists, hailed at first as miraculous breakthroughs but then very rapidly cast aside, only to be taken up again shortly afterwards. These were novelties that have given us a successive stream of tools such as *consumer income, the multiplier, the relation between savings and investment*, all intended to provide an explanation for economic fluctuations or crises, monetary variations and so forth. It is quite right that each *tool* should be put to the proper test, effectively acting as a measure of the logical expertise of the worker assigned to the task, and only the tools that have seriously proved their worth will remain operative. But what I want to mention is the utilization of hypotheses or schemata[4] that stand roughly midway between the drastically simplified abstract hypotheses and the uniformities put forward to describe the manner of the variation of a given phenomenon (for instance, the price of a good) at a given time and place. These "halfway house" hypotheses are less simplified than the traditional type, and they do not aspire to describe any factual state of affairs that existed empirically at some time or place. They are what I would call theoretical-historical schemata. They have a touch of the theoretical about them, in the sense that they do not claim to depict any precise moment of the unfolding of events over history, yet at the same time they have a touch of the historical about them in that they seek to summarize the characteristic patterns and tendencies of institutions that once genuinely existed and are deserving of study on account of their noteworthy impact on the destiny of mankind in certain periods of time.

These are the schemata that seem to underlie the sequence of economies starting from the ancient hunting systems then proceeding through the stages of sheep and animal rearing, agriculture and industry, which according to some scholars represent the successive moments of the economic life-story of mankind. Others have directed attention to the succession of types of labor organization, with a sequence beginning from slavery and serfdom, later moving towards the guilds, corporations and free labor, followed by a renewed period of associations, either free or public. Additional historically oriented portrayals of the successive types of economic activity include primitive communism, the early medieval court economy, the economy of the medieval city state, individual property (craft work), simple capitalism (manufacturing industry), complex capitalism (trusts, cartels, branching companies) and state collectivism. But it can be seen immediately that these are not schemata likely to be scientifically fruitful. They are not tools that can be expected to act as the driving force of scientific investigation, because they lack sufficient simplicity and cannot easily be delineated in precise terms. We can define the hypothesis of free competition (the situation whereby the market is populated by an abundance of producers and a profusion of consumers so that the presence or absence of some individual player among either of these groups exerts no appreciable influence on the price of the goods traded), or we can define the monopoly hypothesis or that of production with increasing or decreasing constant costs, because these are simple premises that give rise to quantitative calculations in terms of pluses or minuses, and they allow the arguments to be based on a given number of unknowns. But just imagine trying to define the economy of hunting, fisheries, sheep rearing, slavery, medieval corporatism, serfdom or, for that matter, primitive or modern capitalism! The resulting descriptions will necessarily be complex, with a string of *but*s and *if*s and considerable reservations about times and places. None of them will be of any use for a quantitative analysis supposedly underpinned by logical reasoning. Anyone attempting to write out clear-cut premises for one or the other of these schemata would find it well-nigh impossible to convert the material into anything even remotely resembling the logical procedure based on premises, corollaries, lemmas and theorems that can be found, to cite just one example, in Pantaleoni's *Principî*.

Are these schemata helpful for historical analysis? Here it is experience that counts. The authors of the schemata utilized them to classify events and economic institutions. Those who followed in their wake revised the classifications, aping the same format and, so they claimed, achieving greater perfection. But what they created were scarcely more than playthings, soon cast aside in favor of new and prettier toys, as is the way with children. History does not lend itself to being reduced to schemata and uniform types. The schemata would have to be unnumbered if they are to have any real spice of their own. History is made up of individual facts, single events, not of types. To be sure, the historian must have an idea, a guiding thread that prompts him to choose the individual facts he deems to be most important amongst the innumerable facts and trivia that are devoid of any real importance or any importance at all. But the idea that guides the historian is not an abstract schema set up purely for classificatory purposes. The guide-motif, the common thread that runs throughout his work, is the impulse that stimulated men to operate, to struggle, to live and to die. Neither slavery nor craft work nor capitalism can act as a guide-motif, for these are simply descriptive terms referring to external modes of living. But these modes themselves draw their *raison d'être* from far deeper sources. It is man who creates an enterprise, reduces his fellow men to slavery or frees himself from such a condition, tills the land or leads his flocks to pasture because he is driven by the thirst for wealth, by the urge to dominate, by the word of Christ who has proclaimed all men to be equal before God, by the aspiration to freedom and to the achievement of moral perfection. Ideas and sentiments, both rational and irrational, are what guide men from one type of economic organization to another. The types and classes and forms explain nothing at all. They are memory aids, didactic expedients devised in order to help men to find their way around in the maze of facts. They are not history. They are jettisoned as soon as it becomes clear, by putting them to use, how limited and how pedestrian is the advantage that can be obtained.

Notes

1   For an application by Pareto of the *coeteris paribus* method, cf. *supra* essay V on [L. Einaudi,] "Le premesse del ragionamento economico e la realtà storica", *Rivista di Storia Economica*, V, n. 3, settembre 1940, pp. 179–199.
2   [Editor's note] Implicit reference to Einaudi (1936e).
3   [Editor's note] Implicit reference to Einaudi (1921).
4   It seems that the word *schema* can be utilized to indicate a hypothesis which, although assumed by the scholar as purely abstract and thus arbitrary, aspires at the same time to portray a section or an aspect of reality. All the hypotheses used in pure economics can likewise be described with the same term "schema", because an investigator only very rarely adduces hypotheses merely in order to delve into a schoolroom example or for ratiocinative purposes. Moreover, if and when he does, he expressly states that this is what he is doing. The term *hypothesis* should be used when focusing, above all, on the abstract aspect of the investigation, whereas *schema* should be used when the aim is to draw attention to the suitability of the hypothesis for portraying some empirical or historical truth.

II On some abstract hypotheses concerning the state and on their historical value

[9–10–11.] Can the schemata used successfully in economic science be used without further ado to explain and systematize facts of a different kind? The following argument has been adduced in a published work:[1] since prices are private and public, and since charges and taxes are none other than the price of public goods produced by the state and supplied by the latter to citizens, why should one not use those very same hypotheses of monopoly (the monopolistic or absolute state) and competition (the cooperative state) that served so well and so usefully in economic science? And indeed De Viti adopted these two investigative tools elegantly and successfully. His success was perhaps due, above all, to his extremely cautious utilization of these tools, deploying them in cases where they were genuinely of aid in clarifying the problems at hand – namely, in setting out the approach to the individual problems. What is characteristic in De Viti's treatment is not so much the fact of dividing up public economy into the two schemata, as, rather, his argument that the problems of public finance (or – to use the expression De Viti himself favored – the problems of *financial economy*) are economic problems, which should be discussed with the same criteria as used in economic science. Proceeding case by case, without becoming overly embroiled in the complexities of the two political schemata (the monopolistic and the cooperative state), he discussed the individual financial problems as if they were price problems, using now the monopoly hypothesis, now that of free competition, depending on which option was best suited to deal with each particular problem.

While use of the two economic schemata for some types of financial problems may seem to act as a clarification, which of the two words is best suited for declaring their substance? Hypotheses or schemata? Are they merely hypotheses thought up by the mind of the scholar in order to derive theoretical laws that are true *sub specie aeternitatis*, or also schemata – tools – for an approximated interpretation of historical reality?

Given the need to define the hypotheses taken as the starting point, let the *monopolistic state* be the one in which the dominating class exercises its power, in monopoly conditions, exclusively in its own interest, without taking into account the interests of those who are dominated. This means that the dominating class produces the public goods that redound to its own exclusive or predominant advantage and passes on the cost exclusively or predominantly to the dominated class. In so doing, the dominating class endeavors to convey the illusory persuasion that the public expenditures are set up in such a manner as to be of greatest advantage to the dominated and that taxation is structured in a way that will inflict the least burden on the latter.

If the systematics of the financial system of a state of this kind were to touch on the matter of taxation only in terms of the popular wisdom embodied in the ancient adage of "plucking a chicken without making it squawk", or, alternatively, if the conjectured description addressed the question of expenditure only in terms of how to maneuver things so that expenditure useful for the dominating members is camouflaged as expenditure useful for everyone or for the whole group – well, I would hesitate to say that this would be a feature of any particular type of state. Indeed a similar approach has on occasion been adopted by legislators who were acting and wanted to act and were convinced they were acting in all people's interest and in the interest of each individual (the cooperative state) or of the whole community (the modern state). And in any case, the limits on the workings of illusions are so extensive and so powerful as to render the field of action of that system practically infinitesimal, even in a more decidedly monopolistic state.

But while the observation is historically founded, the same cannot be said from a logical perspective. The distinction between the monopolistic state and the cooperative state does not entail the assertion that such states ever genuinely existed at some time and place or other. This would mean falling into the error of mistaking reality – which is always complicated and a one-of-a-kind in the sense that it does not admit of repetition – for an abstract schema or a theoretical model, which can serve to explain some particular aspect of reality. On occasion, in the past, some fault-finders hastily put together a series of sniping criticisms, reviling the analysis of finance carried out with the criterion of schemata or theoretical models of an economic nature – such an analysis, they claimed, did not produce a true likeness of reality. The snag is that by launching this critical attack, they revealed their ignorance concerning the intrinsic nature of scientific investigation in the field of our abstract sciences. And what they failed to realize is that those who theorized the above-mentioned types of state did not aim to address a historical problem, but rather a problem of logic, which I would term a problem of *tools*. According to this approach, a criterion is not adopted for the purpose of historical investigation of events that genuinely occurred, but for the purpose of sifting through historical facts and events in order to extract only those that are judged to be intrinsically suited for characterizing the concept itself. Therefore, in characterizing the monopolistic type of state, attention should concentrate only on the facts without which that specific type no longer exists or is transformed into a different type or its opposite, taking into account that the facts themselves may be absent from the opposite types, without this necessarily implying the nonexistence of such types.

It can be argued, for example, that the theory of fiscal illusions is an intrinsic aspect of the limit case of the monopolistic state, whereas it is alien to the other two limit cases of the cooperative and the modern state. Not that illusions cannot equally well arise in matters concerning revenue and expenditure in the other two types of state as well, but it is only in the monopolistic type that such illusions acquire greater weight and thus give rise to a real trend, a *system*. Historically, it is not so much the question that the fiscal system of a given state in a given era may have a greater or lesser abundance of illusionistic institutes, but rather the issue of whether, in an overall perspective, the fiscal system draws closer to or moves away from the limit case in which the illusions become the system.

The types of modern or cooperative state may, as a matter of fact, live without creating fiscal illusions. Indeed, the fewer the illusions summoned up by such states to buttress their legislative and administrative weaponry, the greater the level of perfection they achieve: and both the governing and governed parts of the social body are afforded an undisguised crystal-clear view of the advantages of public expenditure and the burden of taxes necessary to sustain the expenditure. On the other hand, it is equally true that the system of illusions does not stand in contrast with the monopolistic type of state, as described above.

An essential characteristic of the logical tool known as the *monopolistic state* would thus appear to reside in its use of fiscal illusions, *aimed* at facilitating the pursuit of the intrinsic goal of the ruling class – namely, that of exercising power in its own exclusive interest without any concern for the interests of the dominated. What kind of historical experience provided the background from which the indication of the aforesaid aim was drawn?

***

[12.] Great sovereigns have given various descriptions of their mode of governing, with delineations far removed from the intrinsic characteristics of the monopolistic state. Consider, for instance, the reference to Henry IV, in the words of Sully:

> since God is the true owner of all kingdoms and since kings are merely their administrators, all kings must, in the eyes of their people, represent Him whose position they hold, reflecting his qualities and perfections. Above all, they will not reign like him save insofar as they reign like fathers.

The examples of fiscal illusions can be found in the writings of the greatest theorist on this subject,[2] drawn above all from the times when the French ruling classes – and to some extent the Bourbons as well – of the later eighteenth and early nineteenth centuries, and also the democratic classes of the Umbertine era, were preparing the ruinous murky affairs of the last of the Valois or the revolt of the Fronde or the 1789 revolution, or when the Bourbons were digging a veritable abyss between themselves and the rising bourgeois energies that were intensified by the ferment among the peoples of the south. And here I stop, as the obscurities of the budget in the Umbertine era are depicted with somber brush strokes, overlooking the fact that in Italy, no-one was deceived by Magliani's expedients cobbled together with crude white basting thread, and the measures he introduced were hotly debated all over the place. By virtue of these discussions, Italy reached the memorable date of 1914 endowed with a financial apparatus which, although unprepared, like the other financial systems, for the sudden colossal effort of the world war – in the event, an effort accomplished with success – was nevertheless solid and honest and clear.

I do not intend to venture too far in the use of the other investigative tool known as that of logical and non-logical actions. However, I feel I can state that the system of fiscal illusions cannot be described as intrinsic to the generic type of the monopolistic state. At least three subtypes need to be distinguished:

a)   the type in which the dominant class consciously exploits the dominated, by performing only those specific actions that will serve to perpetuate its own power;
b)   the type in which the dominant class behaves in the same manner but unconsciously, by non-logical routes;
c)   the type in which the dominant class exploits the dominated in such a manner as to prepare and bring about its own ruin, by adopting non-logical routes (the logical routes can be disregarded, because no political class hastens consciously towards suicide, unless, that is, reference is being made to cases – excluded here by definition – of sacrificing oneself for the benefit of the majority or the collective community).

The instances of illusion usually adduced in the treatises addressing these issues are taken from this historical armory of the days when the existing type of state was a close approximation of the last subtype (c). The study is extremely impressive, both from the historical and theoretical point of view, but it is the study of a rather particular subtype. As regards France, it does not give us a picture of finance in the time of Henry IV with Sully, nor in the time of Louis XIV with Colbert, nor during the period of First Consul Bonaparte, nor the finances of the Restoration, in other words, of the eras when France was great and restored the fortunes that had been compromised during earlier periods of depravity or decadence or crazed delusions of *grandeur*. As far as Italy is concerned, I confess that I have difficulty in identifying the era to which that subtype (c) belongs. Earlier, I made so bold as to suggest that the portrayal of Umbertine finance is little better than a slanderous parody, and the brooding tones of Bianchini's depiction of Bourbon finance deserve to be carefully reviewed, at least with regard to extensive periods of the eighteenth century and, with intervals, also for the years between 1815 and 1860. But Tuscan finance under the Lorraines was a model, and since nothing is known of finance under the Medici, there is little justification for referring to the latter in disparaging terms simply on the basis of tittle-tattle spread by chroniclers. The balance sheets and accounts published by the Venetian Republic show a picture of rigorous administration of public revenue. Prato and I published the Piedmontese balance sheets from 1700 to 1713,[3] and they are a testimony of austere modes of behavior and great results achieved with measured expenditure: indeed I could, if I had the inclination or the time to do so, provide a precise statement, right down to the last denier – today we would say the last centime – of the tributes and charges collected, the expenditures and the technical means applied by the

Treasury to ensure fluidity in the Sabaudian states from 1714 to 1798. The need to ensure that proper information circulated publicly and that details on financial control were widely available was fulfilled according to the criteria and manner of proceeding of the time. Instead of printed statements of account distributed to members of parliament and the members of budget commissions, the budgets and the final balances were drawn up by hand, debated at ministerial meetings, checked by the General Control Office and by the Court of Accounts. But while the form was different, the substance was identical, and I would hesitate to say it was any less effective. Only the very slightest traces of exploitation of the dominated by the dominators can be perceived. Restrained salaries were paid to ministers, ambassadors, high officials, and this can be explained not so much by the enduring presence of the institutions – for these were no longer fully in tune with their time – as, rather, by the feudal sentiment, which led the *landed gentry* and the squirearchy to feel it was their *duty to serve* the prince.

Before abstracting from historical reality the specific characteristics proper to the non-cooperative and non-modern types of state – in order to interpret reality itself – it is important to pose a preliminary question: where and when did there exist subtypes of the monopolistic state different from subtype (c), in other words, states hastening to their own downfall? What were the precise characteristics of the monopolistic states of type *a* and *b*, i.e. the self-preserving types? In such states, what was the proportional weight of exploitation of the dominated by the dominators as compared to the weight of protection, whether purposeful or unintended, of the interests of all individuals or of the group? Conjure up in your mind the instances of so-called monopolistic states *which persisted for a prolonged period of time*, and let us explore the functions to which they destined public resources. If one were perchance to find that in such states, protection of the interests of all subjects or of the group absorbed, and indeed could not fail to absorb, the greater part – let us say, nine tenths or even more – of public resources and that only one tenth was destined to gratification of the dominant class, and if, moreover, this tenth or some other very limited part was the remuneration paid to the ruling class – a remuneration deemed necessary because that class was indeed a ruling class and because any state needs a ruling class, which is chosen or selected as a function of the ideas of the time and therefore may sometimes take on the appearance of being *dominant* – then would we still classify that or those states among the monopolistic states? And if the answer is no, would we assert that the type described as the monopolistic state is characteristic only of states governed to the advantage of dominators *hastening towards their own downfall*? If such were the case, would that type of state still retain the necessary dignity to stand side by side with the cooperative and modern types? Note that any answer to this question would certainly have to bear in mind that the cooperative and modern types are already assumed to be capable of persisting, as long as they conserve their own nature and do not degenerate into the opposite, i.e. into the monopolistic type, thereby precipitating their own ruin. But assuming, for the sake of the argument, that the type of state hypothesized above did indeed continue in existence, what would be its distinctive theoretical characteristics? These are queries to which

I will not hazard an answer, yet a response would be in order before attributing to the logical tool *monopolistic state* the virtue of being the logical key for interpreting and correctly structuring an aspect or a section of fiscal affairs. Here a problem of logic is encountered. Historically speaking, no state was ever a *pure monopolistic* or *pure cooperative* state, and probably no state will ever be constructed in such a manner that would allow it to be assessed as *purely modern*. The objection, I repeat, is of no value as far as the theoretical investigation is concerned. What is important, for the purpose of theoretical investigation as well, is that when characteristics are posited independently of real circumstances in order to define, let us say, the monopolistic state, such characteristics should be in line with the nature of a state of this type. Should this kind of state act in order to provide for its own self-preservation – yes or no? If it acts in pursuit of this goal, via a logical or non-logical route, can it conceivably fail to provide *overwhelmingly* not just for the power of the dominant ruling class but also for the well-being and security of the governed? Were the state in question to neglect to do so (subtype c), is it then racing towards suicide or not? In order to legitimize the investigation, would it be sufficient to assume hypothetically that the monopolistic state is one in which the dominators exercise power in their own exclusive interest without any concern for the interests of the dominated? I mean, would this be sufficient if the experience of history were to show that in cases where the hypothesis was close to becoming actual fact, the state was indeed hastening towards ruin and destruction, whereas in cases where the state remained in existence, the reality was different from the hypothesis and, despite the apparently monopolistic forms, it was actually closer to the theoretical hypothesis of the cooperative state?

Note that it is not a question here of denying the investigator the right to posit whatever abstract hypotheses he judges to be best suited to the line of argument he is developing. Whenever a scholar asserts that his premises of a monopolistic or cooperative or modern state are purely abstract and whenever, accordingly, he bases his arguments exclusively on such premises, then the whole subject remains in the field of abstractions. And if his arguments have been cogently developed, the laws deduced therefrom are valid. If, on the other hand, the overall thrust of the examples adduced, together with the exclusive characteristics – or at least the major tendencies asserted to hold for the different types of state – allows the legitimate contention that the premises posited do not have the mere character of abstract hypotheses but aspire in their own right to be schemata or models capable of interpreting an aspect of reality, then the logical requirement that a schema or model should be molded on reality inescapably makes itself felt. The abstractly possible must also coincide with an empirically possible, a historically possible; furthermore, the various different schemata or types of state cannot be attributed a content divergent from that which is appropriate for the social nature of man. Therefore it would appear that events belonging to different times and places cannot be listed indiscriminately without careful scrutiny designed to set each fact in its own proper setting and to ascertain its true meaning. Only thus can the risk be averted of attributing to the *enduring* so-called monopolistic state characteristics which probably – I am not saying definitely, as the investigation has yet to be undertaken – are an intrinsic feature exclusively of the suicide-prone monopolistic state, of the type, for instance, exemplified by the decadent monarchy of Louis XV and XVI, by Napoleon in the period from the Spanish and Russian campaign up to Waterloo, by Tzar Nicholas II and other autocrats of that ilk, whose overweening pride and ancestry blinded them to any awareness that they were teetering on the edge of the abyss.

***

[13.] Even more profound doubts are raised by the hypotheses of the cooperative and the modern state. In both types of state, power is exercised – according to a system that allows for alternation at the helm of government – by whichever of the political groups is regarded by the collective community, at any given moment, as best suited to the production of public goods. But in the *cooperative* state, the political group that identifies with the governed population aims essentially to promote the advantage of its members considered individually and, if not of all members, at least of the greatest possible part of the aforesaid population; in the *modern* state, on the other hand, the political group is concerned, above all, with the advantage of the whole group, of the national community considered as a totality.

It is worth noting that the distinction between dominators and the dominated no longer exists either in the cooperative or the modern state. There is, to be sure, a ruling political class, but regardless of how it is chosen – whether by general elections, by co-opting, by inherited position, by self-designation – it operates in the exclusive particular interest of all people or of the greater part of the individual citizens (cooperative state) or in the interests of the collective community (modern state).

***

[14.] It is my contention that once the premise of the lack of contrast and separation between the dominators and the dominated has been laid, the distinction between the two types of state is logically absurd, precisely because it refers to the *state* and to men inasmuch as *they belong to the state*. To suppose that the ruling class of a cooperative state can concern itself only with the interests of the citizens as individuals, even if they are considered in terms of the totality or majority of individual citizens, means supposing that the ruling class acts as if the state did not exist. This, in turn, would be tantamount to considering the citizens of a state as a mere conglomeration of atoms each completely distinct from all the others, gathered together purely by virtue of the technical prospect of achieving certain particular advantages without causing harm to anyone and, more successfully than would be the case, if they were to act individually and separately. But this is absolutely not the case. The state is not a mere joint-stock company. Because of the state, citizens cease to be individuals; they become something other than that which they were previously; or rather, since there has never been a time when they existed outside the confines of a state, they become something other than what one might, with some stretch of the imagination, picture them to be if they were outside of the state. Their personality is no longer that of man, but of man living in an organized society that assumes the form of a state. It cannot be imagined, even for the purposes of a mere logical tool of investigation, that man in the context of the state could remain an individual considered as a single *individual*, i.e. as an *abstraction*. This is inconceivable even if it were assumed simply as a logical tool of analysis. It is equally far-fetched to imagine that a head count of individuals can be taken and that this would yield a picture of the existence of totalities or fairly large majorities.

The truth is that we do not know what entities termed *isolated men* really are. They could be comparable to Robinson Crusoe, living on a desert island, but lacking any awareness of what their life would have been like in society and not linked to it, as was Daniel Defoe's Robinson Crusoe, by the desire to go back and be part of it once more. The only men we have ever known, either historically or through tales related by wayfarers, are men living in society and sharing life in common with other men who have been made into real men, rich in culture and inner energy, driven by passions of dominion or fame, or endowed with humility and love for their fellow men: in other words, men and not automata such as those imagined during the Enlightenment. The *person*, the *individual* within man becomes more varied and is enriched through living together with other men, and *society* or the *collective community* is not something that exists in its own right as distinct from the men who compose it: on the contrary, it exists only insofar as it transforms men and converts them from forlorn wandering atoms or mechanical automata into real men.

Therefore the concepts of *those who belong to the public group* and that of *the public group considered as a unit* are meaningful only if they are considered as indissolubly bound to each other; these concepts become utterly meaningless if an attempt is made to sketch them and outline them discretely.

I stated earlier that the investigative tool needs to have some semblance of reality if it hopes to be genuinely productive. And this reality is not that of one man, a hundred men, a million men, each considered in his own right and carefully numbered. Rather, it is that of man living within the community, transformed by the community, cherishing goals that are such only insofar as he, the individual man, belongs to the community. This is not to say that attention should never focus on the interests of the individual: it is indeed possible to dwell on the particular interests of each person, but in this case, extreme caution should be exercised, and the individual sphere can legitimately be addressed only with regard to private affairs in which the state does not intervene. But if our thoughts turn to goals that are pursued through or within the state, then *ipso facto* we are thinking of goals that are an intrinsic feature of man inasmuch as man is part of the collective community. These are goals that may prove advantageous to individuals not so much if considered singly, but rather as members of the collective community. In the state, there no longer exist particular interests distinct from the interests of the collective community; instead, the two spheres are merged, and the interests of each can be pursued only if the interests of the other are pursued. And it is no coincidence that the ruling classes have a manner of speaking which, although often displaying improper use of language, is a signal of their awareness of the indissoluble bond between private ends and collective ends (in the sense of ends that are intrinsic to the collectivity as a unit, as a set). Thus if we seriously envision that the idea of the cooperative state can be brought about, *ipso facto* we behold the realization of the modern state.

***

[15.] The state can, admittedly, pursue ends pertaining to individuals, considered discretely, who live within its own land. It can deliver Tom's letter, and in so doing it renders a service to Tom and not to Dick. But this is purely a technical point: it is an expedient that is considered advantageous from an economic or some other perspective in order to achieve ends that could equally well be pursued by individual action. The same is true for rail transport, tram routes, postal transport or telegraphy or telephone communication, street lighting, vocational training, etc., etc. This is a technique adopted by all states, not just the cooperative state. If the state decides to build a road, the benefit of which will be reaped by individual homeowners who would have been unable to build it merely by setting up a common agreement – and one may assume that the homeowners served by the road are likely to be more or less the exclusive beneficiaries – then, once again, the state intervention is a mere technical expedient to achieve, or to achieve more successfully, an aim that individuals would be unable to accomplish or to accomplish perfectly on their own. And it is an expedient used by all types of states; it is by no means an essential characteristic of the cooperative state. That is to say, once again the so-called cooperative state cannot, as long as it is a *state*, restrict itself to ends considered as advantageous to single individuals or even to a majority of individuals. A state that restricts itself to the pursuit of ends advantageous to individuals, even if the advantage is in favor of a majority of individuals, has no independent life of its own. It presupposes the existence of another state, the so-called modern state, which pursues ends that are designed for the community as a whole. *First* comes the existence of the state, which assures the life of the collective community, defends it against enemies that threaten from outside, preserves it and sustains it against the forces of domestic disruption (enhancing it via the judiciary, security, education). All these ends are intrinsic to the one and indivisible community, and they cannot be appreciated unless it be through artifices that are conventional precisely because they are not ends representing an intrinsic goal of individual men, capable only of economic evaluation. *Then*, the state, already formed and strong and enduring, can afford the luxury of coming to the aid of single individuals, taking on tasks and pursuing ends that individuals would never be able to accomplish on their own, or would do so only imperfectly. To cite just a few examples: building local roads, seeking colonial outlets for daring farmers and merchants and industrialists, organizing postal and railway services. The pure cooperative state is acephalous, and it has a life purely complementary to that of the modern state.

An example adduced by Fasiani is instructive.

> During the wave of pacifism that swept throughout Europe shortly after the
> 1914–18 war, various authors denied there was any advantage in colonial
> conquests, since the cost of the enterprise exceeds – or so they say – the value
> of the flow of revenue that can be obtained from the colonies. Let us not
> concern ourselves here with the fact that such a conclusion was completely
> arbitrary and devoid of any serious foundation. But the very way the problem
> was addressed shows that the authors who held this view had in mind exclu-
> sively an organization where power is exercised in the interest of all those
> who belong to the public group, but with a focus on the particular interests
> of each individual or at least the majority. It is only in this perspective that
> the problem of conquest can assume the aspect of a balance between the sac-
> rifice individuals are called upon to bear and the advantage they can draw
> therefrom. But in an organization where power is exercised with concern for
> the interests of the public group considered as a unit, the problem is rather
> more complex. Conquest is no longer a question of debits and credits in the
> individual's balance sheet; instead, it influences the fate of the public group as
> such: the group's opportunity for expansion, its military and political power,
> the formation and decadence of its imperialism. It is no longer the interest of
> the single individual that is at stake, but that of the group considered as a unit.[4]

Let us suppose that we have overcome the difficulties of evaluating the costs
and gains of the colonial undertaking and have reached the conclusion that the
balance is likely to result in a serious loss for the entrepreneur (state or company),
while the verdict remains uncertain for the individual settlers who followed in the
entrepreneur's footsteps – especially since the issue of their individual balance
sheets has so far not been investigated at all. Let us also suppose that we have
overcome the difficulty of evaluating the aims of power and expansion pursued
by the state seen as a unit that initiates the colonial enterprise. I would argue
that the first budget, regarding the cost of the enterprise compared to the flow of
income that can be obtained, is not the budget of a state; indeed, I would add that
it is of almost no interest to the state. Conceived as a balance sheet of economic
debits and credits, a colonial enterprise of this nature is typical of a company with
shareholders bent on pursuing the company's own ends of enrichment. But if we
wish to conceive of the colonial enterprise as an attribute of the state, it would
appear to be a characteristic of the monopolistic state, whose dominant group has
set its sights on the colonial conquest as a means of enriching itself and its own
affiliates or hangers-on. Seen in this perspective, a colonial joint-stock enterprise
is something that can indeed be set up in order to increase the income of the
shareholders to a greater degree than the latter would have been able to achieve
if each of them were to make a colonizing sortie independently and separately,
venturing into new or barbarian countries. But a joint-stock company is not the
state: the latter, in order to be such, must pursue the intrinsic ends of men inasmuch as they live within the political community of the given state. What would

be the balance sheet for the individual, in terms of the achievement of ends such as security, justice, defense or national power, public hygiene, i.e. of ends which since the beginning of time have always been characteristic of the state, of any state seeking to ensure its own conservation? If the organization under discussion here is planning to embark on a colonial enterprise only in terms of the balance of costs and return on expenditures, that organization is not a *state*: it is simply a colonial company, which I would define as being *without a charter*, because all the old charters of concession involving colonial conquests imposed obligations of expansion, military power, or political influence in favor of the motherland. If a colonial organization is truly a state, and if it stands for or is the long arm of the state, it necessarily pursues ends pertaining to the group, aims that are intrinsic to living men and, more specifically, men who live within the national community of the motherland. Basically, then, the cooperative state either is not a state or it is one and the same as the modern state; moreover, whatever its name, it is simply called a state and it pursues its own intrinsic ends.

***

[16.] On the other hand, the intrinsic ends of the state cannot be viewed as exclusive ends of the group considered as a unit. Whereas the cooperative state is acephalous, conceived as it is in the form of an entity that pursues only the ends of the single individuals of whom it is composed, the modern state, which is conceived as an entity that exclusively pursues ends pertaining to the collective community considered as a whole, is a monster. The hypothesis presupposes an absurdity: that there can exist a state which pursues its own interests in favor of its collective community without any concern for the interests of the living men of whom it is composed. The heart of the matter is that if the aim is to acquire knowledge of reality, it is inconceivable to assume that in the modern state the interest of individuals is in any way of secondary importance as compared to the interests of the group considered as a whole. To imagine that financial activity in such a state can be pursued even if it does not increase the individual well-being of the totality or the majority of its members is to make a hypothesis that has no interconnectedness with reality whatsoever. To start out from the premise that there exists a *unit* called the state, and that the governing class can, in its exercise of power, deal exclusively with the interests of this entity instead of concerning itself with the particular interests of all those who belong to the public group, means starting out from an unreal premise. Effectively, it means awarding the status of a theoretical-historical premise to what consists of little more than the declarations or raving rant of politicians who are in search of a pretext to justify their own caprices. For within the context of the cooperative or modern state, there exists not even the slightest tendency towards *the 'state' as a unit* conceived as something distinct from the citizens of that state. Now, in seeking to flesh out these somewhat shadowy reflections, it is helpful to move beyond the field that is characteristic of the two types of state, cooperative and modern, and envisage instead the actual existence of a different entity situated at a level above men. This implies entering into the field characteristic of the type depicted as the monopolistic state. If it is true that man does not exist in isolation, if it is true that the two, three, one thousand or one million individuals making up the community have no existence if considered separately, if it is true that the two, three, one thousand or one million individuals are the way they are because they live in society, if it is true that one cannot speak of the interests of individuals except insofar as individuals form part of the collective community, if it is true that speaking of the interests of the collective community is meaningless unless these interests are also those of its components, then it is true that the dualism between individual and community is conceivable only if the community is embodied by someone, an individual man or a group of men – in other words, is embodied by the ruling class. Thus after chasing out the concept of the monopolistic state, here it comes again through the back door of the higher entity, an entity that is different and transcendent, to be expressed with the phrase of the *state conceived as a unit*.

Let us at this point divest the argument of its crudely economic terminology. The state is not a body that pursues economic ends, or *interests*, in the sense in which the latter word is commonly taken – namely, as something measurable in pounds, shillings and pence. The state, or rather men who live in political society pursue economic, moral and political ends in consonance with their collective life as part of the state. To assume they can make a distinction among the ends that can be pursued by the state, differentiating such ends into those that can bring them an advantage if they act as single individuals, versus those that benefit them only if they act as part of the whole community, means resuscitating the dualism between individuals and the state that was shown to be erroneous during the above discussion on the cooperative state. In fact, the dualism between individuals and the whole takes on an even more terrifying and dangerous appearance here, since it is grounded on the premise of a state that is concerned only with the collective community and provides only for the whole community, with no concern for the men who form part of it. This conception is not modern: it is as ancient as the Greek tyrants, as Louis XIV's *l'État c'est moi*; it is a return to the pagan deification of the state above the individual. Christ would have come down to earth in vain if we were not convinced that the state has no other purpose than that of the moral and spiritual elevation of man living in the society of his fellow men. The elevation of the individual man cannot occur other than within the state; it derives from the necessary contact of every free man with all other free men, and from their reciprocal emulation. There exist no ends of the state that are not also the ends pursued by men, by all men, dead, alive and as yet unborn. In organized society, living men acquire an awareness of the indissoluble link that binds them to the past and future generations. It is not the state as an administrative body that casts its mind back to the deceased and forward to the coming generations; rather, it is men who, having entered into associative life and having become different, express by means of the state their will to pursue ends which go beyond their own transient life: rooted in the past, they reach out to a distant future. How could men who live in an isolated manner, even if they live side by side with millions of other men, think of – and provide for – the pursuit of ends that have a bearing on deceased persons? Men themselves, living together, are indeed the state. Men, and not something transcendent above them and beyond them, even though we may decorate this something with the name of the collective community or the group or the state. To find a type of state that exclusively pursues the ends of the community taken as a whole, as a unit, we have to retrace our steps back through the aeons of time. But perhaps not even in Egypt or ancient Persia can one find something resembling the monster that is presented under the ostensible designation of the modern state. Even in antiquity men believed in something. Even when men were erecting the pyramids, and were bowed down by the sheer burden of fatigue, they believed this would more easily allow them to be carried up towards heaven – as men, and not in the guise of their mythic collective unit. Thousands of martyrs have died over the millennia in protest against the transcendental idol of the state placed above and outside of the men who compose it. A great saint and memorable statesman, Thomas More, went to his death on the scaffold because he refused to recognize the state as having power to judge over affairs of conscience. Do we wish to admit today that there can exist a *modern* state which pursues ends concerning the group alone, and thus that such a state can, in the name of the group, order man to violate the commandments dictated by his conscience? To be sure, a monster of this kind may have existed, but it is neither a modern state nor one that is compatible with the freedom of man. The *modern* state is, and cannot be other than, one that purses ends of moral and spiritual elevation of mankind and which, *for this reason and for no other reason*, also pursues the end of the economic well-being of the men through and in whom the state itself is manifested. Not the elevation of hypothetical savages living isolated in the forest, but men living in the society of their fellow men.

***

[17.] We have replaced the notion of the state in which power is exercised either in the interest of the entire body of members belonging to the public group – although a focus on the particular interests of each individual or at least of the majority is still maintained (the so-called cooperative state) – or with due concern for the interests of the public group considered as a unit (the so-called modern state) with the alternative notion of the state in which power is exercised for the sake of the moral and spiritual – and therefore economic – elevation men living in society. Admittedly, by so doing, we slip away or climb up from the conception of the dualism between the monopolistic and the cooperative state (the latter with its modern variant) and move instead towards a dialectical contrast between the state and the non-state. A chasm thus opens up between the state that hopes to live and endure and the non-state that both clashes with and brings about the disintegration of the former. Without specifically intending to do so, theoreticians who created the abstract figure of the monopolistic state have condensed in that figure all the forces which at any given historical moment undermine the existence of the state and lead to its downfall. A monopolistic state that is truly such and which displays the characteristics that genuinely distinguish it from the cooperative and modern state can be identified only as the above described subtype (c), where those who govern through non-logical routes exploit the dominated in such a manner as to prepare and bring about their own ruin. A state where such a circumstance does not come about may be absolute or oligarchic, monarchical or republican, ruled by one, few or many, but it cannot be described as monopolistic unless a demonstration can be given – and this would be a remarkable demonstration, indeed – that its ruling class exercises power in its own exclusive interest without any concern for the interests of the dominated. But this is the *non-state*, which has always existed and will always exist alongside the *state*. At all times, at every moment of history, there is a danger that the forces of dissolution may prevail over creative and organizational forces and that individual egoism may prevail over the common good. As long as the intellectual and economic forces that elevate men continue to be alive and vigorous within a country, the *state* exists and endures, strives and prospers. When the forces that degrade man rear their ugly head and gain the upper hand, the external form of the state may in appearance seem to continue, but it is form devoid of content. No sooner does it start to be challenged than it dissolves, exposing its real nature as a *non-state* for all to see. The western Roman Empire of the fourth and fifth century was dissolving internally, and since it was being undermined by a predominance of disruptive forces, those in positions of power diverted to their own advantage the taxes paid by the majority instead of deploying them for the common benefit. When the barbarians burst onto the scene, they did no more than observe and *take note* that the disappearance of the state had already come about.

The distinction between *state* and *non-state*, which belongs to the sphere of reality and history, has a much more far-reaching significance than the abstract distinction between the monopolistic, cooperative and modern state. At all times, at every moment and in all places, one finds, say, forms of taxation that accompany the state in its rise to power but which are both an effect and a precondition for its growth. At all times, there are tributes that have done their part in impelling the non-state along its fatal path towards the abyss, and are both the cause and the manifestation of its decadence. In all cases, the effects of the former type of taxes have been and will be different from the outcome of the latter type, and the different effects have been and will be at one and the same time both the effect and the cause and the manifestation of the prosperity of states and the ruin of non-states. Individual facts are illuminated and shown to be intertwined in the light of the historical distinction drawn from reality. In contrast, where highly elegant theoretical demonstrations are linked to abstract definitions on points that are refractory to abstraction, such definitions lose some of their splendor of everlasting truths. If the aim is to construct systems, why not base the construction on reality, which is always one and the same – namely, struggle, effort, the overcoming of stumbling blocks, achievement – amid lapses and back-sliding – of the highest ideals of life?

The distinction between the monopolistic and cooperative state can be viewed as a *definition-based* distinction, which overshadows the truly fundamental characteristic – namely, the coexistence of the two types at all times and places. It is this coexistence that explains the alternation of political classes and the decadence of the ruling class, and which underlies the rise of new social forces. The new forces that come to the fore are little by little welded into a novel political grouping, capable of taking over the reins of power and implementing it for the moral and material advantage of the subjects making up the collective community yet these new forces already have, inbuilt within them, the seeds of egoism which *over time* will result in power being exercised in the interests of the dominators, leading to the ruination of public affairs and dooming the dominant group itself to destruction.

The dialectical contrast between state and non-state, the two eternally coexisting forces that are locked in a struggle for predominance, is, if seen in a different perspective, the eternal contrast between God and Satan, between good and evil, matter and spirit. Or, rather, it is that contrast that is ingrained within us, which causes us to suffer and rejoice, saving us from death and doom in favor of life which is constant struggle and striving, constant effort.

The merely definition-based and abstract distinction between the monopolistic and the cooperative state risks being inadvertently linked to the concept of a state distinct from the society of men within which the (monopolistic or cooperative) state effectively lives, although such a connection is by no means logically necessary. That is to say, there may be a risk of associating this kind of distinction with the idea of a state living outside of human society; furthermore, the risk may arise irrespective of whether the argument focuses on the concrete presence of a minority of dominators bent on exploiting the collective community to their own advantage (the monopolistic state) or on the existence of a ruling class aiming to work towards the advantage of men gathered together in society, i.e. of the community as a whole or of society considered as an entity in its own right (cooperative or modern state). The state thus transcends and stands beyond and outside the society, regardless of whether it seeks to exploit or secure advantages for society. The state, which by its very nature is endowed with the attribute of coercion, imposes specific behavioral rules on all citizens or on the group in question – namely, the rules judged by the state itself to be in the best interests of society, and these rules are forcibly imposed on all people or on the whole group, even when the state believes they will work to the advantage of all people or of the whole group. In this perspective, the tasks of the state would appear to be limited to objectives that must be achieved by the force of the law. This engenders a contrast between state and society, a contrast that sets the merely coercive and juridically formal action of the state in opposition to the spontaneous, free, ethical and religious action of society. To be sure, this contrast can indeed be taken as a response to some practical requirements of collective life, but it stands in contradiction to the substance of the fundamental requirement characterizing life in a community – namely, the need to look to the state as a manifestation – likewise free and spontaneous and ethical and religious – of men gathered together in society.

In actual fact, however, it is the distinction between state and non-state that responds to this fundamental requirement. What the distinction tells us is that the state is none other than that which men gathered together in society want it to be. When men have certain religious, political or economic ideals, when they have knowledge of the most suitable routes for putting these ideals into practice, then by the same token they choose the coercive or free tools that are best suited to accomplishing these ideals. In many respects, the distinction between coercion and freedom is merely formal. If men believe that a certain goal, such as national defense or justice or security – which they, by their common consent, deem a desirable objective within their community – can be achieved only by juridical coercion, and if they therefore submit to such coercion, again by their common consent within their community, then can it be asserted – simply because they have submitted to the coercion – that they have not spontaneously opted for this goal? Can it be asserted that this goal is not moral and does not respond to an elevated ethical ideal? Is it not the case that the will of the state is identified with the will of men gathered together in society? Does the concept of the state not implicitly embody identity between two sets of actions: on the one hand, the actions men gathered together in society agree to perform by recourse to coercion, if for no other reason than that of making such actions perfect and fully in accordance with their end, and on the other hand, the actions men perform – equally spontaneously – which remain beyond the bounds of the coercive constraint? In the state, properly speaking, the limits on its action are not imposed by any force extraneous to society itself; rather, they are determined by men themselves, who have freely made their own decisions and resolutions based on customs and on ethical, religious, political or economic considerations, all of which can vary at different times and in accordance with changing historical circumstances. There exists no recalcitrant minority and dominant majority: the rule called for by the majority does not become law until the minority, after appropriate debate and decision making, actively endorses the rule, after realizing that further opposition would be antisocial and destructive.

The distinction, or rather the contrast between state and society, between statal coercion and the spontaneous will of men living in society, does, on the other hand, arise in the *non-state*. It is the manifestation of the decadence of the ruling class – a decadence that may only just have set in or, alternatively, may already be fairly advanced. If the ruling class is not identified with the elect class,[5] but tends instead simply to become a dominant class, then this may lead to a clash with the state governed by men no longer identified with the other men living in the same society. Struggle and even violent unrest may ensue, aiming to place a limit on the action of the state. Accordingly, there is a need for a distinction between, on the one hand, the numbered and limited actions that are an intrinsic feature of the state and which have a coercive nature and, on the other, the various free spontaneous actions that men living in society perform in order to pursue ethical, religious, political and economic ideals. But such a distinction, and indeed the very concept of the clash, is rooted in human imperfection: it is the manifestation of an evil, barely perceptible or profoundly serious, that makes men poorly suited to engaging in perfect forms of collective life. In a society of perfect men, no contrast would subsist, and the problem of placing limits on the coercive action of the state could not even be raised, as men would entrust the state only with all the tasks which they would, by their common consent, believe to be appropriate for pursuing ends that could not be fully or more suitably achieved outside of the confines of coercion. Other ends would continue to be the object of free spontaneous action, either individual or associative. In that perfect society, there would not even be any need to make enquiries among men on sundry occasions in order to ascertain the limits they seek to place on the action of the state, for they would be guided by a spontaneous unanimity rooted in historical experience, in tradition, in the wisdom of the intellect, which would counsel them on the limits that should constrain the state's action as a coercive organ. Freedom of conscience, of thought, the right of the individual to worship God or to pursue the quest for truth are, within the state, properly speaking, placed beyond the bounds of any limitation by external coercive powers. In that state, there rises and towers over all else an ever wider sphere of subjective rights of the human person, rights the state is not empowered to violate.

The *state*, for the very reason that it is the continuous creation of men living in society, is not omnipotent, nor is it omniscient. It is merely a tool men utilize to achieve certain ends they themselves have resolved to pursue; it towers over other issues or is almost hidden from view, depending on the extent to which such ends acquire or lose importance in the mind and the will of men. And if, effectively, in every historically known human society the problem of limits does arise, and conflict between state and society does come into existence, at times muted and barely perceptible, at other times harsh and violent, this is due to the fact that in concrete human historical societies, the forces of concord exist side by side with forces of disintegration: there is a constant struggle between good and evil, between the greater good and the lesser evil, between ethical ideals and purely economic ends, between the state and the non-state.

Notes

1 Antonio De Viti de Marco in *Principii di economia finanziaria* (definitive ed., Torino, Einaudi 1938). The two Devitian hypotheses were supplemented with a third by Mauro Fasiani in *Principii di scienza delle finanze* (Torino, Giappichelli 1941). The critical examination of the three hypotheses conducted in this essay has no direct reference to their formulation in the afore-stated treatises but offers a reconstruction which conveys the present writer's interpretation.
2 Amilcare Puviani, *Teoria delle illusioni finanziarie*, Palermo, Sandron, 1903.
3 [Editor's note] Einaudi (1907, 1908), Prato (1907, 1908).
4 Mauro Fasiani, *Principii* cit: vol. I, pp. 47–48. For the definitions of the two types of state, ivi, p. 42.
5 [Editor's note] Here Einaudi inserted '(cf. below a.p.)' directly into the body of the text, with a blank space after 'a.p.' that probably had to be filled with the reference to the new numbering of the page of the ex § 21 containing the Einaudian reflection on the theory of elite.

III On value judgments in economic sciences

[18.] Can an economist who has dared to venture beyond the confines of merely definition-based premises, or who has been so bold as to peer into the reality that lies behind the definitions, be accused, on these grounds alone, of adopting an anti-scientific mode of proceeding?

If it is true that the *non-state* coexists mainly with the *state*, the economist – who by definition knows and investigates the links between the two – is led by the very nature of his scholarly assignment to seek to highlight the reasons that prompt the shift from the one to the other form and which result in the dominance of one type over the other. Where there exists a state endowed with the characteristic of indefectibility and where, accordingly, the will of the ruling class is by definition the same thing as the *will* of *all people* and, at the same time, of the *collective community*, then the economist, whose very task is to foster debate on these problems, cannot be other than the voice of *all people*, the voice of the *community*. He cannot say: *I just listen and record the facts.* For he is necessarily part of the collective community and therefore by definition he speaks on behalf of and in the name of the community. This, in turn, means that if he listens to opinions and proposals he regards as unfounded, he cannot decline to counter such arguments with other arguments and seek to ensure that his will, which he knows to be more enlightened, becomes the will of the collective community. If he knows that the *datum* he should take as his starting point in his investigation is incompatible with other *data* which, equally, have been established by the political class, or with which he is acquainted by virtue of his participation – his necessary participation – in that political class, then he cannot abstain from declaring this incompatibility; moreover, he must seek to induce the political will, which is his own will, to modify one or the other aspects of the data. He decides in favor of one or the other decision for some reason he considers to be valid, and the reason that is valid for him – which he has to make public – is, according to the opinion of economists adopting the utilitarian line of argument, whatever reason brings advantage for everyone or for the collective community, or alternatively, as stated by many, and in the opinion of this writer, it is the imperative of the moral and therefore also material elevation of man. It can indeed be admitted that the concept of the advantage for all people or for the community, as well as the concept of moral elevation, both lie beyond the realm of science and are scientifically indefinable political formulas or political myths. However, these are forces, data or premises the scholar must take into account and which determine or explain the datum posited by the ruling class.

When Demosthenes persuaded the Athenians – alas! too late – to rule that the *théoricon* and, more generally, any budgetary surpluses should be devolved to the war coffers instead of being distributed among all the citizens as a gift, he succeeded in his intent only because he cleverly conjured up before their eyes the threat of imminent danger from Philip of Macedonia's armies, which risked undermining the freedom of the city. The sequence –

- the freedom of their city represents the greatest good in the eyes of the Athenians
- freedom is threatened by Philip the Macedon
- without appropriate preparation for war, the threat represented by Philip cannot be averted
- this preparation requires pecuniary support
- the limited means available entail abandonment of distribution of the *théoricon* to citizens who are clamoring for festivities and entertainment
- festivities and entertainment are a lower-valued good compared to the freedom of the city
- therefore it is necessary to make a change: war instead of festivities and entertainment

– cannot be mutilated merely because the economist believes he should start out from the decision that has already been made by the citizens' assembly (festivities and entertainment or alternatively preparation for war), and he dare not acknowledge that the choice in question was made because the citizens' assembly, belatedly won over by Demosthenes' eloquence, had allowed itself to be persuaded that the festivals were the real evil and that preparations for war were right and just. Everything that happens is the fruit of judgments, of acts of will carried out by men, whether it be festivals or entertainment, taxes on the wealthy or the poor, high or low levels of taxation, taxes that are transferred in one way or another and affect this or that group of citizens. And the economist who observes and records and analyzes and ascertains links among decisions, costs of public services, and types of taxes, is actually observing and recording and analyzing what he himself, together with all the others who constitute an indissoluble part of the collective community has judged to be right and desirable. A chemist cannot make hydrogen and oxygen be what they are not, and there is no point in formulating favorable and unfavorable judgments on that which is and which remains so independently of his will. But the economist, together with others and – based on his greater knowledge – more so than others, does indeed make the data of his problem into that which they are. It is his will that has contributed to the choice of services, and it has done so because he knew what the uniformities deriving from the decision would be and what different uniformities would ensue from a different decision. Why did the political class, and he too – he who stood at its forefront – prefer one particular sequence of uniformities over the other? Because he believed that the freedom of the city (devolving the *théoricon* and budget surpluses to the war coffers in order to fight against Philip of Macedonia) embodied, at that time, the forces of good, while festivities and entertainment embodied the forces of evil. *Théoricon*, budget surpluses, freedom and enslavement of the city, good and evil are all facts or concepts that are inextricably intertwined, and there is no plausible reason why scientific research should come to a halt when faced with good and evil, or when beholding the ideals and reasons of life, almost as if these were *untouchable* concepts. One might say, at this point, that the scientist should bow his head reverently before something his mind cannot grasp – something on which only mystics or philosophers have pronounced words of illumination. Or perhaps, the idea could be voiced that the specific task of the economist begins, in accordance with the legitimate canons of the division of labor, only from the moment when decisions have been actually made and recorded. It is then that the economist has to take stock of the situation, starting out by acknowledging that men have made this or that decision, with all that follows. But if *what follows* turns out to influence choices that have already been made, if the results of such choices and the choices themselves have an effect on the actual reasons for the choices, then how can one say this is where science starts, and before this there is . . . what? Outside of the scholarly environment, there exist no constraints of academic courtesy which forbid a teacher to usurp another's territory; scientific curiosity knows no limits to its questions on the *whys and wherefores* of things.

***

[19.] The economist's attitude of indifference towards the reasons underlying a choice is probably rooted in the premises of classical arguments on prices in a system of free competition. When attention centered only on study of this case, the importance of which was felt to vastly outweigh all other issues, economists believed that the individual's action – which was thus their own action – or indeed any different choice by the individual, would hardly be likely to produce any effect on prices at all. The infinitesimal action of the individual was basically nothing in comparison to the choices occurring on the market, or in comparison to the ensuing price system; therefore, it seemed reasonable to start out from a description of the choices as observed without delving any further into the links among the facts. But this was no longer the case when attention turned to the study of monopolies. Inevitably, an attempt had to be made to enquire what drove the monopolist producer to choose *that* quantity of goods to be produced or *that* selling price. It had to be admitted that the monopolist producer grounded his actions in the search for maximum net profit, although it was hard to say whether such a motive should be construed as laudable or repellent, or good or bad. It was thus recognized that the theory of the monopoly price did not start out from mere observation of a certain choice, but rather from the premise that a given choice in favor of a certain quantity or price was motivated by the aim of achieving a particular end. Without that motive and that end, the choice would have been different. Today, at a time when such a study takes into account cases of imperfect competition or partial or bilateral monopolies, economists have found it necessary to devise fairly complicated arguments concerning the attitude of the small number of competitors or rival monopolists and to analyze the hypotheses each of these players makes concerning the actions of all the other players. Chess players do not move their counters only on the basis of moves already made by the other players (i.e. choices already made) but they try instead to guess what their rivals may have in mind and what future moves they may be planning. A general on the battlefield who is trying to fathom his adversary's probable motives will make conjectures on the enemy's next steps and will then prepare his own line of attack accordingly. Modern economics increasingly bristles with studies on predictions of other players' actions (*anticipations* has become a very frequent word – too frequent, in fact – in books and essays in the field of English pure economy) and thus on the resulting variations in the actions of the individual under study. Admittedly, this does not substantially change the overall nature of the problem, as the economist basically endeavors to picture for himself the overall set of circumstances composed not only of past and present choices but also of those likely to be made in the future, which influence choices and prices and all the economic magnitudes involved. But while there is no difficulty in limiting debate to choices that have already been made, resting content with arguments based on the observed state of affairs, is it equally easy to predict future choices without using imagination to reconstruct the motives men are likely to have for opting to go in a certain direction in preference to another? Are we not going to be induced, almost forcibly, to re-enact the entire causal chain which, for reasons of the division of labor, we severed at a particular point? The very fact of free competition, a typical representation of the automatism of millions of producers and consumers, each having only a tiny impact – such that the action of a single individual can be regarded as hardly likely to influence the actions of others and the price variations on the market – is indeed a marvelous artifice. That automatism, that unplanned motion of millions of atoms, that unpremeditated meeting of contracting parties, none of whom knows or is concerned with the action of others, is in actual fact the fruit of a concerted effort, of a careful continuous action designed to make sure the premises of that automatism and of that apparent disorder are not foiled. The concerted effort and the action are called civil code, commercial code, law, judges, debate in journals, in newspapers, in parliament, in professional meetings and conferences, all of which pursue the goal and wish to achieve the result – succeeding on occasion in the past and here and there to varying degrees in the present as well – of preventing the rise of monopolies, of inventing surrogates for competition where it has proved sluggish, and of abolishing or limiting anything that might induce the creation of monopolies or quasi-monopolies. Concerted effort and action are studded with passions and actions aimed at acquiring dominance over others or freeing men from some yoke – at downgrading or elevating.

***

[20.] The conventional view which holds that the pure economist studies the more general uniformities of first approximation of the price system under free competition, while the applied economist devotes himself to the uniformities closer to concrete reality and may thus enquire into the forces that limit competition, and the politician and the scholar of law set out the principles or formulate the legislative or administrative rules needed to eliminate or reduce the limitations on competition, is a conventional way of thinking that has an indisputable practical utility, but nothing more. The more our representation of reality shifts from the instant snapshot to the more prolonged cinematographic take, from static to dynamic depiction, the more we find ourselves faced with an ever greater and increasingly interlocked and intermingled maze of completed decisions, future and expected decisions, consequences of decisions that have been made and reasons behind future decisions. Any attempt to treat each of the aspects of a single problem separately is thus flawed and often becomes illogical.

***

[21.] To be sure, the independent treatment of no more than one of the aspects of the whole problem may well be perfectly legitimate. Anyone who wishes to study the price laws operating under free competition has thousands of reasons for not wanting to be disturbed by the relentless cries of those who would like to force him to declare whether, in his opinion, free competition is a good or bad thing, whether it ought to be considered by the liberal or socialist or conservative or catholic lawmaker as something to be tolerated or not, whether it is destined to disappear over the course of history and whether, if it should perchance disappear, it might then be capable of rising up again. A person who wishes to study the laws of taxation in a hypothetical situation he has defined in extremely precise terms is right to chase the disturbers out of his home, especially if they are demanding that he pass a historical or moral or political judgment on the regimes of monopoly or competition he has chosen as the premise of his investigations. Faced with this kind of onslaught, any scholar has the right to rise up.

The right to an uprising does not, however, imply the right of excommunication against other investigations. Whoever studies the manner of action of the ruling class, here meant as the group of persons who possess the qualities, whatever they may be, felt to be necessary at that particular time in order to exercise governance of the state, is perfectly justified in limiting his study to the "ruling class", taken in that specific sense and in no other. But he does not have the right to forbid fellow scholars from studying the very same ruling class using a different definition, which may, for instance, genuinely legitimize use of the terminology of the elect class,[1] even though in other contexts, such terminology might be regarded as improper. Plato defined the elect class as composed of but a few "divine men [. . .] who have succeeded in maintaining themselves pure and free from corruption". Citizens should seek out such men

> far and wide, over land and sea, partly to reinforce the elements of wisdom embodied in the laws of their land, and partly to correct any defects that

may be harbored within the laws. Perfection in the republic is not possible unless these men are observed and sought, or if the search is inadequately performed.

The conception of the ruling class as groups of men who aspire to the conquest of power, or who succeed in achieving and retaining a position of power for a considerable period of time, is a dominant conception in the classical works by Gaetano Mosca and Vilfredo Pareto, but it is by no means the only one possible. For in addition to such a class, there not infrequently exists another group of men who do not aspire to power and who, not infrequently, are persecuted by those who hold the reins of power. The Christians of the first two centuries, the great philosophers, the wise and virtuous men of all ages constitute this group. It is they who have moral power and at times they are far more powerful than those who wield political power. It is they who make up the elect class. Only very seldom is the elect class called upon to govern states or awarded a preponderant and decisive role in government. In these rare cases, prosperous, peace-loving and stable states arise; they are, in the main, states where the moral law is observed and where relations among social classes are not troubled by discord and envy, the nation's economic conditions are achieving progress – with progress understood as a situation in which men are discontented only because they still yearn to elevate themselves – and public finance is structured in such a manner as to rest upon universal consent.

Why should it be a foregone conclusion that among the many species of ruling classes and formulas adopted by the latter to govern peoples, one particular instance is barred from becoming an object of scientific study – namely, the form of government which, by obeying the moral law, assures the persistence and resurrection of peoples thanks to the eternal formula of the Decalogue, and which would thus seem to be the only type of class entitled to be characterized by the term "elect"? Why – setting aside these extremely rare almost legendary cases of states governed by a class of the elect – should scientific study not focus on the perennial, sometimes unnoticed but constantly active work of the elect class? For it is the efforts of the elect that shake the complacent dominion of the ruling classes who effectively hold the reins of government of the states: but these ruling classes will be unable to endure if they lead states to doom and destruction and sow the seeds of civil unrest and military defeat. Is study of the elect class not just as relevant and no less possible than study of the merely ruling class? Does it not embody the study of that which endures alongside that which is transient, study of the forces and ideas that guide mankind towards lofty realms alongside study of the forces and ideas that drag man down? Certainly, defining what constitutes the lofty realms and what the blighted depths are is a challenging task, but difficulty has never discouraged investigators imbued with a love for scientific research. Severe disrespect would be shown towards the human intellect if it were to be declared incapable of distinguishing between God and Satan. Anyone who, while abhorring considerations alien to science, nevertheless believes that from a scientific perspective it is perfectly warranted to conduct an investigation into the alternation of the ruling classes who are at the helm of power, and into the links connecting the composition of the ruling classes with the type and duration of the existing state and with the quantity and quality of revenue and public expenditure, must likewise acknowledge the legitimacy of certain other investigations: for instance, such a scholar must believe that science is warranted in conducting an investigation into the existence, within the overall community, of elect classes distinct from or intermeshed with the ruling class, or into the links that bind together the class of the elect and the ruling class, or on the persistence, decadence, dissolution and resurrection of the state, or the contentedness or discontent, prosperity or ruin of the collective community.

It would hardly seem that *elect classes, persistence, decadence, dissolution, resurrection, contentedness, discontent, prosperity, ruin* (b) are trickier concepts to define or describe than *ruling class, power, interest in conquering and retaining power* (a). Nor would it seem that research into the bonds existing among the facts in (b) is of a different essence as compared to the nature of the bonds among the facts in (a). If it is true that the links in (a) are explained by those in (b), and it is only by contrast or reaction that the facts in (a) explain those in (b), then it has to be concluded that while both are scientific, investigation (a) lies at a lower level than (b).

***

[22.] A scholar's right to limit his studies to an investigation into price laws under full or limited competition or under a monopoly or oligopoly thus does not entail the substantially quite different assertion that science comes to an end at this point and that attempts by other scholars to examine whether the implementation of full competition or monopoly does or does not conform to a certain ideal of life strays beyond the realm of scientific enquiry. Likewise, the scholar's right to limit his investigations to the question of tax law in the regime of an arbitrarily defined monopolistic state by no means entails the right to deny the scientific nature of an enquiry into the rather different subject of whether that definition conforms to the facts, or into the rationale of other definitions of types of states. The transition from insurrection to excommunication is not warranted, because this would mean that the hypotheses of free competition or the monopolistic state are mere fantasies begotten by the imagination of the lone economist in search of subjects for an academic exercise. If such were the case, if the *ifs* introducing the economic line of argument were absolutely arbitrary, then the economist could indeed say, here *science* comes to an end, everything that lies beyond this point cannot be the object of science, because I myself have created the problem, I myself have created the data, and I am not required to be accountable to anyone for the whys and wherefores of my creations. But this is not the way things are. The *ifs* that form the premises to the economic arguments are not lone and arbitrary creations. They are drawn from reality. It is a reality that encompasses passions, sentiment, political, religious and moral ideals, conceptions of good and evil, the interests of one's family, class allegiance, the sense of place and of belonging to an area, relations among the classes and groupings making up the collective community, the laws of the land and customary law and so forth. This reality, so many-sided, multifaceted and changeable, is extremely challenging to investigate. Yet there is no plausible reason why it should not form the object of an enquiry which is every bit as scientific as that built up by economists around the simplified hypotheses of free competition or monopoly, or by fiscal scholars around the hypotheses of monopolistic, cooperative or modern states. Let us suppose that men become convinced that a regime of free competition is intolerable for moral reasons, that it is an affront to human consciousness. Let us further suppose that this conviction gains such extensive credence and universal acclamation that it genuinely induces men to suppress all trace of the free competition regime. The overwhelming majority of economists would end up jettisoning the premises of a line of reasoning that appeared to be totally devoid of any connection with reality. What interest could there be in studying laws relating to non-existent facts? In a previous essay,[2] I wrote that if the disappearance of free competition were to come about in favor of a collectivistic or communistic type of regime, economists would cease even to exist. Other investigators would take their place: I do not know who or with what range of expertise; they would probably be pen-pushers writing descriptions of public accountancy or aspects of administrative management. This is an eloquent testimony of the close bond between reality and the nature of the science whose creation is made possible, at different times, by none other than that very reality itself.

All that would remain, to keep up the tradition of economic science, would be a scattering of scholars, whose particular frame of mind would make them amenable to working on quintessentially theoretical problems. I doubt there are many genuine creators among them. Cantillon, Ricardo, Gossen, Jevons, Walras, Pareto, Marshall – to reel off a random selection of the great minds – were drawn to economic science by their feeling of *human* involvement in the problems they found themselves addressing. Had their initial burst of enthusiasm been purely intellectual, then it is quite likely that other more elegant problems would have attracted them; for instance, the tricky issues involved in the calculation of probability, or in infinitesimal calculus, or in theoretical physics or rational mechanics. But it cannot be ruled out – indeed, we can but hope against hope – that the odd handful of brains, predisposed, by virtue of their innate structure, towards solving problems that belong to the loftiest realms of theoretical speculation, might through one of the many quirks of fate be enticed towards those fields of pure economic science in which problems of this kind do arise and call for a solution that so far has not materialized. This small handful of brains, a minority to be sure, will always exist, under any regime whatsoever, whether it is a regime of free competition or communistic, based on laissez-faire or on state intervention, free or authoritarian. It is a minority that will forever dwell on certain problems, in every age, even if the world perchance were to undergo a drastic change and all men were to live in a Russian kolchoz or in medieval monasteries or in a communistic phalanstery or in an anarchical society, without state and without *carabinieri*. And these problems would be focused on the four or five abstract issues capable of prompting the constructive anxiety and power of analysis of the intellects who delight in reasoning for the pure pleasure of engaging in reasoning. Perhaps no more than half a dozen or a dozen solitary theoreticians would further pursue their debates on those abstract problems or would continue the practice of exchanging the results of their meditations through journals and academic proceedings designed to be read by the members of their small gatherings. But what does that matter? The progress of science is achieved precisely through the lone minds that engage in thought! Once they were called Cantillon or Ricardo and they employed the tools of ordinary logic; later, it was figures such as Gossen, Walras and Pareto who used the language and the tools known only by the initiated. But prior to that time and subsequently as well, their writings were never addressed to the powerful and the multitudes. These thinkers could afford to ignore the surrounding world; often they took little interest in the social mechanism that granted them their daily bread. They could rest content with thinking and with knowing that one day or other, years or decades or centuries later, others would perhaps derive some fruit from their meditations that would be of advantage to mankind. And even if no such fruit were to be forthcoming, is truth not beautiful in its own right?

The majority of those who call themselves theoretical economists do not, however, have the wings to rise to such lofty heights or the self-sacrifice required to devote the full range of mental powers they have derived from nature to the solution of some – perhaps trivial – abstract problem that once aroused their curiosity. These economists who make up the "majority" do not aspire to, or, given the nature of their intellect, should not seek to put forward hypotheses that are not grounded in reality. What arguments can be proposed if one starts out not from hypotheses posited by a researcher but from ordinances or commands issued by the governing powers? A society can indeed live on the basis of a Conventual or charitable or collectivist framework, but in such a society the scholar of economics is unlikely to gather an abundant harvest of analyses from the regulations or administrative circulars or ordinances promulgated by the guardian father or by the alms-giving bursar or by the Minister for the Economy. It would suffice to take note of the economic paragraphs contained in St. Thomas' *Summa* or in the regulations drawn up by the Jesuits for the American Indian reservations in Paraguay.

Interest in the scientific treatment of economic problems pertaining to reality springs exclusively from the possibility of subjecting to critical analysis the data of problems we have to address as part of general experience, whether it be the experience of the guardian father or the alms-giving bursar, or the collectivist minister of production or the entrepreneur operating in a regime of competition, monopoly or oligopoly. Such figures provide the investigator with the raw material, but the investigator does not embrace the data other than merely as a starting point – as an incitement to deal with the problems in a manner that will prove fertile for the advancement of science.

***

[23.] Imagine there is a state in which the ruling class exercises power exclusively in pursuit of the moral and intellectual – and thus also material – elevation of the vast majority of the population or, wherever possible, of the entire community; let us now also imagine that one of the dominant concepts in such a state is that of exempting from tax not merely a physical but also a social minimum of existence. Should we then say that the *scientific* approach to the problem of exemption of the social minimum consists merely in taking note of the opinion expressed on this matter by the ruling class, i.e. in considering it merely as a *given*? Is it true that any attempt to go beyond the mere fact of taking note, any attempt to comprehend the *moral value* of the minimum that has been accepted, oversteps the boundary of scientific enquiry? I am not in any way suggesting that the appropriate route would genuinely involve seeking to determine whether it is truly reasonable to launch a quest for the true or just or perfect social minimum. Indisputably, there exists no perfect criterion of justice in such a controversial matter, and my quiz-zical reflections on the myths of justice in taxation would have been quite in vain had I believed that construction of some other myth of that ilk would be perfectly logical. But in actual fact, we are dealing with a quite different issue. Let us sup-pose that at a given moment of history, the law-making body of the land, being greatly responsive to the opinion of the ruling political group and the general sentiment of the people over whom the politicians rule, and wishing to take into account price and income levels as well as the cost of living, has established that the social minimum of existence on which tax exemption should be granted is 6000 deniers[3] a year per family. Should we then state that anyone who proposes to study only the uniformities of the financial phenomenon is in no way expected or entitled to address the question of how to define the best social minimum of existence – in other words, that he is not required to perform a critical examina-tion of the solution adopted – and that a scientist should unquestioningly accept that solution as a *given* of the problems he specifically deals with? Should we then state that one *must* look skeptically on the politicians' solution, viewing it as a judgment which 'can be good or bad, just or unjust, sensible or foolish, to the satisfaction of this or that fiscal scholar', but which 'for the scientist' is merely 'a *fact*, a *given* of the problems he is dealing with'.[4] Definitely not. There is abso-lutely no logical necessity that obliges a scholar to strip himself voluntarily and gratuitously of the attributes of his scientific manhood. Those 6000 deniers a year per family are certainly not the Ultima Thule of his research. Precisely because they are a *given* of the problem he has to study, they have no particular dignity. The scholar can turn them over and over in all directions, and after studying the effects of the datum, he can trace its origin with the aid of other data, whether pertinent or not to his own field of investigation. To take an example, if by study-ing the effects of applying the *datum* he were to note the following uniformity, as follows: "Given the 6000 deniers of tax exemption for each family, there will be a deficit of 5000 out of 30,000 million in the state budget at the time and place involved", would this not lead to another uniformity: "since the situation of a defi-cit of 5000 out of 30,000 cannot last, it is necessary for other data of the problem to change: either an annual debt of 5000 million will have to be contracted, or expenditure will have to be reduced by an equal amount, or else, if both routes are unacceptable to the opinion of the governing rules classes, the minimum will have to be modified, reducing it, say, from 6000 to 4000 deniers"?

Possibly, the premise the lawmakers took as their starting point is not exactly that of a state dominated by the multitudes, or of a tax-free minimum income level. They may instead have started from the opposite perspective – namely, that of a state dominated by a select few, where the tax-exempt band concerns taxpayers with a higher income, for instance, those with an income above 100,000 deniers. An economist would struggle to detect and analyze the forms in which the afore-stated premise would effectively be asserted, cloaked as they would be in something that would have every appearance of standing for the opposite state of affairs: at no time and in no country does there exist such a thing as an overt practice of taxing only the lower income bands and making incomes tax-free if they are above a certain limit. Contriving such a setup would require a remarkable assortment of most ingenious stratagems. But the economist would also analyze the premise and would delight in applying his implacable logic to pursuit of the substantial truth beyond the veil of the mendacious appearances.

Once the premise had been ascertained, the analysis would proceed in the customary manner. What would be the consequences of the system on the formation of the taxed and the tax-exempt incomes? What would be the consequences on wealth distribution? On state finances? On the political structure of the state? What relations would there be between the more numerous tax-paying class and the most restricted class not subject to taxation? Economic relations of massive fortune and political-social relations of hatred and envy, on the one hand, or of fear and scorn on the other? Hatred, envy, fear, scorn – these are concepts that are not easily measurable, and they do not lend themselves to precise definitions, but there is no reason in the world why it shouldn't be possible to analyze them with decidedly scientific criteria.

If the analysis leads to the conclusion that the state is hastening on the way towards its own ruin, would this not be a demonstration that the ruin is the consequence of the fiscal and political premises posited by a different type of men holding the reins of government, – men who in common parlance are distinguished from others of their ilk by the term oligarchic-plutocratic?

Certainly, in order for the analysis to be carried out properly, the economist or, shall we say, the theoretical investigator must be prepared to look beyond the premises posited by politicians, but not beyond the methods that are his customary working tools – namely, positing one premise, which is necessarily abstract, integrating the first premise with a second, then a third, a fourth through successive approximations. He will no longer posit the third or the fourth or subsequent premise in his capacity as a pure economist, yet he will still be acting as an analyst and as a man who is developing a series of arguments, i.e. as a scientist.

***

[24.] Does this not demonstrate that the 6000 or the 100,000 deniers established, as a hypothesis, by the ruling class holding power in government is by no means the *given* of the problem for the scientist and, by the same token, that the so-called *opinion* or *judgment* of the ruling class is something that he himself contributes to shaping and modifying, he the scientist, through his analysis of the effects on the state budget that ensue or would ensue from the adoption of this or that minimum? Has the scientist, in so doing, strayed beyond the bounds of his own field? Has he given counsels? Has he proposed remedies? Has he become the advocate of perfect justice in taxation? Has he contended that his judgment prevails over that of the ruling class? Not yet. He has simply made an appeal from the ill-informed pope to the well-informed pope.[5] He has simply illustrated a few further uniformities which, like the others, also seem to be of a strictly scientific nature. He has said: if this is the *given*, if this is the premise, then these are the consequences; if the *given* changes in a given sense and to a given extent, then these are the different consequences. If we suppose that the equilibrium of the budget is another datum, what follows is that the *equilibrium of the budget* and *6000 deniers of tax exemption* are, in those particular circumstances of time and place, two incompatible items of data. At this point, it would seem that the definitive judgment is once again left up to the ruling class. But this would be a rather inaccurate way of expressing the situation. A ruling class that governs not in its own interest but in that of the elevation of the men who make up the collective community does not, indeed cannot, pass judgment arbitrarily. It passes judgment in the manner that the judgment *must* be passed, based on the end which the ruling class *must* by its very nature pursue. Otherwise we would no longer be operating under the hypothesis of a ruling class which, etc., etc. (as above). Let us therefore suppose, as in fact we must, that it is the scientist who, knowing *all* the knowable data of the problem at hand (the need for a social minimum of existence, budgetary requirements, the structure of taxation, the possibility and advantage of varying the amount of public and private expenditure and, above all, the aim of human elevation), thus foresees, anticipates and calls for the solution of the problem which will eventually be given by the ruling class after repeated experiments. Now, if we make the above supposition, in effect we are denying that science is merely something that restricts itself to taking note of the premises established by the ruling class. By subjecting the first provisional solutions to critical examination, and by examining and clarifying their effects, the scientist carries out an operation which apparently is one of criticism, but is actually designed to acquire knowledge on the uniformities underlying the behavior of the data he examines case by case and also as a whole. If he has knowledge of a greater number of data than those known to the ruling class, should he pretend to ignore such data? What are these blinkers that certain scientists who call themselves pure would like to don and which would preclude them from looking beyond the opinions expressed by the ruling class? He addresses no harsh words to these politicians, but he openly also takes into account the data which, although known to himself, are disregarded inadvertently (in the case of the modern state) or out of self-interest (in the case of the monopolistic state) by the ruling class itself. Sometimes, in his anxiety to fulfill his own duty, he forgets to couch his conclusions in the hypothetical *if* form, thus giving the impression he is giving counsels and commanding or judging. But in actual fact, whatever the form of his argument, he is fulfilling his duty, which is to endeavor to take into account all the data available to him when addressing the problem. If the data are scanty, the proposed solution will be imperfect; if there is an abundance of data, he will be in a better position to move towards the perfection he rightly aspires to achieve.

The real distinction is not between science and non-science, but between a science that starts out from the premises posited by the ruling class and a science that *also* inquires into the question of the further premises that may underlie those of the ruling class.

A scholar who goes no further than the judgment passed by the ruling class, in the manner of Pontius Pilate, is washing his hands of the real scientific problem. If he assumes that the 6000 deniers of the social minimum of existence is the *given* of the problem he is not allowed to criticize, because it embodies the opinion held by the governing ruling class, then he is not engaging in any scientific enquiry. What he is doing bears a different name: he is serving someone and deserves the title of the *emperor's advocate*.

***

[25.] As a matter of fact, the scholar does not deserve to be belittled so indecorously if all he is doing is highlighting the impossibility of the coexistence of two or more aspects of the data put forward by the ruling class. By so doing, however, he has to all intents and purposes become *critical*. By illustrating the reciprocal incompatibility of numerous issues raised simultaneously by the legislator, critics are unavoidably doomed to overstep the limits they themselves had set on their investigation. Moreover, they perceive no limit whatsoever that might constrain their analysis. If it is obvious that a scientist will establish a relation between the datum of *6000 deniers a year* and the data concerning the *state budget*, average income levels and the economic composition of the social classes, why should it not be equally natural to set the datum of 6000 deniers in relation to other *data* or forces which may be more relevant from a historical perspective? Why not, for instance, in relation to the consequences of the policy of *panem et circenses*? Is it not the case that exempting not only the *physical* minimum of existence but also an additional minimum, called *social*, amounts to recognizing the principle that the most numerous classes of society should enjoy public services without paying anything at all to the state? Let us set aside the circumstance that the social minimum of existence is generally a misnomer, because the most numerous classes pay more than enough consumption taxes to cover their debt towards the public affairs; let us instead take the idea seriously that the minimum is genuinely respected. How can the scientist fail to ask himself the following question: what consequences are going to derive from this *given* in terms of the amount of public expenditure and the distribution of public spending? What kind of pressure is going to be exerted by taxation on the classes who have been left to shoulder the overwhelming portion of the burden? What will be the effects on production and savings? What would be the effects if the *figure in question* were different, greater or smaller? What are likely to be its effects on the *morale* of those who are reaping the benefits and of the taxpayers themselves? In other words, on their feelings and attitude towards the state? What kind of reaction will the principle that a man who earns no more than 6000 deniers a year is entitled to free state services provoke amongst those who earn 7000 or 8000 deniers a year? What effect is it likely to have on the demand for public services the state will be expected to provide for the social groups which, in principle, have the right to free services? Might it not be the case that the state will little by little become transformed from the type represented by the Periclean state to that of Athens, which was the designated victim of Philip of Macedonia, or from the type embodied by the Roman republic to that of the Rome of the late Empire? The scholar does not yet, at this point, pronounce value judgments stating that the Periclean city is preferable to the Demosthenic model, or the Roman republic to the Diocletian Empire. But is it not the case that the above-stated queries genuinely belong to the field of scientific enquiry and of the quest for theoretical-historical uniformities? From *a* there follows *b*, from *b* there follows *c*, and *c* exerts an effect on *b* and also on *a*.

* * *

[26.] The above argument should by no means be taken as implying that a scholar should address all of these issues and that by tracing a path leading from one to the other he should arrive at the point where he beholds the *causa causarum*. A man of science who seeks to plumb the depths of a given field of enquiry in order to demarcate the field of his investigation as precisely as possible is certainly doing the right thing in saying, I cherish no aspiration to go any further. This is the manner of operating characteristic of serious-minded scholars, and they deserve praise. But the division of labor is one thing; excommunication is quite a different matter. It is one thing to say, I will go no further, but it is quite another thing to add, that which lies beyond is not science. Taking the intentional will of the ruling class as a *given*, and starting out from that *given*, can certainly be seen as correctly setting the boundaries of the line of reasoning that is being pursued. But it is not correct to add that *given* is a *prime* and whatever lies beyond is not the province of science. Unintentionally, purely by clarifying the effects, I contribute to modifying it, I set quite profound changes in motion. By highlighting the links connecting *that* datum to other data, which may or may not be dependent on the judgment of the politically influential ruling class, I demonstrate that there exist certain laws, certain uniformities which make *that datum* reveal its true nature – transient or stable, apparent or of substance.

It may be the case that the scientist has ceased to belong to the ranks of pure economists, i.e. that at a certain point of his investigation into the links among the data known to him or among the premises he has posited, he has shifted from the field of pure economics to another closely related sphere. In so doing, however, he has by no means ceased to engage in purely scientific work. He has not yet formulated any value judgment. If, having reached the threshold of the moral necessity to declare his position on the matter at hand, he then holds his silence, certainly he is justified in declaring that he has fulfilled his mission, or at least its most arduous and noble part. Suffice it to reflect on the typical attitude of politicians when they attempt to demonstrate that measures designed to favor particular interests actually lead to economic benefits for the collective community. Is it a question of a protective excise duty, which, to the detriment of the majority of consumers and producers, is advantageous for one particular industry or sometimes even one particular entrepreneur? The politician is always going to say that the excise duty will help create jobs for the workers, set the country free from foreign bondage, and ensure that gold stays within the national boundaries. If an economist, performing an objective analysis of the measure, demonstrates that employment among workers is, instead, likely to be reduced, that foreign bondage is a non-existent myth and that the quantity of gold existing in the country will certainly not be increased by the excise duty, he will at one and the same time have fulfilled his specific scientific duty and upheld political morals: for it is immoral to deceive public opinion by misleading people into believing that a certain measure is in the public interest, whereas in actual fact it is merely at the service of a private advantage.

Similarly, there may be occasions when the ruling class is pursuing the aim of extending the metropolitan or colonial territory and thus tries to popularize this intent by claiming that the conquest will bring a wealth of far from trivial economic advantages for the most numerous classes of the population of the homeland. But now, let us consider the *ifs*. What happens if an economist, probing into the likely consequences of the conquest, comes to the opposite conclusion? What if he demonstrates that the conquest will, on the contrary, result in a far from trivial economic burden? What if he shows that the expansion will require the homeland to make tough and prolonged sacrifices and that even if it does eventually prove possible to achieve the aims of extending civilization which figure prominently on the list of public declarations made by the advocates of the undertaking, the ones who will actually reap the benefits will be the native populations? Those who are confident it will bring benefits to the homeland should not overlook that the native populations will receive the gifts of education, hygiene, technical advancement, whereas the colony will yield advantages only to a handful of traders and agricultural entrepreneurs from the fatherland. And what happens if the economist points out that the eventual outcome of the conquest, even though genuinely carried out with the intention of promoting the spread of civil life, will be that of prompting the colonial populations to aspire to independence and thus to seek *de facto*, if not formal, separation from the metropolitan homeland? Let us suppose that all these hypotheses are indeed put forward: will it not be the case that the economist, having rigidly abided by the rules of his own field of economic analysis, has thus engaged in political action of the most elevated morality? A colonial enterprise spurred by the hope of economic gain leads before long to economic disenchantment, and therefore it is soon feebly abandoned at the halfway stage or, alternatively, even in cases where it is brought to completion militarily, it is not followed by the necessary lengthy and costly task of economic and political construction. But if on the other hand, in accordance with the economist's conclusions, it is begun with a clear awareness of the issue of the present costs and sacrifices and the extremely far-off indirect

advantages, its chances of success will be much greater. If a person builds knowing that he himself will not reap the benefits of his undertaking, but rather that the
benefits will accrue to his distant offspring and above all to populations unknown
to him and living in foreign lands, that person is building for eternity, that person
is shortening the time to success, that person is truly generating greatness for the
mother country.

An economist who, faced with a proposition put forward by a statesman, coldly
investigates its likely effects and studies the relations it must necessarily enter-
tain with other propositions and other institutions, and who does not strive to go
beyond this framework, can thus be regarded as a real high priest of science. An
enquiry into truths, not a list of counsels: therein lies his commitment, and a more
demanding and more challenging mission would be hard even to imagine.

***

[27.] By enquiring into truths, the scholar inevitably asks himself the following
question: is it possible for me to avoid subjecting to criticism the opinions, beliefs
or decisions made by the ruling classes, since in the cooperative or modern type
of state – where the state is the echo of the will of the governed as interpreted
by the ruling class – this means criticizing the opinions, beliefs and decisions of
men living in society? What seems to be certain is that given certain ends, certain
choices are made, and given other ends, other choices are made. And is it not the
case that whoever investigates the links between ends and choices is engaging in
scientific activity? Economists may indeed opt to expel this investigation from the
territory they have begun to cultivate; however, as there exists no plausible reason
for setting the boundaries of any scientific territory according to one line rather
than another, there may be someone whose curiosity is aroused by a different
range of phenomena. Thus an enquiring mind little swayed by any urge to take up
a position in this or that particular column of the table of scientific classifications
may quite legitimately study the links between ends and choices, if for no other
reason than to investigate whether by consecrating himself to a particular science
he might not be performing a sacrifice to an idol devoid of soul.

The fate of economists is bound to the type of society where men make their
choices freely within the limits established by such aspects as institutions, age-old
traditions and customs; the cultural background, the law, the climate, the political,
social, religious and moral framework; the indefinite and multifarious prolifera-
tion of desires in relation to the incomes of the different social classes. To state
that choices are determined by the ends men themselves have selected amounts to
stating that they are a function of the various and multifarious factors that make
up the ends, and since the factors and choices stand in a relation to one another
that may be of a quantitative nature, there appears to be no decisive reason why
economists should limit their investigations to the fact of *choice*. For the sake of
the argument, let us designate those who enquire into the theoretical laws and
into the empirical uniformities that ensue from the fact of *choice* as *alpha* economists and those who, while likewise investigating the laws and the uniformities

which, through choices, have the effect of linking, say, customs, laws, institutions or income distribution to prices, will be designated as *beta* economists. But the difference will be merely a question of the division of labor, devoid of any substantial content.

***

So far, neither economists of yore nor latter-day economists nor, more generally, scientists, have concerned themselves with any problem of value. The economist's stance can, recapitulating the arguments put forward so far, be outlined in the following manner:

The economist not only has no need to address the problem of the value of the ends man sets himself in his economic action; rather, quite the opposite is true, as it is appropriate, on account of methodological considerations involving a correct approach to the problem, for the economist not to issue value judgments. Does an individual person, or a man of government, seek to achieve an end? The economist is impassible to the value, dignity or morality of the end in question. The problem he is dealing with is quite different; or rather, the problems he is dealing with are quite different:

1) Once the aim has been set, are the means mustered by the individual or by a man holding government office appropriate for achieving the end? Are they the least expensive? Are there no alternative means? Which among the numerous alternative means is the most effective for achieving the end?

2) Given the means, what are the alternative ends that can be achieved by employing those means or various combinations among them?

3) What are the results which, according to the economic analysis, are shown to ensue from the action designed to achieve the chosen end or ends? Do the results genuinely conform to the expected or declared outcome? Do the secondary or final results differ from the immediate outcome? Is *ce qu'on voit* identical to *ce qu'on ne voit pas?*[6]

Once the economist has analyzed the above-stated problems or others of the same type, he has accomplished his mission. Which, especially if it is a case of ends set by those holding government office, is a dangerous mission. Generally, the economist succeeds in demonstrating

- that the means employed are not suitable for achievement of the end;
- that the end achieved is judged by the overwhelming majority of men belonging to the collective community as harmful, unwanted or the cause of costs that exceed the advantages obtained.

By giving this demonstration, the economist falls out of favor among men who hold the reins of government or among groups in the community who wield power either by virtue of their wealth or their numbers.

In demonstrating his arguments, the economist has pronounced no value judgment. He has restricted himself to stating that from *a* there follows *b*. If you are
seeking to achieve *b*, then your aim has been achieved. I do not know, in my
capacity as an economist, whether *b* is a good thing or a bad thing. Deciding is a
task that falls to the whole man, not to a slice of man – a slice called economist.

At this point, since the economist himself is likewise a whole man, and indeed
cannot fail to be such given his profession as a scholar, and given his customary
practice of apprehending the motives and ends of his actions, he as an economist
has the duty to speak out – a duty that behooves him as a man and indeed as one
whose awareness precedes that of other men. And if he believes his convictions
to be true he has the duty to say: I want or I do not want *b*, because *b* aligns with
that which is good or with that which is evil; I want or I do not want to use the
means appropriate for achieving *b*, because that particular means represents good
or evil, respectively.

Alternatively, prompted by prudence, a highly honorable motive according to
the dictates of morals, the economist can refrain from this final step of his line of
reasoning. He can, in other words, remain silent and abstain from overstepping the
limits of the task assigned to him. No-one can reproach him for such a position;
he cannot be chided if he artfully opts not to choose as the object of his analysis
only those cases in which he can declare that the action of a man in government is
appropriate with regard to the desired ends, or those in which the results obtained
are considered by the majority to be honest and desirable. His moral conduct
will be irreproachable only if, adopting a casuistry-based method, he applies his
reasoning, within the limits of his knowledge, to survey the whole range of cases.

***

No doubts can be raised on another issue concerning moral judgments. The question arises of whether, once the economist has completed his analytical task of
highlighting that what follows from *a* is *b* and not *c*, so that *a* is an appropriate
means for obtaining the end *b* and inappropriate for obtaining the end *c*, and once
he has stripped himself of the mantle that robes the economist and has become
a simple man again, a whole man, he can justifiably pronounce moral judgments
on *a*, *b* and *c*. That he can – and indeed *as a whole man* he must – express these
value judgments is perfectly plain and there need be no discussion on this point.

What does need to be addressed is a rather different problem. The issue is
whether an economist, *specifically as an economist*, should issue judgments on
values and whether he should do so on the basis of the tools that are proper to his
discipline.

It is important, first and foremost, to underscore a crucial requirement of economic science. This science would cease to exist if it were to forsake reasoning
with its own methods. Although the appearances may seem to suggest otherwise,
economists do not study true reality, nor will they ever be able to do so, for only
reality in its entirety can be considered as true reality. It may seem strange to find
that none other than economists – they who are accused every day of restricting

their focus of investigation to the material aspects, i.e. to that which is – actually do not and indeed cannot set out to study the reality of that which is, or even only that particular aspect of reality consisting of the economic aspect. And yet, such is the case. Economists aspire to acquire knowledge on reality, they strive to draw as close to it as possible, but they know they will never reach it. They know that if they sought to tackle reality, they would achieve nothing. Reality is too complicated, too variable, dependent on too many unknown, unspecifiable, unmeasurable factors. Every attempt (the German Historical School, the American Institutionalist School, the statistical-empirical or descriptive approaches) has ended up as a failure. Not so much in the sense of a failure in relation to the results effectively obtained, which often made a substantial contribution to the advancement of scientific knowledge, but rather, in relation to the broader ambitions that had spurred the innovators – namely, the thirst to discover the laws regulating the real economic world.

Therefore, economists *do not* study reality, as historians do; instead, they create abstractions. They start out from hypotheses, from premises. Such hypotheses or premises are far from arbitrary: they are drawn, to the best of the economists' ability, from reality. Economists posit that men act on the basis of a simple hypothesis. The hypothesis in question is *not* the egoistic or utilitarian assumption of the greatest *economic* advantage for man. That is a hypothesis which, today, *no economist whatsoever* would consider taking as his starting point. It has been found to be unnecessary for economic reasoning. Nor, for that matter, is it the hypothesis of a material economic end that can be evaluated in monetary terms. This too is a hypothesis that has been discarded, because it is not sufficiently general and it is a poor fit to reality. More simply, what is taken as the starting point is the hypothesis of *an end*, an aim, a result to be achieved, whatever it may be material or immaterial, egoistic or altruistic, individual or based on the family, the species, the nation and so forth. *An end.* Even the end of relinquishing wealth, even the end of destroying wealth. And it becomes immediately clear that there is never just a single solitary end: more often than not, *the ends* pursued by men are legion and vie with one another for dominance. And in no way can they be considered finite; on the contrary, they are indefinite, so that no sooner has one group of ends been satisfied than another series pushes to the fore. At the same time, it likewise becomes clear that for each end, and for each quantity of ends, the appropriate means vary: there are some means that are of aid in achieving a given end or group of ends but are of no avail for others, while in certain cases a number of different means can be used, but they are in competition for the achievement of a range of ends. Further, it becomes equally clear that the means are always limited: men do not have as many means available as the ends they would endeavor to accomplish if they could rely on having sufficient means to hand.

This is the premise from which economists start out in forging economic science: a choice among limited means to achieve an end that is itself the upshot of a preferential choice among ends to be achieved with those limited means. Once economists have reached certain very general conclusions on the basis of this premise, they construct the theory of prices, production, remuneration of production factors, money, taxation, commerce, international trade, etc., etc.

In so doing, they have no need to pronounce value judgments. On the contrary, woe betide them if they were to countenance the use of value judgments in their investigations. Woe betide them if they allowed themselves to stoop to *this is the way you have to behave,* or if they were to become entangled in some investigation that sought to find out how men behave rationally starting from the premise of choice among limited means in order to achieve various different ends. An economist, as such, is not entitled to say what ends should be reached. The ends are set by men and the ends can vary, from a moral point of view, over an amazingly wide range. The aim of *getting hold of some poison* can sometimes be pursued with the intent of committing murder or suicide, whereas on other occasions it might be needed to save a sick person, if given at the appropriate dose. The aim represented by *gun* could embody the desire to defend oneself against wild beasts or murderers, but conceivably also to commit murder or to fight the enemy, rightly or wrongly. Not that the economist is genuinely indifferent when faced with all these actions – but he has to make every effort to remain indifferent if he wants to fulfill his precise duty, which is that of acquiring knowledge on the result of applying limited means for achievement of the ends pursued by man. If an economist fails to conduct his investigations with the methods that are proper to pure logic, he is betraying his duty. He is allowing not just the problem, but the solution as well, to be dictated to him by one over whom he has the duty to be the master. But when a person ought to act in a certain way, out of obedience to others, or obeisance to the command of a higher or transcendent authority, or the commandment of conscience, then it is pointless to draw a comparison between that action and another. The person *is obliged* to adopt that course of action, and there are no two ways about it. What use is the economist?

If on the other hand, as in the manner of the economist, it is assumed that the line of reasoning is going to start out by contemplating the different possible choices among the means available for achieving various ends, but then a man holding government office comes along, saying the goal the group of men I have under my command are required to achieve is the conquest of a foreign country (a colony or whatever), then the economist finds himself starting from a premise he himself has not posited. But in any case, he calculates its cost in men and in money, the repercussions on the social fabric, the variations in relations among different classes, the rise of new feelings which may be of glory, plunder, hatred, envy, oppression of the weak, indifference to bloodshed, abstention from present pleasures for the sake of future advantages, conversion of the heathens, propagation of hygiene, culture and civilization among barbarian peoples, etc., etc. In short, the economist carries out observations, follows lines of reasoning and reaches conclusions. If his investigation has been truly rigorous, if he has put on display absolutely everything he has found out and subjected to analysis, then the economist has no need to say you must or you must not conquer. This idea of "must or must not" is the logical univocal conclusion of all that he has ascertained by his reasoned arguments, dissimulating – indeed ignoring – the conclusion he would have reached right from the very start had he been prompted by the command to act for the good.

This indifference, which is the essence of the scientist's garb, is the most fundamental – indeed I would say the one and only – defense available to economists in their attempt to impede charlatans and lackeys from bursting into their field. Charlatans and lackeys have a priori knowledge of what *must* be done. The formula that can save the world, cure society of all its ills, is in the hands of the charlatans; meanwhile, the lackeys, slavishly serving the powerful, have invented the principle that justifies the good or evil actions the powerful intend to carry out. What tool is available to economists to defend themselves – and thus all other men as well – against charlatans and lackeys? Precisely that of adopting a position of indifference vis-à-vis the ends. Yes, that's fine. Let that be the end to pursue. What are the other ends that have to be forsaken if the idea is to reach that goal set by the charlatan or the lackey? How many, and which, limited means possessed by men have to be consumed for this purpose? What economic, financial, social consequences can be foreseen? In other words, in what way is there likely to be a variation in state budget, in the weight of taxation, the purchasing power of the currency, relations among social classes, income or wealth distribution? What new senses of solidarity or discord, love or hatred, emulation or envy can be expected to arise in the society of men if people seek to achieve that particular end? The economist, having terminated his investigation, will utter no value judgment, and to anyone lending an ear, he will say, "*ora per te ti pasci*".[7]

***

Basically, it may be noted, he will have pronounced the best value judgment his specific sphere of power could allow him to pronounce. He will have enlightened public opinion. His work is parallel to that of the moralist whose teachings indicate what is good. By educating the public, the economist will have enabled the population to follow the moralist. If he had been oblivious or had little awareness of the truth, the man would probably have followed the charlatan or the lackey. Once enlightened, *perhaps* he will follow the route towards the good. The economist is not to blame if the work he accomplishes is not always a fountainhead of the good. Sometimes, men desire evil against the light that comes from science and against the command that comes from morals. Well, so what does that matter? Economists and moralists will continue to do their duty, each in conformity with their own specific *ufficium*. The moralist teaches how to recognize what is good and what is bad. The economist investigates into the logical consequences of the various species of actions performed by men to reach out towards the different goals, the different ends they may set themselves.

There is little point in the one doing the work of the other, for they would only cause inconvenience to each other. The moralist would taint his teachings with considerations of a contingent nature – whenever the good enjoys the status of an absolute value, then that is what must be done. The economist, troubled by the premise that a certain action is men's bounden duty, would no longer investigate the consequences of the various different actions men could undertake instead of doing their bounden duty; consequently, the economist's arguments would no longer be of any interest to the majority of men, who would almost certainly relegate these arguments to the status of non-sense put forward by charlatans and lackeys.

What is important is that the economist, conducting his line of analysis as an economist and not straying from his specific field, should always keep in mind that he is a servant of truth alone. Provided he bears this in mind, it is quite certain that his arguments will never lead to results contrary to morals; indeed, he will supply morals with excellent argumentations for rendering its commands more accessible and persuasive to men who need them.

Unfortunately, some economists – none of the major figures – are not always mindful that they are servants of the truth, and so they become servants of the prince or the demos. They feign to be scandalized when others, momentarily forgetting their specific task as economists, pay lip service to morals – the realm of truth – or to truth – the realm of morals – and expostulate about biased opinions, myths, metaphysics. Therefore it is important that rather than explicitly pronouncing value judgments, an economist should allow such judgments to spring forth almost involuntarily from the abstractions, from the theoretical premises, from the arguments and from the statistical and empirical evidence that his duty bids him to present.

It is imperative for an economist who is someone's servant to be enmeshed in the web of his own premises and, crucially, for it to be demonstrated that the premises do not conform to reality or that his line of reasoning is flawed in some link of the chain of arguments, or that the ends pursued are in contradiction with one another or the means proposed do not lead to the desired end.

***

So is the conclusion negative? Is it the case that economists or, more generally, scientists do not pronounce value judgments? Are the latter the privilege of the whole man who, as a historian or philosopher, meditates on the problems of life and prescribes to himself the commandments of good and evil, selects the ends to be achieved and, given the ends, establishes which among the means are in conformity with morals, such means being the only ones that can be used? In other words, is there a dualism between two types of figures: on the one hand, a scientist who concerns himself only with the congruence and the adequacy of the means available to achieve the end and with the possibility of reaching the various different ends in relation to the existing means, versus, on the other hand, a philosopher who constructs a hierarchy among ends and the morally allowable means and then bans any means judged to be immoral, without concerning himself with their economicity?

I am merely raising doubts: far be it from me to claim I have a solution to the problem. If a scientist working in the field of the moral sciences set out only to solve abstract problems, there could be no dualism, properly speaking, since the studies would be conducted on different planes and there would be no necessary logical contact between them. It would be up to the scientist to deal with abstractions, the arbitrary section of a complex reality – in fact, one of the multiple aspects of reality – while the historian and the philosopher would have the task of dealing with reality taken as a whole. There would be no need for the two orders of research to meet. And yet, might it not be that the abstract method adopted in research determines the aim and content of the study rather than being a mere tool for conquest of the truth? And is this maybe a tool that economists, and other categories of scholars as well, utilize not so much because it is the only existing tool but simply because – given that immediate observation and analysis of the full extent of reality has been shown to be impossible – they have had to be content with tackling the study of reality cut up into segments, into sections, with successive attempts to grasp now one aspect, now another, of reality itself? This notwithstanding, since the aim of their research is one and one alone – namely, knowledge of the full extent of the whole of reality – it is logically inconceivable to argue that there is a fundamental, irreducible dualism between the logical position of the scientist, who aspires to acquire knowledge on reality through abstractions that successively draw closer to reality, and the historian-philosopher who aims to engage with the world of the whole of reality. Accordingly, this scenario cannot be portrayed as a contrast, but should instead be seen as different modes of conquering truth. The mode adopted by a scientist is tentative, he proceeds by hypothetical propositions and by demonstrations contained within the limits of the hypotheses he has made, but the hypotheses are not the fruit of mere fantasy. *Hypotheses non fingo*, Newton said. Economists do not feign absurd hypotheses; the hypotheses are drawn from contemplation of reality and seek to aid in its interpretation. If a historian and a philosopher wish to know the whole range of realities and do not disdain any means to reach the desired knowledge, if a moralist, if a priest, if a prophet issue an order for observance of the good and condemn evil by starting from the supreme ends of life or from the word of God, then they too, basing their proclamation on the experience of the past, or on intuition or interpretation of reality along with awareness of mystery, are seeking to achieve the very same knowledge of truth.

Moreover, dualism cannot be founded on the contrast between the rational and the irrational. Dualism cannot validly be explained and legitimated by a trite appeal to the fact that men often do not behave rationally and that, on the contrary, they reject supposedly rational behavioral rules and espouse irrational rules, which appear inexplicable in the eyes of the scientist. For a scientist's aspiration is that men's behavior should be prompted uniquely by a procedure of reasoning.

***

Here it is certainly the scientist who is in the wrong, inasmuch as he overlooks the limited character of the knowledge that can be acquired with his methods of research, which are necessarily abstract and therefore partial. One might ask, is the irrational something different from those aspects or sections of reality that escape the scientist's observation? What multitude of things are unknown to scientists and perhaps will never be known to them! Therefore scientists are hesitant and prefer *if*-clauses and restrict the validity of their arguments and their conclusions to the validity and the scope of the simplified premises they have posited as the foundation of their research. But in no way do they claim, on such grounds, that their conclusions suffice to set rules for human action: they are well aware that above and beyond the premises they have posited there exist factors that are partly unknown, perhaps destined never to be known and measured, which nevertheless exert an influence on the actions of men.

If others – historians, philosophers, moralists – endeavor to go beyond the limit of knowledge attainable through reasoning, and if, by the study of history, intuition or contemplation of human nature, or by a flash of genius or a revelation from the beyond, others are induced to take a step forward in the knowledge of reality, to dictate the eternal rules of good and evil, to indicate the ways of life, then a move of this kind by no means genuinely gives rise to a dualism between science and philosophy, between science and history, between science and morals. There can be no dualism where the common aim is discovery of the truth. In the quest to achieve his aim, a scientist proceeds with reasoned arguments, calculations, experience, and the truth he discovers is certain within the limits set by the premises of his arguments, by the rigor of his calculations and the precision of experience. In the field of the moral sciences, a scientist can determine only the laws that regulate rational human behavior – that is to say, behavior endowed with the rationality that consists in the presence of means appropriate for the ends that man endeavors and is able to achieve, given the means available. Can it be claimed that a philosopher or a moralist are using behavioral rules inspired by any other principles? Philosophers and moralists can say that among the ends of life, the accumulation of wealth has no place or has a secondary place, and is restricted to certain categories of men. And indeed, no economist has ever stated the contrary; rather, economists restrict themselves to clarifying which laws can be regarded as prompting men to engage in rational behavior, to the extent to which men do indeed strive to accumulate wealth. A moralist can, sometimes at the risk of his life and often of his peace of mind and freedom, strongly condemn the existing distribution of wealth and its detrimental use by the rich; he can order the rapacious wealthy to return their ill-gotten gains. But his condemnation in no way contradicts the teachings of economists, whose statements are limited to demonstrating that since the distribution of wealth is what it is, the inevitable consequence is that the goods chosen by men are what they are and the costs and prices are this or that. The economist adds, however, that if the pattern of wealth distribution were different; if, for instance, there were appropriate laws limiting monopolies, privileges and the natural or artificial favors which have the effect that some of the population grow rich while others become more and more impoverished; if, insofar as possible, the purchasing power of the currency unit stayed constant; and if, furthermore, the new generations of the less fortunate were given extensive chances of elevating themselves through study and internships, then demand and production would obviously be directed towards a quite different range of consumption goods, and the economic structure of society would be different, the relative weight of the various industries would no longer be the same and production costs and the prices of goods would likewise be different.

Moralists can correctly teach that happiness, the moral standing of human behavior and the spiritual plenitude of life do not depend on the range of goods possessed; a moralist can point to the examples of Spinoza who built up his philosophical system while earning a living cleaning diamonds. And, again, the moralist finds no contradiction in an economist who restricts himself to observing that given the frailty of human nature, the overwhelming majority of men are not spurred to lift up their face from the rough earth towards the sky: they cannot be expected to elevate themselves to a higher level of spiritual and moral life if, in order to obtain the wherewithal for physical life, they are obliged to cope with grinding drudgery day by day and if, due to the paucity of their earnings, they are forced to live huddled in repulsive promiscuity in unsanitary hovels. Accordingly, the moralist finds no contradiction if, in such conditions, the economist points to technical progress as the most suitable tool both to reduce the daily toil suffered by men seeking to eke out a living and secure the goods they need for their existence and also to make a greater amount of time available that would allow men to aspire to produce goods of a higher order, which elsewhere[8] I called leisure goods. Admittedly, the opportunities offered by technical advancement do not in themselves imply the certainty that man will devote his time – a factor that has thus become available to him – to procuring goods of a higher spiritual order; rather, it can well be said that the abundance of material wealth generates sloth and vices. But if attention turns to the squalid life imposed on the multitudes as a result of their utter destitution, as compared to the vicious life favored by the lucky, then the latter option seems less necessary and universal, and it is the task of moralists, politicians and ministers of the Church to provide guidance, through education and example, that will direct the opportunities arising from technical advancement towards pursuit of the good.

Thus it is not a question of contrast and dualism between science and philosophy, or between science and morals. Since philosophy, morals and religion are all likewise striving to find truth, they cannot spurn the chance to draw advantage from the rich content of arguments, experiences and calculations that science offers them. A philosophy based exclusively on intuition and on illumination springing from a spark of genius would seem stunted, for if philosophy is indeed justified in prying into the unknown, the irrational or mystery, it must however rest on the solid ground of knowledge of reality. Only science offers this starting point, develops the investigative tools required for the discovery of truth, slowly but surely restricts the field of the irrational, albeit by successive achievements each of infinitesimally tiny value, and in so doing offers philosophers, moralists and politicians the opportunity to endow with richer and more persuasive content the rules they establish for human behavior. Learning how to use the power of reasoning, to contemplate the external world with open and discerning eyes, to replace mere intuition and wonderment with critical reasoning and to move towards an attitude whereby impulsive – i.e. irrational – behavior gives way to a different behavioral mode in which human action is preceded by conscious specification of it aims: does not all this constitute the true value of science? By exerting influence over men in this manner, science acquires a content that is not exclusively abstract and formal. Rather, its content is substantial. It influences the teachings of philosophers and moralists, the action of politicians, historians' interpretation of the events of the past. Philosophers and moralists no longer set out the aims of life on the basis of intuition and illumination; instead, prompted by scientific advances, they take the precepts of reason into account. Science thereby contributes, within the limits of its nature, to building up the spiritual and moral edifice within which man lives; it helps to determine the value of human actions and to draw a line between good and evil. Thus even the very separation between the whole man and man as a scientist, between reality and abstraction, between concrete action and pure reasoning is shown to be an abstraction. The extremely close link between thought and action, between reasoning and behavior, between logic and morals was already admirably stated in the words of Pascal: 'L'homme est visiblement fait pour penser; c'est toute sa dignité et tout some mérite; et tout son devoir est de penser comme il faut'.[9]

Notes

1 [Editor's note] Here Einaudi refers to his reflection on and reformulation of the theories of elites (E. 1936a), further developed in the concluding chapter of *MPJT.*
2 [Essay n.] V on *Le premesse del ragionamento economico e la realtà storica.*
3 I use the denier [i.e. penny (translator's note)] as the unit of money of account, because, due to its association with bygone times, it no longer has any connection with the monetary units in use today, and therefore it is unlikely to give rise to any impression of being too much or too little.
4 M. Fasiani, *Principii di scienze delle finanze*, vol. II, pp. 59–60.
5 [Editor and translator's note] Einaudi seems to allude to the attempt made by Luther prior to his excommunication: before leaving Augsburg, he left an appeal from Cardinal Cajetan to the Pope: *a papa male informato ad papam melius informandum* ['from the Pope ill informed to the Pope to be better informed']. Nevertheless, the expression also means the instance to re-examine the facts when one cannot do an appeal to a higer authority.
6 [Editor's note] Implicit reference to Bastiat's essay *Ce qu'on voit et ce qu'on ne voit pas.*
7 [Editor and translator's note] Untranslatable. Literally, 'and now nourish yourself for yourself'. The meaning deducible from the context is probably the following: [the economist, having done this analysis, says] 'and now it's up to you'.
8 [Editor's note] Here there is a note ['cf. *supra*'] which implicitly makes reference to the rewriting of Einaudi (1942c) (some pages of this rewriting are missing).
9 B. Pascal, *Pensées*, d'après l'édition de M. Brunschwig, sec. II, n. 146. [in French in the text] [English transl.: Man is obviously made to think. It is his whole dignity and his whole merit; and his whole duty is to think as he ought (Pascal 2003: 45)].

Bibliographical note

[. . .[1]] And since not all the motives behind choices can be measured quantitatively, what impediment can, in the name of science, prevent the investigator from pronouncing a judgment on the relative dignity of the various different motives and the various ends pursued by man? Necessarily, if he does not wish to relinquish the use of reason, the investigator is ultimately led to formulate moral judgments on the motives behind his own choices, decisions and private and public actions. Why should science keep silent on this point, which is so closely linked to the choices that have been made? Why should economists, with a snarl on their face, gruffly bark out their repartee: do it yourselves, you politicians, do it yourselves, all you men: go ahead and create a liberal or communist or plutocratic-protectionist society and I, dispassionately, objectively, will study the relations among the facts, whatever the latter may be, that you have created? No, dispassionateness and objectivity do not exist in human affairs. An economist who knows what kind of rules govern a liberal or communist or plutocratic-protectionist economic society cannot have failed to make his choice, in accordance with his ideal of life, and it is his duty to declare the reasons underlying such a choice. Whoever, as is the case of this writer, abhors the communist or plutocratic-protectionist ideal cannot refrain from declaring himself to be a champion of the liberal[2] ideal, and this vision of life cannot but exert a major influence on his treatment of economic problems. Almost all economists, even those whose sympathies lie with the workers or the socialists or with those who advocate state intervention, basically desire that the fundamental principle of men's free choice of their own ends and thus also men's own consumption patterns should be respected. And since this principle is incompatible with the persistence of a communist or plutocratic-protectionist system, such economists implicitly want society to be organized according to a liberal system. Why should they scrupulously abstain from displaying this belief that they hold? The classics were deemed to be great partly because they held a belief and carried out abstract investigations that endured over time because the premises of their investigative activity were laid by the faith they held in a certain social order. If they had held a different belief, they would have established different premises; as a result, their arguments would probably have been sterile, just as those based on utopian ideals proved scientifically sterile, or just as the arguments of thinkers who, like Marx, derived the premise of the labor-value from the goal of inducing the multitudes to rise up against the capitalist myth, did not fulfill their scientific promise. If the premises and arguments of economists were productive of great scientific outcomes, credit should at least in part be given to their ideals of life. Consciously or otherwise, they possessed and possess a certain ideal, which still underpins their thought and mode of reasoning today. Why should this be shrouded from view, and why should there be a desire to mask the profound links that define the relation between what a man wants and what he does? Between ideal and action? What are these *facts*, which are supposed to strictly delimit the field of enquiry of *science*, if not the outcome of human action, that is to say, in the last analysis, the outcome of the ideals that move the human spirit?

Notes

1 [Editor's note] The *incipit* of this text has something missing. As explained in the Editorial Foreword, the Bibligraphical Note was to be inserted at the end of the volume in which the present essay was to be published. Einaudi was planning to introduce this text with some comments concerning the development of the text and its modifications, the critical assessments and debates sparked by his writings, and their various republications. In actual fact, this incipit was the continuation of the phrase: 'But the difference will be merely a question of the division of labor, devoid of any substantial content' (p. 82).

2 I refer here to *liberalism* and not *liberism*, as liberism is a rather more restricted concept, although it is quite frequently compatible with liberalism and has a concrete content in terms of its application, in particular, with regard to certain commercial problems and customs duties. Liberalism implies an ideal of life and springs from absolute moral imperatives; liberism fulfils the more modest function of enumerating the *hindrances* and objections imposed by human nature against the implementation of lines of reasoning that are in themselves correct and which would lead to certain forms of state intervention perfectly compatible with the liberal ideal. Liberalism is an ideal of life; liberism is a mere contingent practice deriving above all from political-moral considerations.

Afterword
Freedom and taxation between good and bad polity and the economist-whole-man

Paolo Silvestri

1 The *schemata* of the state and the search for a liberal good polity

The sections of part II of the present essay (§§ 9–17), On Some Abstract Hypotheses Concerning the State and on Their Historical Value, are those in which Einaudi redefines his position in the Italian tradition of public finance by engaging in a comparative assessment of his position with that of De Viti De Marco and Fasiani and, in turn, went back over the earlier discussion with Fasiani on the types of state but set it as a background and gave a more explicit account of his perspective, with particular reference to the last two chapters of *MPJT* – 'The Supreme Paradox of Taxation' and 'Historical Schemata and Ideal Schemata' – which constitute a fundamental step in his long (and unconcluded) quest for *buon governo* (*lato sensu* taken to mean good polity, thus good government and good society), which is here re-examined and developed further through the dialectical opposition between non-state and state.

However, it is important to underline straightaway that Einaudi's critical enquiry was guided, as he wrote in the old abstract, by the attempt to put forward a critical view of the 'concept of a state which, in pursuit of its own ends, focuses only on the individual or only the collective community' (Editorial Foreword, par. 3). Given the fact that the different approaches developed by the Italian tradition of public finance can be understood within the dichotomies individual/collective, voluntary/coercion, economic/political (Bellanca 1993, Fausto 1998), such a statement by Einaudi remarks his intention to redefine his position in this tradition, where the cooperative and the modern type of state seems to be stylized so as to represent the limits, respectively, of the individualistic and the collectivistic approach.

The second part of the present essay also constitutes a central node (in all senses) of the entire evolution of Einaudi's arguments. Thus on the one hand they are the premise for his subsequent reflection on value judgments, while on the other, they give a special significance to the previous sections, where Einaudi ponders on the nature of the hypotheses of economic science in general. More precisely, Einaudi was seeking to formulate a critique of 'some abstract hypotheses concerning the state' – "monopolistic", "cooperative" and "modern" state, as formulated in Fasiani's *Principii di Scienza delle finanze* and presented by Einaudi as a further development of De Viti's monopolistic and cooperative state – by insisting on their "historical value" – that is to say, on their fertility, or lack thereof, depending, respectively, on their ability or inability to interpret reality and history.

In order to criticize Fasiani's abstract hypotheses – and, *de facto*, to rewrite DeViti's hypotheses as well – Einaudi proceeds by developing a lengthy series of reasonings, the main stages of which can be summarized as follows:

1) Reduction of the breadth of Fasiani's type of monopolistic state to a particular subtype – namely, to the type of state that is constructed on a system of 'illusions' and has within itself the germs of its own 'ruin' (§§ 11–12);
2) Critique of the dualism between the cooperative state and the modern state and of the implicit dualism between 'individual' and the 'whole', insofar as in the first type, the state would seem to disappear by dissolving into individuals, while in the second it would be the individuals that would disappear, cancelled out by the state (§§ 13–15);
3) Revelation of the true identity of the scheme of the modern state as defined by Fasiani, which is now shown to be none other than a monopolistic state, or a 'monster' in the definition of which Einaudi saw, as pointed out in the Introduction (par. 3.3), a representation of the corporatist organicism of the fascist state (§ 16);
4) Replacement of the three types of state by the dialectical opposition between 'non-state and state' – in the Einaudian vision this opposition coincided with the distinction between bad polity and good polity – 'which belongs to the sphere of reality and history', inasmuch as such an opposition would be more 'fertile' than the merely 'definitional' distinctions among types of state, because it is based on an anthropological foundation, which is human freedom, always poised 'between good and evil' (§ 17).

As we have already mentioned in the Introduction (par. 3.4), most of the arguments developed in this second part, and even the title of the present essay were already anticipated in Einaudi's review of Fasiani's book, where Einaudi focused on the epistemological nature of the types of state used by Fasiani – highlighting their theoretical-historical ambiguity as well as the internal contradiction of the monopolistic and the cooperative type – and compared them to the historical schemata of good/bad polities developed in *MPJT*.

Both in the first edition and in the rewriting for the present essay, Einaudi seems inclined to consider these points once again, and, above all, to further develop his historical schemata of good/bad polities through the (new) dialectical opposition between state and non-state. Moreover, the nature of this dialectical opposition was further explained in the rewriting by adding a reformulation of the pages *Individual, Society and State* (ISS) (sent to Solari) at the end of § 17.

In any case, the thoughts and second thoughts that led from *MPJT* to the present essay introduced an important modification: from a historical foundation to one that would be more explicitly anthropological, although likewise labelled as "historical" and "real". In this regard, it should be emphasized straight out, that this "history" and "reality" should not be taken in the ontological sense, but rather in an anthropological perspective. This change of orientation seems to be further emphasized in an additional passage that was inserted not far from the conclusions of § 12 where Einaudi writes that

> the abstractly possible must also coincide with an empirically possible, a historically possible; furthermore, the various different schemata or types of state cannot be attributed a content divergent from that which is appropriate for the social nature of man.
>
> (p. 54)

Perhaps the best way to gain insight into this second part without losing one's way in the prolonged meanders of Einaudi's arguments is to bear in mind from the outset the *telos* which guides the strategy of his line of reasoning, which emerges clearly in the synthesis provided in the last section (§ 17). In my view, it is necessary to pay particular attention to four passages of this section, which will be recalled and analyzed in the following paragraphs.

The first passage summarizes Einaudi's replacement strategy, which may also be interpreted as an attempt to claim the epistemological legitimacy of his approach or even its superiority compared to the approaches adopted by De Viti De Marco and Fasiani:

> we have replaced the notion of the state in which power is exercised either in the interest of the entire body of members belonging to the public group – although a focus on the particular interests of each individual or at least of the majority is still maintained (the so-called cooperative state) – or with due concern for the interests of the public group considered as a unit (the so-called modern state) with the alternative notion of the state in which power is exercised for the sake of the moral and spiritual – and therefore economic – elevation of men living in society. Admittedly, by so doing, we slip away or climb up from the conception of the dualism between the monopolistic and the cooperative state (the latter with its modern variant), and move instead towards a dialectical contrast between the state and the non-state. A chasm thus opens up between the state that hopes to live and endure, and the non-state that both clashes with and brings about the disintegration of the former. Without specifically intending to do so, theoreticians [as De Viti and Fasiani] who created the abstract figure of the monopolistic state have condensed in that figure all the forces which at any given historical moment undermine the existence of the state and lead to its downfall.
>
> (p. 61)

Einaudi's line of reasoning thus has the aim of 'replacing' the three schemata of the state with the 'dialectical contrast between the state and the non-state'. It should be noted that the reference to De Viti and Fasiani, which I have inserted within square brackets, was contained in the first edition of this essay but then eliminated by Einaudi himself during the rewriting. However, he had also eliminated almost all the quotation marks which indicated the citations drawn from Fasiani's text, and in some cases, he had also reformulated/reinterpreted the citations in question. Moreover, he eliminated sizeable portions of §§ 9, 10 and 11 of the first edition, which were explicitly devoted to the earlier debate with Fasiani. The reason for his interventions can be found in the first note of the second part where Einaudi makes it clear that what he was giving was his own free 'interpretation' and 'reconstruction' of the schemata of De Viti and Fasiani (note 1, p. 65), which had eventually resulted in the attempt to replace them with the 'dialectical contrast between the state and the non-state', good and bad government, or also good and bad polity – and in this regard, it seems to me to be significant that although in the present essay Einaudi reduces the monopolistic state to a figure of the non-state, he later re-read DeViti's type of the monopolistic state as a figure of 'bad government' (Einaudi 1950a).

This rewriting-reinterpretation of the thought of De Viti and Fasiani is, in my view, an important modification. Einaudi seems almost to attempt to distance himself from the earlier exchange of ideas with Fasiani and to reveal his position more openly, more so than he had done in the first edition (also spurred by Solari's comments on the notions of state and non-state used in the first edition) and to give a more explicit account of the methodological, institutional and anthropological foundations of his liberal conception of the good polity.

The second and third passage are a specific development of the reflections on good and bad polities. In particular, the second passage reflects Einaudi's awareness that institutions are founded on moral and spiritual forces and, therefore, cannot be reduced to their (legal-political) 'form':

> the *non-state* [. . .] has always existed and will always exist alongside the *state*. At all times, at every moment of history, there is a danger that the forces of dissolution may prevail over creative and organizational forces, and that individual egoism may prevail over the common good. As long as the intellectual and economic forces that elevate men continue to be alive and vigorous within a country, the *state* exists and endures, strives and prospers. When the forces that degrade man rear their ugly head and gain the upper hand, the external form of the state may in appearance seem to continue, but it is form devoid of content. No sooner does it start to be challenged than it dissolves, exposing its real nature as a *non-state* for all to see.
>
> (p. 62)

The third passage is an implicit quotation of the fundamental reflection developed in *MPJT* with reference to the central role played by fiscal systems, thus at the heart of virtuous or vicious circles, both in good and bad polities:

> the distinction between *state* and *non-state*, which belongs to the sphere of reality and history, has a much more far-reaching significance than the abstract distinction between the monopolistic, cooperative and modern state. At all times, at every moment and in all places, one finds, say, forms of taxation

that accompany the state in its rise to power but which are both an effect and a precondition for its growth. At all times, there are tributes that have done their part in impelling the non-state along its fatal path towards the abyss, and are both the cause and the manifestation of its decadence.

(p. 62)

The fourth and last passage refers to the anthropological background of the dialectical contrast between state and non-state:

if the aim is to construct systems, why not base the construction on reality, which is always one and the same, namely, struggle, effort, the overcoming of stumbling blocks, achievement – amid lapses and back-sliding – of the highest ideals of life?

(p. 62)

The purpose of the following paragraphs is to provide the reader with a perspective designed to illuminate the meaning of these complex passages and, therefore, of the *telos* and argumentative strategy adopted by Einaudi. They are organized as follows. I will mainly focus on Einaudi's way of engaging with the Italian tradition in public finance, on the reflections developed in *MPJT* that led to the present essay, and on his attempt to go beyond the so-called economic approach to public finance and taxation (par. 1.1). I will then try to shed light on Einaudi's concern as to Fasiani's hypotheses of state, with specific reference to the relation among theory, interpretation and communication of historical reality (par. 1.2). Since the whole of the second part, which eventually results in the thematisation of the 'dialectical contrast between the state and the non-state', could appear rather difficult to grasp, if not indeed obscure to those who have little familiarity with the Einaudian quest for liberal good polity[1]– a quest that sought to maintain the economic, legal and political aspects of a good polity as a cohesive whole by virtue of an anthropological foundation – and since the theme of 'dialectical contrast between the state and the non-state' is conceived and developed by Einaudi only in the present essay, whereas the theme of good/bad polity formed the object of much earlier and also subsequent reflections, it will also be necessary to examine this fundamental and foundational background of Einaudi's thought. This will also shed light on his attempt to consider the relation between the individual and the collective community in dual and non-dualistic terms (par. 1.3).

1.1 Engaging with the Italian tradition in public finance: Within and beyond the economic approach

Einaudi's attempt to redefine his position in the Italian tradition of public finance by considering his views in relation to (or through a reinterpretation of) De Viti De Marco and Fasiani is first of all highlighted by the opening question that replaced the old *incipit* of this second part: 'can the schemata used successfully in economic science be used without further ado to explain and systematize facts of a different kind?' (p. 49). This was a revisitation of the problem which had long been a source of ceaseless debate in the Italian tradition of public finance – namely, the question of whether and to what extent it is admissible to study public finance with the categories and with the tools of economic science, or whether it should not be studied, rather, from other perspectives: political, sociological and/or juridical.[2]

In the Italian tradition of public finance, Einaudi is usually classified in the "school" or among the proponents of the economic or "hedonistic" approach to public finance (later taken up again by the *public choice* approach), as Fasiani himself had denominated it in an article which offered an important reconstruction of the Italian tradition of public finance (Fasiani 1932–33). However, these labels cannot be taken for granted without reservations and distinctions:[3] one need only think of the differences compared to De Viti De Marco,[4] to whom Einaudi is most frequently associated, partly by virtue of his preface to De Viti's work *Principii di economia finanziaria* (1934),[5] which was later translated into English (De Viti 1936, E. 1936b).

Very briefly, what could be said is that although Einaudi was aware of the limitations of the economic approach to public finance (and to the study of society in general), he preferred it to other approaches, though not because the expediency-based judgments of *homo oeconomicus* were *the* privileged reference point on political-financial problems. Rather, he believed that the expediency-based judgments of *homo oeconomicus* supplied, at least as a *first approximation*, a better *interpretation*, and therefore a better explanation of the sense of the observed phenomena and reality.

Indeed this was the aspect Einaudi most appreciated in De Viti De Marco's position within the history of public finance: through the introduction of the two schemata of the monopolistic and cooperative state he had achieved the, by no means insignificant, advantage of having brought order into chaos by throwing light on the confused jumble of financial facts. Consequently, these two schemata served to *interpret* history and reality, helping to orient politicians' choices (E. 1936b).

In the first edition of the present essay (§ 9), Einaudi had taken up some of these issues again, adding a specific reference to the reasons that had led him to 'prefer' the economic approach:

> by opting to treat the problems of finance as economic problems De Viti found himself facing criticism from those who held that financial problems are predominantly of a political, sociological or legal nature. Since the science of finance is and for the foreseeable future is likely to remain an abstract science and must necessarily live on schemata that are fairly close to reality, and since the economic schema is, among the many that have been devised, the only one to have so far produced a construction having some degree of logic and order in itself, as well as an acceptable content of quite well demonstrated theorems, I too prefer the economic schema and I await such a time as different schemata may begin to bear fruit through the efforts of others.
>
> (E. 1942–1943 [2014a]: 36)

However, in the rewriting process, this passage was eliminated. A number of different reasons may have contributed to this elimination, but judging by the actual question itself raised in the incipit, the explanatory note added at the beginning of the second part, the overall set of changes introduced in this part – including the last pages added to the concluding § 17, where the issue of coercion is explicitly faced by Einaudi reformulating the pages ISS sent to Solari – one gains the impression that Einaudi genuinely intended to make specific observations on his reinterpretation of (and therefore also of his position in) the Italian tradition of public finance. Such observations had been awarded significant prominence in his reflections on good/bad polity developed in the conclusions of *MPJT*.

Now, only in appearance does Einaudian reflection on good government stand in continuity with that which, as early as *MPJT*, he had renamed the 'political schemata' of De Viti (but also of Pantaleoni [1883]). In effect Einaudi had set out on the path of seeking to 'construct' his own 'political schemata', meant as pertaining 'to the *polis*, to the city, to the realm of public affairs' (E. 1959: 257). The Einaudian construction of political schemata, construed as subsitutive or a surrogate of the economic schemata in order to explain the *polis*, was designed not only to bridge a gap in the aforesaid schemata but also to provide a response to a considerably broader problem, to which the economic schemata likewise gave an inadequate answer. Specifically, this was the problem of individual *liberty* in relation to the legitimate authority of the ruling power to impose taxation[6] and, more generally, in relation to the legitimacy of the institutions and of the ruling class that represents, acts and speaks in the name of such institutions.

In other words, Einaudi's historical reflection and his attempt to building up political schemata of good/bad polities start from the limits of the voluntary exchange paradigm, as a specific (economic) reformulation of the benefit-received principle in taxation,[7] in order to address the inescapable question of the legitimacy of the power to tax and the tax-coercion, and is developed within the framework of the always problematic anthropological tension between law and freedom, institutional and individual, formal (legal, political) frameworks and informal or "invisible" foundations of good/bad societies and good/bad governments (Silvestri 2008a, 2012a, 2012b).

In particular, Einaudi's reflection on good government in *MPJT* starts out from the attempt to overcome what he called the 'supreme taxation paradox'. This was the problem of the 'inapplicability of the Mengerian table' to public finance, i.e. of the difficulty in applying the theory of weighted marginal utility to public goods (E. 1959: 246–247) – a complication that was partly due to forms of individual behavior which, in modern terms, evoke the problem of the free-rider. Taxation descends directly from that paradox, because the 'sanction of the ultimate taxation paradox is coercion' (E. 1959: 248). The shackles of the paradox 'can be broken by building a table in which certain men, who compose the entity called "state", register the decisions that "should be" – according to the judgment of the "state" – the citizens' "rational" decisions *vis-à-vis* public goods' (E. 1959: 250). In this manner, Einaudi was gradually outlining something which, again if cast in modern terms, would be likened to a principal-agent relation between citizens and their agents or the ruling class (Forte 2009: 104).

So far, one may feel that Einaudi still remained within the economic approach. And in effect this approach was never rejected, if for no other reason than because means-aim rationality, which Einaudi saw above all as the virtue of prudence, continued to represent both an important node of interaction between public and private and, also, a regulatory criterion of the manner of action of the (good) politician.[8] But on the other hand, Einaudi developed new reflections that led him to go beyond the mere economic approach.[9]

With reference to the issues taken up again and implicitly or explicitly reformulated in the present essay, Einaudi's reflection in *MPJT* (1940a [2014a]: 116–147) can be summarized in the following points (Silvestri 2015):

1) through a reformulation of the Italian theories of the elites and legitimacy, the introduction of the distinction between elites and "elect class", and a specific re-articulation of the nexus between rule of law and rule of men[10] (Einaudi 1936a, 1940a [2014a]: 138–139), a reflection partly recalled in § 21 of the present essay, Einaudi reached the conclusion that the so-called tax-coercion would not be necessarily perceived as brute coercion if power (and the power to tax) is founded on shared and recognized values and on a shared sense of reciprocal trust and mutual recognition, or, as he calls it, reinterpreting Wicksell's (1896) [1958] approach, on an atmosphere of 'compromise and mutual recognition' (E. 1940a [2014]: 139–141) – first of all, in a democratic process, between majority and minority – or, as he writes in the present essay, on a process of 'identification' between governors and governed (p. 64). This constitutes the social capital on which any society is founded and through which societies overcome social dilemmas such as that of public goods and the free-rider.

2) to better understand the fiscal phenomenon, Einaudi examines it through a historical-anthropological, almost ethnographic, study or, as it were, following the principle *ubi homo, ibi societas; ubi societas, ibi jus; ergo ubi homo, ibi jus . . .* and *ubi homo, ubi societas* and *ibi tributum*. In this manner, he detaches tax obligation from any legal imperativism of his epoch – mainly based on the notion of state sovereignty – in order to understand such obligation within the framework of the always problematic anthropological tension between law and freedom, institutional and individual. Such a historical-anthropological research revealed the existence of 'spontaneous oblations' or 'voluntary donations' or fiscal gifts to the *res publica* (such as the *liturgyes* in the Periclean Polis). The fiscal gift portrayed by Einaudi is a fundamental figure of free and non-constrained contribution that goes beyond the mere costs-benefits calculus of the individual tax burden and benefit. At the same time, however, Einaudi highlights not only its potential for enhancing the social bond but also its structural fragility and ambiguity, for the gift is always susceptible of being perverted into a form of harsh competition[11] as well as of undermining the social bond itself (E. 1940a [2014a]: 116–128). This means that the two ideal-typical extremes, taxation as pure exchange and taxation as pure gift, must coexist in order to preserve the dynamics of the fiscal systems.

3) Einaudi observed the *simultaneous* presence in the Greek poleis, as in any city, of *virtuous and vicious circles* that he assumed as a descriptive and normative theory of "prosperous" and "decadent" societies, where the path toward

prosperity or decadence is often triggered when such circles go beyond or below a certain threshold. Such virtuous/vicious circles mainly depend on societal and political (horizontal and vertical) relations of reciprocity, understood and developed by Einaudi through a reflection on relational passions: 'ambition' and 'emulation', on the one hand, and 'fear' and 'envy' on the other. In the case of Periclean Polis, such relations arose among those who perform the *liturgyes* (mainly the rich) and between them and other citizens. Virtuous and vicious circles are at the core of an 'extremely delicate' social equilibrium, where the tax system plays an important role in distributing burdens and benefits among citizens – that is to say, the tax system is 'the condition, the effect and the sign' of a good (or bad) society (Einaudi 1940a [2014a]: 127).

This tenet, which was implicitly recalled, as seen, in § 17 of the present essay, is truly crucial for an understanding of the logic of that which Einaudi further develops as 'the dialectical contrast between state and non-state'. In turn, this tenet was later formalized through the theory of the *critical point* (see, above all, Einaudi 1949a) – namely, the "point" when a virtuous circle turns into a vicious circle, the good become evil, the state become non-state, or vice versa – which is mainly a theory of the unpredictable relation between individual freedom and (formal and informal) institutions.[12] Emblematic, in this regard, is Einaudi's reply to Solari. The latter claimed that the notions of "state" and "elite" as used by Einaudi could reintroduce a concept of an 'ethical state' (see Editorial Foreward, par. 5), and exhorted Einaudi to clarify the relation between 'individual, society and state'. Einaudi explained that 'society can be more or less than the sum of individuals'. The 'state' is only a 'means', among many 'forms' through which men gather in community or society. Through these means, men may, however, 'elevate' or 'degrade' themselves, depending on 'concord or discord', cooperation or conflict, 'emulation or envy' among them (ISS: 5–7). Or, as he wrote elsewhere, with an implicit reference to his doctrine of the struggle (see par. 1.3),

> there is no theoretical rule which tells us when diversity degenerates into anarchy and when uniformity is a prodrome of tyranny. We only know that there exists a critical point such that, when it is passed, every way of life, every custom that had up to that point been a means of human elevation and refinement becomes an instrument of degeneration and decadence.
>
> (E. 1949a: 231)

4) The ruling class, provided that it is recognised (and rules) in the name of shared values, is a figure of thirdness that works as a coordinating mechanism; it also (or alternatively) fulfills the function of breaking up vicious circles,[13] and/or acts as a symbolic guarantor of the equilibrium of the system and its *legitimacy*, including the legitimacy of taxes. As Einaudi writes in the concluding words of *MPJT*:

> if it's a question of coercing people into paying taxes, then any old despot is perfectly able to do that. But the leader chosen by the *valentior pars* of the citizens [. . .] intends to elevate the mortals of the earthly city to the divine

city, where the word 'tax' is unknown, because all the people know the reason and the value of the sacrifice offered on the altar of the common good.

(Einaudi 1940a [2014]: 147)

These points also allow us to make an assessment of Einaudi's position in the Italian tradition in public finance.

The Einaudian theme of the relation between freedom and the legitimacy of the institutions and the ruling class marks a first element that differentiated Einaudi from De Viti, but also from Fasiani. While in De Viti there is no specific reflection on the ruling class and the elites (Forte 2009: 103), Fasiani takes up again the political-sociological theories of the elites that can be traced back to Moschian–Paretian views (Mosca 1982, Pareto 1916 [1964]), adding a special reinterpretation of Puviani's (1903) theory of fiscal illusions[14] within the framework of the schema of a monopolistic state. In any case, Fasiani's reference to the theories of elites is merely functional to the construction of the types of states as limit cases, and not a true development, and even less an approval of these theories. Einaudi, on the other hand, turned away from these theories, developing a critical reflection of his own on the problem of authority and legitimacy and, therefore, of liberty (Silvestri 2012a: 74–88).

In this regard, one should not neglect the sense of the Einaudian citation of the formula embodying the foundation of legitimacy of Henry IV, where the king states that he is acting as an 'administrator', 'representative' and place-holder of god (p. 51). Einaudi drew this formula from Fasiani (Fasiani 1941, I: 77), but he deployed it against Fasiani to draw attention to the observation that some historical experiences of apparently monopolistic (or absolutist) states were not negative and that their legitimacy was not necessarily the fruit of "illusions" produced by the ruling powers themselves. For Einaudi, these foundations were not necessarily to be regarded as exclusively rhetorical strategies (in the negative sense of the term rhetorics), or as illusionistic strategies for the legitimation of power. Rather, they express the foundational beliefs of a given historical and cultural context, though they may also be criticized and they may change over time. Accordingly, it becomes easier to understand Einaudi's endeavor to downplay the significance of Fasiani's monopolistic state, which rested on a system of illusions: such a state was now reduced to certain historical cases in which public discussion and criticism was absent (p. 51–53) and which, precisely for this reason, were destined to fail.[15] In the background of this critical assessment Einaudi gave of Fasiani's approach, one may also perceive the principle of liberal thought which, ever since the time of Hume, has always held that government is founded on opinion and therefore, in the long run, it cannot endure if the men who form it and the methods they apply are not accepted by the majority of the ruled.

Einaudi's attempt to go beyond the economic approach seems to be remarked in the context of the critique of the dualism between the individual and the state, where he maintains that 'the state is not a mere joint-stock company' (p. 55). Here Einaudi seems to assume the cooperative and the modern types of state as, respectively, the individualistic or self-interest approach, and collective approach to public finance.

By claiming that 'the state is not a mere joint-stock company', Einaudi's line of thought moves in two directions. On the one hand, he draws attention to the problem of the state an 'artifice', thus as as a founding legal *fiction*, or, as Solari had perceived, as a 'more or less fictive personality' (Lett.: Solari to E., June 27, 1943), by virtue of which a set of individuals perceive themselves, collectively, as a 'political community' and not as a mere sum of individuals or 'atoms' (p. 55), each with their own interests. But on the other, he focuses on the related logic of the collective ends (safety, justice, defense, etc.) which lie beyond the self-interest or the 'balance sheet for the individual' (p. 59):

> these ends are intrinsic to the one and indivisible community, and they cannot be appreciated unless it be through artifices that are conventional precisely because they are not ends representing an intrinsic goal of individual men, capable only of economic evaluation.
>
> (p. 57)

There is a further difference between Einaudi and De Viti with regard to the starting point of the analysis:

> unlike De Viti, Einaudi did not adopt a position whereby his conception of finance descended from a certain definition of the State; [rather, he] preferred to start out from a few ideal schemata of taxation, and to derive the model of the state therefrom.
>
> (Faucci 1982: 124)

It is a difference that is by no means trivial, since the former case implies assuming the point of view of the state, while the latter assumes that of the individual and his freedom.

The difference in the starting point of the analysis also marks the distance that separates Einaudi from Fasiani. It was Einaudi himself who brought the distance to attention, in a note of the first edition, which was later eliminated. In that note, the question was raised as to whether their discussion might not end up being transformed into a 'dispute on the mere didactic expediency' of following one method or the other.[16] But Einaudi probably realized that it was by no means a question of 'mere didactic expediency' concerning the starting point of the analysis, especially since Fasiani's types of state also included the type of the "modern" or "nationalist" or "corporatist" state (these were synonyms Einaudi criticized in the first edition (Introduction, par. 3.3)). Particularly galling was the fact that Fasiani presented the nationalist state as a 'negation and transformation' of the liberal state and as 'the last and most vivid expression of the evolution of European civilisation' (Fasiani 1941: I, 55).

From Einaudi's perspective, the starting point of the analysis not only reflected an inevitable axiological choice by the scholar (as Einaudi pointed out in his review of Fasiani's book), but it could also give rise to communicative-normative effects (as we will see in the next paragraph). In effect building the "type" of the corporatist state during the fascist era could hardly be dubbed a merely descriptive or neutral operation, and even less could it be one of 'mere didactic expediency'.

Naturally, even the very fact of starting out from the analysis of taxation reflects an axiological option – that is to say, it reflects Einaudi's greater attention to the person and to liberty, so that the problem of taxation comes "first" in the sense that the man on the street (to whom Einaudi's thoughts and writings are generally addressed) perceives it as one of the more evident and immediate problems of the presence of the state in his life.

1.2 Hypotheses and schema: Theory, interpretation and communication of historical reality

It is important to note that while Einaudi's discussion with Fasiani had ended up also involving his reinterpretation of De Viti's schemata, Einaudi nevertheless seemed to try to maintain a distinction between the two thinkers, not so much with regard to the content of the schemata, but rather their 'use'. Einaudi underlined De Viti's 'extremely cautious utilization of these tools, deploying them in cases where they were genuinely of aid in clarifying the problems at hand – namely, in setting out the approach to the individual problems' (p. 49). In contrast, the passage in which Einaudi moves on to analyze Fasiani's schemata of states is introduced by the following question:

> while use of the two economic schemata for some types of financial problems may seem to act as a clarification, which of the two words is best suited for declaring their substance? Hypotheses or schemata? Are they merely hypotheses thought up by the mind of the scholar in order to derive theoretical laws that are true *sub specie aeternitatis*, or also schemata – tools – for an approximated interpretation of historical reality?
>
> (p. 49)

The latter question, which (as we will see) rewrote § 11, marked the beginning of Einaudi's critical analysis concerning the "historical value" of these hypotheses – a theme that forms the basis of the whole of the second part. What in my view represents the crucial problem is ascertaining what Einaudi really meant by 'approximated interpretation of historical reality'. This is particularly important inasmuch as the expression "historical value" placed in the title of the second part, but without a specific explanation in the text, seems to conceal an ambiguity: is the role of such schemata one of interpretation and/or communication of the historical situation?

To gain further understanding on this point, and to grasp all the implications of the question posed by Einaudi, it is important to follow Einaudi's various reformulations and second thoughts. The trail of his thoughts starts from his review of Fasiani's *Principii di scienza delle Finanze* (E. 1942a), later taken up again both in the text and in a long note of the first edition (partly also as a result of the subsequent exchange of correspondence with Fasiani: E. 1942–43 [2014b]: 299–301), and later eliminated in the rewriting.

In his review of Fasiani, Einaudi had interpreted these hypotheses as a means of 'achieving greater perfection' in De Viti De Marco's hypotheses of the monopolistic and cooperative states and assimilated them to Weber's ideal types (see Weber 1949), viewing the latter as 'logical tools' for the 'interpretation of economic and social history' (E. 1942a: 35). In effect, Fasiani, while not referring to Weberian ideal types, did regard his types of state as "limit cases" or pure types, because he felt they did not claim to represent a historically existing case of a state. Rather, in his view they simply emphasized some aspect or tendency, with the result that 'all the concrete historical states, whether past, present or future, are a mixed combination' of these limit cases (E. 1942a: 31).

From the time of this review onwards, Einaudi felt that Fasiani's typology of states displayed the characteristics of an excess of generalization: a sort of metatheory which claimed to explain too much and, moreover, without a "necessary" – i.e. logical-deductive – connection with an "analysis of the effects of taxation" – an analysis which Einaudi believed could be carried out without recourse to the typology of states.

In seeking to give a more precise assessment of the epistemological status of Fasiani's types, Einaudi noted, as already mentioned in the Introduction (par. 4.3) that on the one hand they displayed a certain ambiguity – 'something midway between the historical and the theoretical' – and on the other, a sort of internal contradiction or a 'flaw' of self-confutation.

The allegedly ambiguous nature in Fasiani's types of state would later be remodelled when Einaudi had second thoughts on this issue, prompted by the exchange of correspondence with Fasiani that took place after Einaudi's review article. In addition, the 'flaw of their own denial', which is touched on only very briefly in the review, was discussed more clearly and developed in greater detail both in Einaudi's first edition and also in the present essay, where he addressed what he regarded as the central problem – namely, that of the dualism between the individual and the state.

In the exchange of letters between the two scholars, Fasiani maintained that his approach was merely theoretical and therefore could no way be said to have the 'historical character' Einaudi attributed to it. In order to study the 'uniformities' of the 'political-financial life' of states, Fasiani believed it was appropriate to follow a manner of proceeding by abstractions, identical to that usually adopted in economic science to build such lines of reasoning as the 'hypothesis of a subject who seeks to achieve a maximum of ophelimity'. To achieve this aim, all that is required is to gather

> *a part* of the facts, *a small part* [. . .] *one of the tendencies*, or rather, to single out *three of the tendencies* that are manifested in its activity [of the state]. And this, in my opinion, is to be viewed as working on theory and not on history. Whether the trivial facts I remember actually took place in the eighteenth century or in the nineteenth is an absolutely trivial circumstance, just as it is of very little importance in the realm of economics to determine whether hedonistic activities are more abundant in old age or in one's prime rather than during one's youth.
>
> (Lett.: Fasiani to E., June 12, 1942)

At first, Einaudi seemed to be loath to accept Fasiani's claim of the 'theoretical' and abstract character of his types of state. In this regard, the changes Einaudi introduced during the rewriting process, and, above all, the various eliminations that we will examine shortly, are particularly significant.

In the first edition, after dealing with the problem of the epistemological status of the ideal types, which he had renamed 'theoretical-historical schemata' (§ 8), Einaudi turned to § 9 (replaced in the rewriting by the new incipit of part II mentioned earlier) and began by outlining a comparison with the theoretical-historical schemata and the types of state as they were found in De Viti and Fasiani:

> since those who made use of such [theoretical-historical schemata] declared them explicitly or implicitly to be purely theoretical, devoid of reference to any particular factual verification, the schemata proposed in modern times by De Viti De Marco to portray the finances of the monopolistic state and the cooperative state – to which Fasiani has now added the model of the modern state – would appear to be immune from criticism.
>
> (E. 1942–43 [2014a]: 35)

The treatment of De Viti's approach is then followed, at the beginning of the next § 10, by a remark on Fasiani's *Principii* and also a question:

> did Fasiani succeed, with his magnificent recent attempt, in demonstrating that the models of the monopolistic, cooperative and modern state have their own theoretical virtue?
>
> (E. 1942–43 [2014a]: 36)

Einaudi remained hesitant, declaring himself to be 'skeptical' as regards the success of such an attempt, since he continued to believe that the typology of states and the analysis of the 'problems of tax shifting and the effects of taxation' were two independent fields of study that were not necessarily interconnected.[17] On the contrary, as can again be observed in the incipit of § 11 (likewise eliminated), the latter field 'was the only' analysis of pure economics that could be undertaken in public finance. Therefore, Einaudi continued to note a certain difficulty of using such schemata to conduct the delicate investigations on tax shifting.

Now, it was precisely this difficulty that prompted the next question on the nature of these types of states. The question was then slightly reformulated during the rewriting, and it is from here that we started out on our investigation: 'are they merely hypotheses thought up by the mind of the scholar in order to derive theoretical laws that are true *sub specie aeternitatis*, or also *schemata* – tools – for an approximated interpretation of historical reality?' Clearly, this last question, which Einaudi reformulated by adding the word "schemata", takes on a particular meaning if it is taken in connection with the aforementioned eliminations of various parts of the text.

That is to say, one has the impression that Einaudi did indeed want to take Fasiani seriously with regard to the claim by the latter of having been careful to formulate his hypotheses on the state in a suitably theoretical and abstract manner.

However, here Einaudi's attitude was motivated only by the fact that Fasiani's approach would lend itself more easily to criticism if it were to be shown that the types of state do not *also* have a "historical value". Besides, it is likely that Einaudi was somewhat concerned about Fasiani's identification of the types of state as 'purely theoretical, devoid of reference to any particular factual verification', to the point that even the type of "modern state" (read – the fascist state) 'would appear to be immune from criticism', as Einaudi had written in his first edition.

We must therefore return to the question mentioned at the beginning: in other words, we should endeavour to grasp in what sense Einaudi assigned to these schemata or tools the task of providing an 'approximated interpretation of historical reality'.

In appearance, the problem in question would appear to be the classical methodological problem of the realism of hypotheses.[18] But Einaudi was well aware that these schemata cannot be criticized in terms of their degree of realism, or through a 'factual verification', inasmuch as they neither are nor can be a mimetic representation of reality, as indeed Einaudi himself states on a number of occasions in the present essay. Any attempt to criticize the schemata on the basis of a supposed 'true likeness of reality'

> would mean falling into the error of mistaking reality – which is always complicated and a one-of-a-kind in the sense that it does not admit of repetition – for an abstract schema or a theoretical model, which can serve to explain some particular aspect of reality.
>
> (p. 49)

And yet, for Einaudi, 'the investigative tool needs to have some semblance of reality if it hopes to be genuinely productive' (p. 56), or at least, as he says elsewhere, it must maintain some kind of relation or 'interconnectedness with reality' (p. 59). Therefore, Einaudi felt that an attempt should be to maintain this reference to the real situation, if for no other reason than as a tool of a critical appraisal to counter the claim of theoreticalness advanced by Fasiani, or, alternatively, as a means to indicate the 'limits of the concrete validity of theorems that have been correctly shown to be true when examined in their abstract framework', as he wrote in a note to the first edition (E. 1942–43 [2014a]: 302).

However, the insistence on the "*interpretive*" capacity, or on the "fertility" or "productivity" of the schemata refers not only (or not so much) to their relationship with reality, but above all to their ability to *produce* and *communicate* a *sense* and a *meaning*. Naturally, this raises two questions. Who is the interpreter? Who is the interpreter's message addressed to? These are two questions intricately related to each other, and they are dependent on the Einaudian conception of the role (and the responsibility) of economists in the public sphere (see Introduction, par. 1). Without a good understanding of the impact of these questions, it becomes difficult to grasp Einaudi's uneasiness with regard to the type of modern state in Fasiani, i.e. his apprehension that such a type of state could play into the hands of the regime or, at the very least, legitimate it (this concern had already come to the fore in Einaudi's review). Traces of this fear are found, for instance, in the adjective 'monster' used by Einaudi no fewer than three times to characterize the modern state, or in the references to the 'terrifying and dangerous' aspects of the 'dualism between individuals and the whole' (p. 60); they are also found in the statements expressing his worry that the 'modern state' could bring about a 'return to the pagan *deification* of the state above the individual' (p. 60), or that it could be construed as a 'transcendental *idol* [. . .] placed above and outside of the men who compose it' (p. 61). Equally emblematic is the passage where Einaudi writes:

> to start out from the premise that there exists a *unit* called the state, and that the governing class can, in its exercise of power, deal exclusively with the interests of this entity instead of concerning itself with the particular interests of all those who belong to the public group, means starting out from an unreal premise.

To this he added the following during the rewriting:

> effectively, it means awarding the status of a theoretical-historical premise to what consists of little more than the declarations or raving rant of politicians who are in search of a pretext to justify their own caprices.
>
> (p. 59)

To Einaudi's pupil Fasiani, who had adopted the Paretian sociological tools and concepts, this addition (had he been able to read it) would have sounded like the very worst of accusations: that the modern state is, in Paretian terms, a derivation. For as early as in his review, Einaudi had implicitly pointed out that Fasiani had been guided, in his construction of the type of modern state, by passion or feelings. In their exchange of correspondence, Fasiani seems almost to have attempted to sidestep this charge by placing greater emphasis on the scientificity of his procedure. He suggested that 'it is his [Einaudi's] warm regard for me that leads him to find "derivations" [. . .] so as not to have to delve in greater depth into the central question', i.e. the "typology" and, accordingly, the "scientific" way of constructing the types. For Fasiani, in accordance with his Paretian allegiance, the 'Public Finance of all times is an encyclopaedia of "derivations", and I do not for a moment believe that it is destined to change in the future, whether or not "typologies" are used' (Lett.: Fasiani to E., June 12, 1942: 17). In any case, Fasiani claims for his typology the character of a normal procedure of abstraction, which is precisely a manner of engaging in science by starting out from hypotheses. Thus in this passage, Einaudi seems to want to press the point home even more emphatically by reversing Fasiani's accusation – that of supplying by means of those types, "derivations" or justifications of the (fascist) state.

This notwithstanding, it should also be repeated here that the above-mentioned addition testifies emblematically to the presence of two registers in the Einaudian line of argument: on the one hand, the question of the relation between scheme and reality, or of the limits of the "unreal premise" (an expression used in a critical sense against Fasiani), and on the other that of the communicative and constructive force of the sense Einaudi attributes to these schemata. They are two registers that frequently overlap, but are far from coinciding exactly with each other.

On closer inspection, Einaudi's concern as regards the "monster" of the modern state and its possible "deification" or drift towards "idolatry" has to do with the problem of the communicative-normative or performative effects inherent in the discourse of an economist within the public sphere.[19] Thus his misgivings no longer have any connection with the epistemological problem of the relation between scheme and reality, but rather with the question of the relation between the schema built up by an economist and the subjects who receive the message embedded in the schema itself. Regardless of whether the recipients happened to be rulers, the ruled or the lay public, Einaudi's concern was by no means diminished. It is clear that when, after a prolonged analysis of the modern state, Einaudi asks, and then asserts,

> do we wish to admit today that there can exist a *modern* state which pursues ends concerning the group alone, and thus that such a state can, in the name of the group, order man to violate the commandments dictated by his conscience? To be sure, a monster of this kind may have existed; but it is neither a modern state nor one that is compatible with the freedom of man.
>
> (p. 61)

He is not conducting a reflection on the epistemological status of the type. Here the problem is not the 'unreal premise' of the 'modern state', since this 'monster', not only 'may have existed', but it was precisely that in which he was living. One thus has the impression that by resorting to a rhetorical stratagem, Einaudi appeared to be referring to the past, or to the tyrannical states of the past, but he was actually really talking about the present. And of the 'freedom of man' and of his 'conscience' 'violated' by fascism 'in the name of the group'.

Therefore, one can surmise that Einaudi made use here of the argument of realism or of the "historical value" of purely hypotheses as a tool: it offered him a handy device for criticism of the "theoretical" Fasiani.

Nevertheless, given Einaudi's awareness of the unbridgeable gap between schema and reality, and given his conception of the economist in the public sphere, it would appear that his interest focused predominantly on the problem of the meaning conveyed through the schemata constructed by an economist. He perhaps tried to make this clearer at the beginning of the last four pages added at the end of the concluding section (§ 17) of this second part, when he states more specifically,

> the merely definition-based and abstract distinction between the monopolistic and the cooperative state risks being inadvertently linked to the concept of a state distinct from the society of men within which the (monopolistic or cooperative) state effectively lives, although such a connection is by no means logically necessary [. . .] The state thus transcends and stands beyond and outside the society.
>
> (p. 63)

In this case, and once again, the 'connection', the 'link' or the mental association and the attendant 'risk' mentioned by Einaudi do not concern the relation between schema and reality, but rather the dangerous and potential (communicative-normative) effects of the schema on those to whom the economist's discourse is addressed.

Naturally, if one affirms that from the point of view of communication in the public sphere such schemata can exert a negative effect, this also implies the assumption that they could, in different circumstances, have a positive communicative effect. Einaudi asserts this directly, reinterpreting the schemata of De Viti a few years later and resorting once more to the twofold register in which his arguments are framed, as we have underlined so far. The monopolistic state and the cooperative state clearly do not correspond to positions that have been achieved or are achievable in actual reality, but they can serve as tools for the interpretation and proper ordering of facts that genuinely did occur, or also as a guide for practical activity.

> [De Viti believed that there was an historically inevitable transition from the monopolistic state to the cooperative state, yet,] for this historical vision, which fundamentally embraced a perspective of optimism, De Viti's financial economics [. . .] acquires its value not only as a work of science, but also as the driver of actions directed towards ever less imperfect forms of self-government and freedom.
>
> (E. 1949b: 7)

1.3 The anthropological background: The individual and the collective[20]

Although Einaudian search for *buon governo* made reference to some of its classical meanings – *rule of law, government by good ruling class, mixed constitution* – [21] it should also be examined in a broader and more profound sense: as the search for the anthropological and institutional foundations that can give rise either to a good or a bad polity.

Let us dwell here on some of the essential moments of this quest, setting aside the – certainly important – circumstance that Einaudian search for good government was always reactivated *post res perditas*: its most important moments stem from the darkest periods and most tragic events of the twentieth century and particularly of both Italian and his own personal history: the First World War, the ensuing economic and social crisis, fascism, the great depression of 1929 and World War II. This means that the search for the *good* society always starts out from the experience of *evil*, or of a *bad* society.

In 1922, in a profoundly autobiographical work in which Einaudi re-evokes the *ethos* of his family home, he wrote:

> this manner of living that I used to observe in the family home represented the universal habits of the Piedmontese bourgeoisie for the greater part of the 19th century. [These habits shaped] a ruling class that left a profound imprint of honesty, capabilities, parsimony, devotion to duty in the political and

administrative life of the Piedmont which subsequently created Italy itself. [At that time] man, the family, were not conceived in isolation from their rootedness in the land, the home, the local area, and these are sentiments that also engender dedication to the homeland and the spirit of sacrifice which, alone, is capable of nurturing the young shoots that will burgeon into sound states.

(E. 1922 [1988]: 32–34)[22]

This "picture" can also be likened to another topical moment of Einaudi's search for good government, which evokes the *ethos* of those components of the middle class who

deemed that the most consummate art of statesmanship lay in ensuring 'good government' of public affairs, where 'good government' was to be understood as that wise and prudent manner of administrating which they adopted in private affairs.

(E. 1933: 400)

Reading between the lines of these two citations, which evoke a latent analogy between *oikonomia* and civil government, a synthesis of some of the most recurrent problems of political, juridical and economic philosophy can be perceived: the problem of order, legitimacy and obligation; the question of the ruling class and of those holding power in government; the question of the relation between private and public and between society in general and the government; and, last but not least, the problem of individual, family, affective and social relations, the question of values, traditions and the civic virtues on which every social order is built (in dwelling on these issues, Einaudi mentions specific aspects such as prudence, parsimony, a hard-working approach, honesty, a professional attitude, loyalty, trust, spirit of sacrifice). The veritable conundrum of these issues was to become the crux of Einaudian research on liberal good government.[23]

In 1937, Bruguier Pacini, reflecting on Einaudi's 1922 essay, and acutely aware of the "personal" aspect of Einaudian reflection as well as Einaudi's "faith" not so much in the 'heroic virtues of the supreme hours' but rather in the 'modest virtues of everyday life', expressed the belief that those 'homespun virtues', those of the *oikos*, 'were representative of a bygone world, one that had perhaps disappeared for ever'. But he expressed regret that Einaudi was unwilling to 'include in the theoretical schemata' the innovation of the more recent time – namely, the 'corporatist experience' (Bruguier Pacini 1937: 70).

But in actual fact, it should be stated, first and foremost, that while Einaudi did indeed look to the past, this represented an attempt to understand the foundations of a liberal good society and thus to re-establish it on new foundations. In particular, it should not be overlooked that Einaudi's reflection was prompted, initially, by the experience of the collapse of the political, juridical and economic institutions of the liberal state, which had not withstood the impact of the war, the *biennio rosso* (two red years) and fascism.

This experience lay at the root of Einaudi's fundamental awareness that the institutions are not sufficient to guarantee freedom, and that freedom cannot be reduced to the institutions; moreover, even less can it be guaranteed by mere constitutional engineering.

Secondly, Einaudi had long been critical of the emerging corporativist doctrine, and once again his objections rested on an anthropological basis: *in primis*, the defense of freedom and diversity. In a famous preface entitled *Bellezza della lotta* [*The Beauty of Struggle*], Einaudi gave an explicit account of his 'generative ideas'. Against any imposition from on high, or even worse, against any surreptitiously paternalistic attempt, whether brought about at the hand of whichever petty politician happens to wield power at the time, or espoused by socialism or the rising growing corporative doctrine, Einaudi re-affirms

> [the value of the] efforts of those who desire to elevate themselves on their own and in this struggle, fight, falter and rise again, learning at their own expense how to win and to better themselves.
>
> (E. [1923] 2006: 66)[24]

Similarly, in 1925, when he was writing the preface to *On Liberty* by J.S. Mill, 'at a moment when it is vitally urgent that the right of criticism and of non conformism', and all the issues involved in the struggle against uniformity, should come to the fore and be given pride of place, Einaudi took up an even more outspoken position against 'absolute conformism to the nationalist gospel imposed by fascism' (E. 1925).

Thus if we compare his 1922 essay with the last two essays dating from 1923 and 1925, one can begin by noting that Einaudi's anthropological vision rests on a fertile tension between past and future, homing and roaming, tradition and criticism, conservation and innovation, rules and life, law and liberty, wherein the "law" or the institutions take on the form of a particular figure of the limit.

These polarities constitute the background to Einaudi's critique of Fasiani's types of state and also allow insight into his attempt to provide a more explicit account of his position in order to specify the relation between the individual and the collective community in dual rather than dualistic terms. In Einaudi's *sui generis* liberalism there remains a fruitful tension, a duality between individual and institutional which is not resolved into a dualism or a monism. On the one hand, there is, undoubtedly, an anthropological-individualistic foundation of the good society that makes an appeal to the freedom, responsibility and dignity of every individual man (L.R. Einaudi 2010: 319, 320, 322), while on the other there is also an institutional sphere that is, *lato sensu*, foundational of the person (Heritier, Silvestri 2012b). The free Einaudian "man" is indeed an independent (and responsible) being, but he is not one who considers himself as self-founded, self-sufficient or who puts forward the demand to be exonerated from recognition of any limit or constraint. On the contrary, he is not only a man rooted in a community, but rather one who believes himself to be free precisely insofar as he recognizes a limit. The Einaudian man is one who abandons his home, but is also capable of returning home, and who knows that no father, state, corporation, welfare state, branch of knowledge or science can act as shield against the boundless contingencies of life.

It is by no means superfluous to point out that at the origin of the Einaudian conception of struggle and freedom there lay anti-perfectist Christian anthropology: man as a flawed and fallible being, not perfect, yet perfectible: 'a mixture of virtues and vices, reason and passion' (Einaudi 1920b [1963])[25] and always poised between good and evil. Although Einaudi refers only occasionally to this background, it remains as the underlying setting of many of his statements on the fallibility of knowledge and human action. Now, this anthropological background was to be significantly taken up again by Einaudi in the pages added at the end of this second part, at the point where, giving a more precise statement of the meaning of the non-state, it becomes a figure of the ineliminable human condition, with its emblematic 'contrast' between limit and liberty which is rooted in human imperfection: it is the manifestation of an evil, barely perceptible or profoundly serious, that makes men poorly suited to engaging in perfect forms of collective life' (p. 64).

The subsequent arguments concerning the 'society of perfect men' thus take on the character of a counterfactual line of reasoning.[26] It is designed to convey the sense of human tension or struggle towards the ideal, the "state" or good polity, of which the accomplishment of an 'ever wider sphere of subjective rights of the human person' (p. 65) is a fundamental and crucial historical moment.

Moreover, this Einaudian reference to the 'person' as a fundamental juridical concept should not be neglected, since it is linked to the 'moral and spiritual – and therefore economic elevation – of men living in society' (p. 61), which he assumed and explicitly declared as the value reference of his own analysis. On one of the very few occasions where Einaudi ventures a definition of liberalism, he terms it a 'doctrine of limits' as well as a 'doctrine of those who puts the betterment, the elevation of the human person before any other goal'; it is therefore a moral doctrine, 'independent of the contingencies of time and place' (E. 1944a [2001]: 65–66). With reference to the Einaudian concept of the person, it has been noted that

> in Einaudi, the position of a 'tradition', of the realm of the 'ideal', is never separated from the concrete problem of the historical unfolding of that same 'tradition' and its projection towards the future. This is a feature that appears to imply the adoption of an *evolutionistic concept of the human 'person'*, where liberalism has, to put it briefly, an anthropological destination and meaning that concerns the actual ways of exercising and possible forms of human freedom [. . .] It is precisely the concept of the person that is the key that resolves, in evolutionistic and liberal terms and not those of natural law or the moral-religious, the conflict between the foundational exigencies of the social bond and the concreteness of the contingent.
>
> (Heritier 2012a: 277–278, 279)

In effect, the concept of person reappears precisely at the point where Einaudi, criticizing the dichotomy between the individual and the collective community that was inherent in cooperative and modern types of state, endeavoured to address the issue in dual and non-dualistic terms. Recast in modern terms, this could be viewed as an attempt to go beyond the mere opposition between individualism and holism:

> the *person*, the *individual* within man becomes more varied and is enriched through living together with other men; and *society* or the *collective community* is not something that exists in its own right as distinct from the men who compose it: on the contrary, it exists only insofar as it transforms men and converts them from forlorn wandering atoms or mechanical automata into real men.
>
> (p. 56)

In order to gain insight into this logic of '*society* or the *collective community*', Einaudi had already long been engaged in profound reflection on the importance, but also the fragility, of the fictional or aesthetic-legal-political foundations on which society rests. One fundamental moment in this train of thought was his re-reading of Le Play (1877, 1878, 1881), who, in Einaudi's words, investigated the reasons underlying prosperous and stable societies in search of those 'powerful, at times mysterious, forces that account for the greatness and decadence, the permanence and disintegration of societies' (Einaudi 1936a [1953]: 315). This was a reflection that was prompted by the tragic death of his young pupil Gobetti, an event which for Einaudi also acted as a moment of self-criticism, during which he reproached himself for having been overly optimistic in his vision of struggle and, at the same time, naïve in having discounted the problem of 'evil':[27] both in the sense of the ambiguity of "struggle" – for struggle can be not only "fertile" but also "infertile" – but also in the sense that struggle must take place within an institutional framework that has the function of containing the struggle itself and its conceivable degeneration. Hence his reflection on the

> ancient institutions which impose themselves on peoples almost as if they were endowed with a supernatural virtue [. . .] [a] sense of taboo which holds the basic social structure firm [. . .] [institutions and societies are founded on] magic spell [:] all the social world's a stage curtain; and behind it there's nothing.
>
> (E. 1926b: 80)

The difficulty thus lies in finding a way to ensure that the sense of tradition and the institutions can be held together with the critical and revolutionary spirit that cannot go beyond a certain limit, beyond which 'the paper castle, [which] stood firm of its own accord under the shelter of the spell', collapses. Thus meditating on the discussions with his pupil Gobetti, with a classic projective judgment, Einaudi resumed his reflections on the possibility of the good society, here depicted as the 'ideal city':

> [tradition as well as criticism] have just as much right of citizenship in that ideal city he was shaping in his mind, a city that is fine to behold because it is

not rigidly motionless but is continually in transformation under the contrasting pressures of the many forces that act upon it.

(E. 1926b: 80)

Finally, for additional insight into the meaning to be attributed to Einaudian
reflection on the 'dialectical contrast between the state and the non-state', it
becomes fundamental to return to the question raised at the end of the lengthy line
of reasoning that proposed to replace this dialectical contrast with the schemata of
the state put forward by Fasiani (and De Viti):

> if the aim is to construct systems, why not base the construction on reality,
> which is always one and the same, namely, struggle, effort, the overcoming
> of stumbling blocks, achievement – amid lapses and back-sliding – of the
> highest ideals of life?

(p. 62)

By touching once again on the theme of struggle, Einaudi sought to found the
'dialectical contrast between the state and the non-state', on a *reality* which is
not a reality to be understood in the ontological sense, but rather historical and
anthropological. That is to say, it makes reference to the contingent dynamics of
individual and social living and to the concreteness of human freedom and its
always potentially ambivalent effects, poised between evil and good, of which the
oscillation between non-state and state is a manifestation.

2 Excursus

Perhaps the best way to close the previous section and open the next one is to
dwell on Einaudi's preface to the 1959 edition of *MPJT*. It can be considered an
admirable reinterpretation and synthesis of some of the ideas that led his enquiry
into the causes of good and bad polities, prosperous and decadent societies.

At the end of this preface, Einaudi dwells on the developments of welfare economics, as if this theme were a pretext for his concluding remarks. Although he
recognized the theoretical progress and concrete results of welfare economics, he
pointed out that prosperity, i.e. 'welfare', means first and foremost 'well-being';
accordingly,

> [welfare] is not composed of the only wealth that is measurable and summa-
> ble, mentally translatable into money. "Welfare" is different and it is some-
> thing more than wealth; it is a composite of wealth, contentment, good social
> relations, good government, solid – even if small – families, lack of envy
> and hatred among different classes, which is replaced by emulation which
> elevates the mediocre and does not morally abase the great. [. . .].
> [Just as] taxation is not a purely economic fact [. . .] the well-being of a
> political body is not composed only of material goods. Nations, kingdoms,
> empires, grow and decay for primarily moral and spiritual reasons. Tax too is a

factor of stability or decline; and the moment in which tax by a factor of stability becomes a factor of decadence is decisive for the future of the state [. . .].

We are still far from the critical point; and it is worth expressing the hope that scholars' impassioned aspiration towards the creation of increasing well-being for all peoples does not restrict itself to material well-being, for this could signify and provoke envy, hatred and decadence. What is truly required is above all moral and spiritual well-being, such as will signify the emulation of individuals, cohesion within families, and the solid ordering of social classes and orders, for these are the sentiments from which there arise great states.

(E. 1959: XVI–XIX)[28]

With these last words, Einaudi came back home to the *oikos* and *ethos* that he glimpsed as the invisible foundations of a liberal good society.

3 Value judgments, economics, philosophy

In the abstract of the first edition, Einaudi summed up the general claim of the third part as follows: 'the economist's decision to refrain from value judgments [. . .] is legitimate if motivated by the scientific division of labor, but illogical in the perspective of the more general quest for truth'. The main arguments linked to this general claim are set out in the first section (§ 18) of the third part and then explained in the following sections. Before analyzing these arguments, it is worth reading and understanding the nexus established by Einaudi between the end of the second part (§ 17) and the beginning of the third part (§ 18). Insight can thus be gained into the meaning of the changes he himself introduced:

the dialectical contrast between state and non-state, the two eternally coexisting forces that are locked in a struggle for predominance, is, if seen in a different perspective, the eternal contrast between God and Satan, between good and evil, matter and spirit. Or rather, it is that contrast that is ingrained within us, which causes us to suffer and rejoice, saving us from death and doom in favor of life which is constant struggle and striving, constant effort. [Stating the matter in this form, it is clear that we have moved beyond the bounds of economic science and have uttered value judgments.]

[18.] [Can the economist, indeed, refrain from pronouncing value judgments, if the latter are taken as judgments on the moral and spiritual aspects, i.e. on the good and evil inherent in the choices made by men, who, for reasons pertaining to the rational division of labor, restrict their field of enquiry to their specific field of competence? The question is [. . .] whether he should be branded as having engaged in anti-scientific behavior and consequently be excommunicated if he ventures into fields of study that men deem to be out of bounds].

These passages were set out by Einaudi to connect the arguments of the two parts that he reformulated as part two and part three of the present essay. Nevertheless, he deleted and reformulated those passages that I have put in square brackets. The statement on value judgments concluding § 17 was substituted by four sheets (thus the reformulation of the pages ISS). In turn, the beginning of § 18 – as well as any other statement through which he seemed to be more inclined to say that the economist cannot always refrain himself from pronouncing value judgments – was entirely substituted by a new passage aimed at stressing the scientific validity of his analysis and rejecting the accusation of an anti-scientific conduct. Einaudi's effort, in this regard, aimed to avoid complete abandonment of the possibility of conceiving his own research as "scientific", even though this conception of science was completely different from that of Fasiani (and Pareto). Rather, what Einaudi sought to demonstrate was the impossibility of completely rejecting value judgments and of deeming them to lie beyond the boundaries of economics. Highly telling, in this regard, is his cancellation of the statement 'we have moved beyond the bounds of economic science and have uttered value judgments' seems to imply.

The shift of emphasis is relevant. It is likely that Einaudi, mainly spurred by Bruguier Pacini's comments (Lett.: Bruguier Pacini to E., August 2, 1943), understood the ambiguity of his expression on 'pronouncing' value judgments. Thus it is likely that he believed that it was necessary to emphasize the possibility of doing such a scientific enquiry without necessarily 'pronouncing', as he wrote in the deleted statement, 'value judgments [meant] as judgments on the moral and spiritual aspects, i.e. on the good and evil inherent in the choices made by men', and/or he tried to restructure the issue in terms of implicit/explicit value judgments, which is an issue that, in the present essay, was mainly referred to as the economist *qua* economist.

In order to fully grasp the meaning of the third and last part of the present essay – *On Value Judgments in Economic Sciences* – its rewriting, as well as the pages added in the conclusions, it is, in my view, necessary

a)   to interpret the third part as an epistemological justification of the enquiry into the causes of prosperous and decadent (or good and bad) societies and governments, which found in *MPJT* a significant moment, which, in turn, was further recalled and developed in the second part of the present essay in terms of the dialectical contrast between state and non-state;

b)   to grasp the main arguments developed in the first edition and, in turn, to understand them against the background of the Paretian demarcation between science and non-science (see also, Introduction, par. 3.1) in the name of which Fasiani claimed that values and value judgments are outside the boundaries of the scientific enquiry and that Einaudi, in his *MPJT*, held an 'anti-scientific' conduct (p. 66);

c)   to understand the nexus between the demarcation issue and the other issue dealt with by Einaudi – namely, the alleged indifference of the economist towards the motifs or ends of choices made by both the individuals in society and the ruling class, as well as, and above all, towards his own moral ends. This, in turn, raises the issue of whether the economist *qua* economist may pronounce value judgments;

d)   to consider that in the rewriting process which led to the present essay, Einaudi ended up not only deleting those statements in which he seemed to admit that he made value judgments, but also addressing the demarcation issue. In this context, spurred by the dialogue with his interlocutors, he additionally took into account the Crocean demarcation between philosophy and (economic) science (see Editorial Foreword, par. 5, and Introduction, par. 4.3).

Although Einaudi made a considerable effort to tackle all these issues in a coherent framework, the rewriting process and the sheets (COP and DVE) sent to his interlocutors testifiy to the difficulties and 'doubts' he had about his own arguments that developed both in the first edition and in the present essay. In this regard, it is also important to consider that the new conclusions – namely, the last five sections added in the present essay of which the first three were embodied in the sheets DVE and COP, whereas the last two were written independently – are the expression of such doubts. This accounts for the fact that, even after the debate with his interlocutors, the last five sections remained formulated in a dubitative form, as Einaudi himself declares. 'I am merely raising doubts: far be it from me to claim I have a solution to the problem' (p. 87) (thus, in this case, the problem of the distinction between philosophy and economics). This makes the interpretation of the last five sections quite difficult and, in many respects, speculative.

For the sake of clarity I will therefore try to analytically distinguish Einaudi's arguments and doubts into two main topics: the issue of value judgments, which I will further subdivide into the issue of taking a stand and the difficulty of separating the study of means from the understanding of ends (par. 3.1), and Einaudi's attempt to clarify both the distinction between economics and philosophy, and the alleged separation between the economist *qua* scientist and the whole man (par. 3.2).

3.1 The issue of value judgments

In the entire third part, the issue of value judgments, as developed by Einaudi, re-proposes the same difficulty already noticed in Einaudi's preface that I recalled as the nearest antecedent of the present essay (Introduction, par. 4.2), although Einaudi introduces new arguments (and further doubts). Thus the issue of value judgments conceals two different problems, which, in Einaudi's discourse, seem to be somewhat overlapping and kept together by his reflection on the alleged indifference of the economist *qua* economist towards the ends: 1) the issue of whether and when to take up a position with regard to the ends pursued by ruling powers, which, in Einaudi's reflection seems to be a deontological issue and 2) the difficulty of separating rigorously, in the analysis of society, the study of means and the understanding of ends. Let us try to analyze them separately.

1) The first issue comes to the fore through the way in which, in the first edition, Einaudi formulated the problem of value judgments in terms of "duty" or "obligation" or even "necessity" to "pronounce" value judgments. Although some of these words and expressions were deleted in the rewriting, the problem of taking a stand remained.

Einaudi claims that the economist's knowledge cannot be paralleled to that of 'physicists, chemists and astronomers' (p. 38) (as Fasiani, with Pareto, believed).

Economist's knowledge is never neutral with regard to political process and society, even when such knowledge is assumed to be as a mere instrumental reasoning aimed at analyzing the effects of certain policies. First of all, since economist's knowledge is 'more enlightened' (p. 66), such a knowledge will also contribute to changing the initial data of the problem, the 'opinion or judgment' of and/or the aims pursued by the political class (p. 76). Secondly, assuming economist's knowledge as instrumental reasoning, merely aiming at a technical criticism of values, implies the further assumption of the *value* of such reasoning as a means to 'enlighten public opinion' (p. 86) and/or to speak the truth to power. Of course, formulating a technical critique of the ends pursued by the ruling class and taking a stand against power are not exactly the same thing. In this regard, Einaudi's uneasiness seems to be (as Solari understood) an issue of the *deontology* of the economist, given the fascist context in which he was writing, and given Fasiani's claim (Fasiani 1941, II: 59–60) that 'for the scientist' the ends pursued by rulers are merely 'a *fact*, a *given* of the problems he is dealing with' (p. 75). Nevertheless, this disquieting aspect remained one of Einaudi's main concerns, well beyond the debate with Fasiani (Einaudi 1950c, 1962).[29]

The difficulty of the latter issue was reformulated many times by Einaudi in the attempt to keep together two potentially conflicting values, thus to save the dignity and autonomy of the 'priest of science' (p. 81) and, at the same time, to save the "duty" – depending on the circumstances, freedom, responsibility and morals of the economist – to take a stand against power. And it was also reformulated in the recapitulation set at the beginning of the last 15 sheets, thus the last five sections, added at the end of the present essay:

> since the economist himself is likewise a whole man, and indeed cannot fail to be such given his profession as a scholar, and given his customary practice of apprehending the motives and ends of his actions, he as an economist has the duty to speak out – a duty that behooves him as a man and indeed as one whose awareness precedes that of other men. And if he believes his convictions to be true he has the duty to say: I want or I do not want *b*, because *b* aligns with that which is good or with that which is evil; I want or I do not want to use the means appropriate for achieving *b*, because that particular means represents good or evil, respectively.
>
> Alternatively, prompted by prudence, a highly honorable motive according to the dictates of morals, the economist can refrain from this final step of his line of reasoning. He can, in other words, remain silent, and abstain from overstepping the limits of the task assigned to him. No-one can reproach him for such a position; he cannot be chided if he artfully opts not to choose as the object of his analysis only those cases in which he can declare that the action of a man in government is appropriate with regard to the desired ends, or those in which the results obtained are considered by the majority to be honest and desirable. His moral conduct will be irreproachable only if, adopting a casuistry-based method, he applies his reasoning, within the limits of his knowledge, to survey the whole range of cases.
>
> (p. 83 and DVE: 10–11)

This notwithstanding, as we have already seen (Introduction, par. 4.3), Einaudi, as an economist and 'whole man' had already made public his own choice in favour of the values ruling a liberal society. In this regard, it is worth quoting Einaudi's statement once more in order to highlight the subtle shift of emphasis made by the following addition:

> he [the economist] decides in favor of one or the other decision [of the ruling class] for some reason he considers to be valid, and the reason that is valid for him – which he has to make public – is [. . .], as stated by many, and in the opinion of this writer, the imperative of the moral and therefore also material elevation of man.
>
> (p. 66)

In the rewriting, Einaudi added the following passage:

> it can indeed be admitted that the concept of the advantage for all people or for the community, as well as the concept of moral elevation, both lie beyond the realm of science, and are scientifically indefinable political formulas or political myths. However, these are forces, data or premises the scholar must take into account and which determine or explain the datum posited by the ruling class.
>
> (p. 67)

This addition seems to represent, once again, a subtle shift from the first to the second issue.

2) With regard to the second issue – namely, the difficulty of rigorously separating the analysis of means and the understanding of ends – Einaudi introduces his main thesis (§ 18) with the following argument:

> there is no plausible reason why scientific research should come to a halt when faced with good and evil, or when beholding the ideals and reasons of life, almost as if these were *untouchable* concepts. [. . .] perhaps, the idea could be voiced that the specific task of the economist begins, in accordance with the legitimate canons of the division of labor, only from the moment when decisions have been actually made and recorded. It is then that the economist has to take stock of the situation, starting out by acknowledging that men have made this or that decision, with all that follows. But if *what follows* turns out to influence choices that have already been made, if the results of such choices and the choices themselves have an effect on the actual reasons for the choices, then how can one say: this is where science starts; and before this there is . . . what?
>
> (p. 68)

This point was further developed in some of the following sections through (at least) two major arguments.

a) The economist's indifference towards the reasons underlying choices mainly depends on his decision to fictionally put into brackets (or consider as exogenous) the ends of human choices and/or the institutional or moral context within which those choices take place (§ 19). Nevertheless, such indifference is not always possible if the economist seeks to gain a better understanding of some economic phenomena as well as of society as a whole: for this purpose, the economist should at least have an *understanding* of those ends[30] and, sometimes, is forced to 're-enact the entire causal chain [of means and ends] which, for reasons of the division of labor, we severed at a particular point' (p. 69). As Einaudi stated in the summary of the last section (§ 27) of the first edition (see Editorial Foreword, par. 3): 'it is impossible to study choices while pretending to be unaware of the ends from which they sprang'.

b)   The divisions among disciplines as well as that between science and non-science are merely 'conventional' and have no more than a 'practical utility' (§ 20, p. 70), and in any case, do not give any scholar the right to excommunicate other scholars (§ 21). This thesis, connected to the general claim stated in the old Abstract – 'the economist's decision to refrain from value judgments [. . .] is legitimate if motivated by the scientific division of labor, but illogical in the perspective of the more general quest for truth' (Editorial Foreword, par. 3) – was further extended to the reflection on the division between economics and philosophy.

It may well be true that, in this regard, Einaudi held an 'anti-Robbinsian position' (Forte, Marchionatti 2012: 594) without stating it explicitly, but it is also true that, spurred by the debate with Fasiani, Einaudi was forced to develop an anti-Paretian position with specific reference to the demarcation issue, the theory of choice and the separation between economics and sociology (as he explicitly stated in his DVE: see par. 3.2).

To explain this point, it is worth recalling a theme I have already highlighted in the Introduction (par. 3.1). Einaudi consistently sought to deal with the demarcation issue between science and non-science through an attempt to reflect on his own analysis of the values and motifs implied by human choices and the way in which they influence (good and bad) polities, state and non-state. Furthermore, he endeavoured to legitimate the study of the ends within the dominion of economic science – an attempt that may be understood if the following three aspects are awarded due consideration: Fasiani's already mentioned critique of Einaudi's *MPJT* (E. 1938b) in the name of Pareto's epistemology; the fact that Pareto, through the discovery of the pure and 'naked fact of choice' (Pareto 1900 [1953]), re-founded economics by distinguishing the economic field from the social (non-economical) field through the distinction between logical actions and non-logical actions, which were in the domain, respectively, of economics and sociology; and the circumstance that in Pareto's epistemology, there is a structural analogy between the demarcation science/non-science and logical/non-logical categories (Albert 2004).

In this regard, it is symptomatic that, before the recapitulation with which Einaudi started the new concluding sections, he decided to conclude § 27 (which was the last section of the first edition) with the statement:

> there appears to be no decisive reason why economists should limit their investigations to the fact of *choice*. For the sake of the argument, let us designate those who inquire into the theoretical laws and into the empirical uniformities that ensue from the fact of *choice* as *alpha* economists, and those who, while likewise investigating the laws and the uniformities which, through choices, have the effect of linking, say, customs, laws, institutions or income distribution to prices, will be designated as *beta* economists. But the difference will be merely a question of the division of labor, devoid of any substantial content.
>
> (p. 82)

There is no doubt that Einaudi felt himself as belonging to the 'beta economists' category: through his enquiry into the causes of good and bad polities, he felt that such an enquiry would have been incomplete by merely analyzing the 'fact of choice' without taking into account 'customs, laws, institutions' and even those human passions involved in social relations, which Einaudi himself considered as an explanatory criterion of virtuous and vicious circles at the heart of the dialectical contrast between non-state and state.

3.2 Economics, philosophy and the whole man

In the rewriting process, Einaudi extended his reflection on the issue of value judgments, directly tackling the demarcation issue in terms of the separation between science and philosophy. He thus endeavoured to probe more deeply into the alleged separation between the economist *qua* scientist and the whole man.

In DVE and COP, Einaudi explained to his interlocutors one of the major 'doubts' that led him to have second thoughts, which was later reformulated in the present essay (soon after the already mentioned recapitulation put at the beginning of the new conclusions) as follows:

> the question arises of whether, once the economist has completed his analytical task of highlighting that what follows from *a* is *b* and not *c*, so that *a* is an appropriate means for obtaining the end *b* and inappropriate for obtaining the end *c*, and once he has stripped himself of the mantle that robes the economist and has become a simple man again, a whole man, he can justifiably pronounce moral judgments on *a*, *b* and *c*. That he can – and indeed *as a whole man* he must – express these value judgments is perfectly plain and there need be no discussion on this point. What does need to be addressed is a rather different problem.
>
> The issue is whether an economist, *specifically as an economist*, should issue judgments on values and whether he should do so on the basis of the tools that are proper to his discipline.

It is important, first and foremost, to underscore a crucial requirement of economic science. This science would cease to exist if it were to forsake reasoning with its own methods.

(p. 83, but see also COP: 1–2, and DVE: 11–12)

Einaudi's doubts refer to the 'tools' and 'method' that are 'proper' to economics, which, in this context, are respectively the ends-means instrumental reasoning and the abstracting-isolating method as compared to the Crocean philosophy-history.

Before analyzing these points in detail, it is also worth noting that the last passage quoted earlier was, in the COP, followed by a sort of confession by Einaudi to his interlocutors, which revealed that he looked to Croce and Vailati as beacons of guidance. This avowal was later eliminated in the final draft of the present essay.[31] Indeed, a joint reading of DVE, COP and the present essay leads to the impression that Einaudi, on the one hand, was seeking some sort of clarification or feedback from his correspondents on the thought of Croce and Vailati and, on the other, was also trying to use these two philosophers in order to criticize Pareto, most probably Pareto's method and notion of science, as well as his sociological drift.[32] But at the same time, Einaudi also needed to distance himself from Croce, in the attempt to go beyond the Crocean distinction between science and philosophy. As a matter of fact, after the Croce–Pareto debate, this separation had not only affected the epistemology of social sciences in Italy, but also ended up having an adverse effect on the very essence of his debate with Croce on liberism and liberalism, which relegated economic science to a subordinate and instrumental role compared to philosophy (see Introduction, par. 4.3).

Therefore, in the background of Einaudi's rewriting, one also perceives the attempt to go beyond the unsettled issues of the Croce–Pareto debate (Croce 1900 [1953], 1901 [1953], Pareto 1900 [1953], 1901 [1953], Croce 1906 [1961]). The extreme complexity of this debate cannot be analyzed here,[33] but, as far as Einaudi's rewriting is concerned, it is worth at least recalling its central issues.

Starting from the acquisitions of the *Methodenstreit*, thus from the victory of the "abstract" over the "historical" (implicitly recalled by Einaudi: p. 84), the Croce–Pareto debate arose initially as a reflection on the "principle" or founding hypotheses of economic science. But, with a crescendo of mutual misunderstandings, the debate came to a halt on the threshold of a crucial issue: the dichotomy of nominalism *versus* realism.

This dichotomy was later reformulated by Croce through the distinction between pseudo-concepts, or fictional concepts, pure concepts (Croce 1907), science and philosophy, which, in Croce's *Philosophy of the Spirit*, corresponded to economics and logic, and, respectively, to the categories of "Utile" and "True". Pseudo-concepts are characterized by their *non-cognitive* but, rather, *practical-economic* character. They are the *schemata*, laws, models, constructs and abstractions of science and social sciences. They work as names, *étiquettes* and *symbols*: having the function not of acquiring knowledge but of creating an order in the world for practical and operative purposes. The pseudo-concept is not truth but imitation of the truth or concept. The doctrine of the pure concept is, for Croce, *realism*, in the sense that it is founded (= true) reality. It is, however, a doctrine that does not deny nominalism, inasmuch as the name, the fiction, the *étiquettes* and the *symbols*, belong – precisely because they are useful – to the category of the *useful* and not to that of the *true*. But this resulted in the definitive interruption of the communication routes between economics and philosophy, but also between economists and philosophers.[34]

Pareto, on the other hand, many years later and in a different context – a sort of last criticism of 'literary economists' – seemed to want to resume his professed nominalism, or rather push it to the extreme by proclaiming a radical thesis: 'things are everything, and names nothing' (Pareto 1916 [1964], sec. 118).

Although Einaudi did not address the issue of nominalism versus realism, his defense of literary economists, his interest – shared with the philosopher Vailati – in the language of science and, above all, his own conclusions of the present essay would suggest that he was trying, albeit dubitatively, to overcome the unresolved issues of the Croce–Pareto debate.

As to the doubts on the ends-means instrumental reasoning, Einaudi confesses to his interlocutors that even adopting such a tool and even when making 'the utmost effort in order to remain within the limits of his own discipline', as he himself endeavoured to do, the economist might nevertheless have made a 'value judgment, without declaring it' explicitly (COP: 1).

The explanation and the example provided by Einaudi to his correspondents are important. After repeating the claims according to which the boundaries between disciplines are merely conventional and that there are no boundaries to the scientific investigation, he adds,

> at some point in his life, Pareto became intolerant of the limits he gave to himself as an economist and became a sociologist, while preserving the same method of study. Here lies the problem.
>
> (DVE: 11–12)

In this case, by 'method', Einaudi is referring to the Paretian logical-experimental method, which, in Pareto's view, was the only true "scientific" method, where "science" is a) that which investigates facts and only facts and b) the reign of measurable and of factual knowledge ascertained through the logical-experimental method. All the rest is non-science.

To explain where 'the problem' lies, Einaudi reformulates the example of the analysis of the policy of tax exemption of a social minimum of existence, already developed in the first edition (§ 23). He shows how the instrumental reasoning and the possibility of taking values as mere facts can work only up to a certain point of the analysis. As soon as the analysis is expanded to consider other data and, above all, the social consequences of such a fiscal policy, the economist may bump into concepts, "ideas", "sentiments" and "passions" – such as oligarchic-plutocratic or demagogic regimes, 'strong or weak polity', 'prosperous or decadent states' (DVE: 18–19), 'economic relations of massive fortune and political-social relations of hatred and envy, on the one hand, or of fear and scorn on the other' (p. 76), as well as 'social, political and religious ideas' forming a chain of 'reciprocal reactions and counteractions' (DVE: 19) – which are not easily treatable from a "scientific" point of view.

Hence Einaudi's doubts on the economist's reasoning when facing these concepts and ideas that seem to lie on the threshold between fact and value: a) such concepts and ideas do not belong to the reign of 'measurable' and 'calculable', nor can they be subject to a 'cost-benefit' analysis; b) if the analysis leads to the conclusion that the ruling class is ' "leading the state towards its own ruin", isn't it an implicit value judgment?'; and c) 'What does the philosopher [but also the historian, the politician, the moralist, etc.] add so that the judgment [on value] exists'? (DVE: 18–19)

In the final draft of the present essay, the first two issues (a) and (b) were not developed further by Einaudi, even though he continued to believe that implicit value judgments are unavoidable. Significantly, he writes that the question is 'not that the economist is genuinely indifferent . . . [to the ends of actions] – but he has to make every effort to remain indifferent if he wants to fulfill his precise duty' (p. 85) (in other words, if he aims to be *super partes* and not to be confused with charlatans or the powerful. The expression 'he has to make every effort to remain indifferent' replaced 'he must feign indifference' (written in COP: 5). Or as when Einaudi refers to the 'dissimulation' of the economist:

> this idea of 'must or must not' is the logical univocal conclusion of all that he has ascertained by his reasoned arguments, dissimulating – indeed ignoring – the conclusion he would have reached right from the very start, had he been prompted by the command to act for the good.

(p. 85)

In many respects, Einaudi's reflection on the fiction of indifference may be interpreted, as seen in the Introduction (par. 2.1), as an attempt to explain to Fasiani the reasons behind his defense of economic science. Implicitly, it may also seek to vindicate the rhetorical or discursive strategy of the position of indifference and neutrality he adopted during the 1930s against the charlatans and lackeys. Be this as it may, the relevance of his intuition as to the issue of implicit value judgments cannot be overlooked.

The issue of implicit value judgments addressed here by Einaudi is not that of the values which may be implicit in the selection of the problem or in the economist's choice of the object of study. Thus it differs, for example, from the reflection he developed in the essay on Sismondi and in the review of Fasiani's book (see Introduction, par. 3.3 and par. 4.1) – a reflection that can be paralleled to that of Myrdal (1953, 1958).

Here Einaudi refers to the fact that the conclusions reached by the economist through an instrumental reasoning may hide some evaluation that surfaced in the economist's mind during the chain of such a reasoning. This is due to the fact that in his reasoning, the economist may find himself face-to-face with concepts on the borderline between fact and value – as was the case with the aforementioned concepts listed by Einaudi – where the purely descriptive and the purely evaluative part cannot easily be separated. Although Einaudi did not analyze this issue further, his intuition can be paralleled to Putnam's idea of 'entanglement' of fact and value, where such an entanglement is particularly evident in the case of 'thick ethical concepts' (H. Putnam 2002, 2012: 112).[35]

Let us now turn to the question (c) – 'what does the philosopher [but also the historian, the politician, the moralist, etc.] add so that the judgment [on value] exist?' – which concludes the DVE and is further developed in COP. The question is introduced by Einaudi's 'doubt' on whether there is a 'hiatus' between science and philosophy as well as between the 'economist *qua* scientist' and the 'philosopher' (DVE: 15), and whether economist's abstention from value judgment is nothing but 'mere language scruples' given the existence of implicit value judgments (DVE: 18).

In the rewriting of the conclusions, Einaudi conducts an examination of these issues in a wider reflection whose main purpose seems to be the critique of the alleged separation between the economist *qua* scientist and the whole man. In this regard, the path of Einaudi's argument may be understood as follows.

First of all, Einaudi puts forward a sort of last defense of the 'value of science' (p. 90), thus stressing the value of positive analysis and instrumental reasoning (regardless of the existence of implicit value judgments). This, he maintains, holds true even for ethics and philosophy or for normative purposes, as in the case of the analysis of social consequences of certain fiscal policies.[36] Nevertheless, as noticed by d'Entreves, Einaudi ended up emphasizing a prescriptive conception of ethics and philosophy and assuming, contrary to his intentions, that value judgments are 'non-demonstrable' by reason (Lett.: Passerin d'Entreves to E., August 1943). Therefore, d'Entrèves exhorted Einaudi to reflect on Pascal's fragment: '*Travaillons donc à bien penser. Voilà le principe de la morale*' [Let us endeavour, then, to think well; this is the principle of morality].

In any case, Einaudi's reflection on the value of science seems to be an implicit re-elaboration of the plea for the significance of economic science developed in the re-reading of Robbins (see Introduction, par. 2.1). He voiced such a plea despite the fact that his last critique of the alleged separation between the economist *qua* scientist and the whole man goes in a different direction than that of Robbins (and of all those who keep on insisting on such a separation).

Moreover, in this context, Einaudi's assertion of the value of science is also to be understood as a critique of the Crocean distinction between science (the domain of the abstract, belonging to the category of Utile) and philosophy (the domain of reality-history, belonging to the category of True). It likewise constitutes an implicit reply to his correspondents (Introduction, par. 4.3). In Einaudi's view, there is no 'dualism' between philosophy and economics and respectively between the philosopher and the economist:

> since the aim of their [economist's] research is one and one alone – namely, knowledge of the full extent of the whole of reality – it is logically inconceivable to argue that there is a fundamental, irreducible dualism between the logical position of the scientist, who aspires to acquire knowledge on reality through abstractions that successively draw closer to reality, and the historian-philosopher who aims to engage with the world of the whole of reality. Accordingly, this scenario cannot be portrayed as a contrast, but should instead be seen as different modes of conquering truth.
>
> (p. 88)

Moreover, 'dualism cannot be founded on the contrast between the rational and the irrational' since the 'irrational' is nothing but the unknown (p. 88), that is to say, those 'factors that are partly unknown, perhaps destined never to be known and measured, which nevertheless exert an influence on the actions of men' (p. 89). This statement seems also to imply a sort of last critique of Pareto's (and Fasiani's) science/non-science dualism – which Einaudi traces back to the anthropological-hierarchical dualism based on the dichotomy rational/irrational. But it can additionally be seen as an implicit reference to 'the other and perhaps better part' of the whole person, evoking the concluding sentence of § 2: 'the imitators, the servile pen-pushers, incapable of perceiving the links between the two aspects of the whole person, construct insipid theory and supply the counsels they know will find favor with the powerful' (p. 38).

In the conclusion, where Einaudi attempts to sum up the long reasoning, he goes so far as to say that

> even the very separation between the whole man and man as a scientist, between reality and abstraction, between concrete action and pure reasoning is shown to be an abstraction. The extremely close link between thought and action, between reasoning and behavior, between logic and morals, was already admirably stated in the words of Pascal: "L'homme est visiblement fait pour penser; c'est toute sa dignité et tout some mérite; et tout son devoir est de penser comme il faut" [Man is obviously made to think. It is his whole dignity and his whole merit; and his whole duty is to think as he ought.].
>
> (p. 91)

In contrast with the Crocean devaluation of the abstractions of sciences as merely fictitious in the name of a true and founded reality, Einaudi seems to claim that the very distinction between abstraction (science) and reality (history-philosophy) is and cannot but be an abstraction in itself – namely, a product of the language and discourse.

In my view, Einaudi's last reflection on the whole man may also be understood by considering the previous reflection on the alleged indifference of the economist *qua* scientist: however useful such indifference may be as a 'defense' against 'charlatans and lackeys', it is and remains a 'garb' (p. 86); or, as he wrote earlier, 'blinkers that certain scientists who call themselves pure would like to don' (p. 77); or a 'mantle that robes the economist' (p. 83). In turn, this reflection cannot be separated from Einaudi's awareness of the power, effects and ambiguity of language. As he asked his students, in the already mentioned section of *Doubts and Queries*, and at the end of his analysis of the various types of language in the social sciences,

> in the field of social science, is agnosticism [meant as indifference] thus proper to the true scientist, or is it a provisional merely pedagogical and methodological attitude assumed in order to clarify, both to himself and to others, the premises that have been adopted and the arguments developed? Can a scientist not take sides?
>
> (E. 1940b [1945]: 532)

Einaudi appears to maintain that the garb or mantle – namely, the identity of the economist *qua* scientist – is nothing but the fruit of the economist's language and discourse. If the divisions among disciplines are merely conventional, the same holds true for the division between the economist *qua* scientist and the whole man. The *identity* of the economist *qua* scientist may also be *deduced* through a discourse – on "method", "neutrality", "value neutrality", "indifference", "detachment", "reason", "science", "scientificity of economics", etc. – that represents, institutes or robes the economist precisely *qua* scientist (or hides him behind the veil of neutrality). But the freedom and responsibility of the economist as a whole man, or simply the *human*, can never be deduced from such a discourse. The economist is indeducible from economics. This is, in my view, also the message that Einaudi has left us in *Politicians and Economists* (E. 1962), his spiritual testament.

Notes

1 For an overview of the Einaudian vision of good government (albeit only with reference to his articles intended for the general public), see Einaudi (1954). Among the various works designed to grasp the complexity and the wealth of ideas embodied in the Einaudian conception of good government, readers are referred to Forte (2009: 101–142), Forte, Marchionatti (2012: 608–619) and Silvestri (2008a). For a re-reading of Einaudian good government in a contemporary perspective, see the essays collected in Heritier, Silvestri (2012a), with special reference to Forte (2012), Garofalo (2012), Reviglio (2012) and Silvestri (2012a). On the issue of good government in the Italian tradition in public finance, see also Medema (2005, 2009: 77–100).

   Good government is an issue which by definition is interdisciplinary and pervades the whole of the history of western thought – for an initial orientation, see Bobbio (1983); on the issue of good government in the Italian liberal thought, see Silvestri (2011). It has been a constant concern of the various branches of social science, re-emerging and revived in changing forms over time. For a few recent works (in random order) that have addressed the theme of good government or the good society from markedly different disciplinary perspectives and with highly diversified axiological assumptions, cf. Besley (2006), Hamlin, Pettit (1989) and Persson, Tabellini (2003).

2 This problem had already been discussed by Einaudi with his pupil Borgatta, even though, at that time (1920), Einaudi's intention was to defend the economic approach, but without negating the relevance of the other sociological and political approaches. On this debate, see Forte, Silvestri (2013: 252–253). On the political and sociological theories in the Italian tradition of public finance, see Boccaccio, De Bonis (2003).

3 First, because this would be unfair to Einaudi himself, who had a great sense of the uniqueness and unrepeatability of history and of the life of each individual, and for this reason Einaudi believed that the 'name tags' and the 'histories of schools' should be replaced by 'sketches of individual economists' (Einaudi 1953: VII–XIII). And second, because it was the very reflection on the foundations of the good society that had led Einaudi to insist on the fact that economic thought is simply a point of view (of the scholar) on the world. And finally, because Einaudi warned against the "excommunications" pronounced by the various "schools" of public finance (political, economic, sociological and juridical) or by whoever claimed to have a privileged point of view on the world. Therefore, it is in this sense and in a negative perspective, that Einaudi did not look favourably on the "schools" in general.

4 On De Viti's thought see Eusepi, Wagner (2013), Fossati (unpublished), Mosca (2005). On the differences and analogies between Einaudi and De Viti see Forte (2009: 103–104).

5 However, it should not be overlooked that Einaudi was the editor in charge of the publication of De Viti's *Principii* – also as a function of a critique of fascism. This would
   appear to be supported both by the decision of Einaudi himself to publish the work of
   an author who refused to take the oath of allegiance to the regime that was required of
   university professors and also by Einaudi's implicit appreciation of the freedoms that
   existed before fascism (Einaudi 1936b).
6 As known, this is one of the key issues of the public choice school. See Brennan,
   Buchanan (1980 [2000]).
7 On this see Musgrave (1939).
8 On the persistence in the Italian tradition of public finance of the benefit-received principle as a criterion of judgments and control of the action of governments, see Liberati,
   Paradiso (2014).
9 The starting point of Einaudi's analysis is the classic problem 'why pay taxes?', and,
   in this respect, his reflection can be paralleled to the more recent literature on tax
   compliance and tax morale, even though in Einaudi's analysis, the positive and normative aspects of this problem are often present together. This is mainly because of his
   awareness that tax phenomenon is a complex phenomenon in which an in-depth study
   can be performed only by analyzing the political process, legal institutions and their
   moral foundations. But it is also due to the fact that this question involves the foundation of the legitimacy of tax obligation, the power to tax, tax policies and redistributive
   policies. As he wrote, the question 'why pay [taxes?]' arises from a 'spiritual need [:]
   to give an account of the economic social legal political institutions in which we live'.
   If, from the citizen's point of view, the question comes into play when a sense of 'injus-
   tice' is perceived, from a theoretical standpoint, this question is at the origin of almost
   all the 'theoretical [economic, legal and political] disputes' on the 'rational foundation
   of taxation', particularly the disputes between the main theories of taxation and the
   ever new attempts to integrate and/or overcome them (Einaudi 1945b). Such a question, therefore, also entails the issue of legitimacy of the fiscal constitution and, more
   generally, the principles of good governance and of a good society.
       Mainstream neoclassical economics, starting from Becker's (1968) 'economic
   approach [to] crimes and punishments' (also known as "deterrence approach"), followed a completely different path, interpreting the tax compliance issue as a problem
   of rational choice between paying or evading taxes (Allingham, Sandmo 1972). This
   approach has generated the so-called tax compliance puzzle. Since the model predicts
   that it would be rational to evade (calculating the probability of being audited and the
   costs of detention and punishment), it is not at all clear 'why [so many] people pay
   taxes' (Alm, McClelland, Schulze 1992). Criticism of this approach and attempts to
   explain the puzzle have given rise to a considerable literature, often referred to as "tax
   morale" (Torgler 2007), which has partially borrowed the findings of behavioral economics and public goods experiments (Andreoni 1988, Cox 2012, Fehr, Gächter 2000,
   Gintis 2000). This literature aims to explain the taxpayer's compliance by introducing
   motives that are not always related to pure self-interest. These studies have revealed
   the existence of various forms of reciprocity regarding the relations between taxpayers
   and state and among citizen-taxpayers in general: impure altruism (Andreoni 1990),
   respect for social norms and considerations regarding institutional and governance
   quality, as well as other forms of reciprocity based on such aspects as moral judgment
   and perceptions of fairness (Cullis, Lewis 1997), trust (Feld, Frey 2000, Feld, Frey
   2007), civic virtues and respect of procedural justice (Frey 1997), group motivations
   (Alm 2014), reciprocal fairness and shared burdens as the basis of the legitimacy of
   a welfare state regime (Bowles, Gintis 2000). For a recent re-reading of these issues
   starting from the Italian tradition in public finance, see Giurato (2009).
10 On Einaudi's theory of elites and the differences among Einaudi, Mosca and Pareto,
   see Forte, Silvestri (2013), Silvestri (2006, 2009), Silvestri (2012a: 74–88).
       As to the nexus between rule of law and rule of man, Einaudi was throughout his life
   a staunch supporter of the rule of law as a guarantee of citizens' liberty. This is indeed

testified by his insistence on the difference between 'command-rules' and 'framework-rules', or between 'specific command' and 'general and abstract law', 'arbitrary power' and 'law', 'administrative' and 'juridical' action (E. 1994: 30). These differences can be considered on a par with the Hayekian distinction between rules of organization and rules of just conduct (Hayek 1973, 1976). But he knew equally well that the rule of law is a 'necessary condition', albeit not a sufficient condition, for a free society, because 'the life of a man living in society cannot be infused from outside [the legal "formal conditions or guarantees"], but rather must come from an inner creative force' (*ibidem*). Besides, as he writes in his reflection on Le Play's conception of elite: 'in prosperous societies coercive laws are brought into action only in cases where the moral example of the natural and social authorities proves insufficient; furthermore, the multiplication of coercive laws is a sign of a transition of societies from the prosperous and stable type to the unstable and disorganized type' (Einaudi 1936a). In other words, Einaudi was searching for the founding ethos of the laws – namely, that their foundation rests on a fiduciary relationship, or the so-called spirit of the laws. In this perspective, the "social authorities" which, it should be recalled, are defined on the basis of their recognition as being capable of giving "counsel", become one of the possible figures of this trust-based foundation of the institutions without which their legitimacy would be reduced to mere legality or to a mere command.

11 Here Einaudi's reflection on the harsh competition caused by a perversion of the logic of gift-giving is not far from that by Mauss (1990 [1923–1924]), but see also Starobinski (1994).

12 On Einaudi's theory of critical point see Bruni (2015), Leoni (1964) and Silvestri (2012a: 89–91) and, above all, Heritier (2012a). As noticed by Heritier (2012a: 298–299),

'critical point theory is clearly an *epistemological theory of the limits of knowledge*, which set freedom in opposition to the standardising use of plan and program. The defender of freedom knows well that following an abstract normative model is not what confers vitality on society; rather, the concrete exercise of knowledge incorporated into concrete free choice is what constitutes the life blood of faith in the institutions.

In every society, there is a *critical point* that determines whether the effects of the (individual) act and of the (collective) government are "good" or "bad", but where, in a given situation, this critical point lies, and who holds the knowledge of it, is not known at all in concrete terms. That ignorance itself represents knowledge, a limit on the theory of knowledge available, which Einaudi situates as the common epistemological basis for the philosophy of social sciences, politics, economics and law in a key that is *aesthetic and figurative* (as the frequent references to Lorenzetti's frescos of good and bad government show). The kind of knowledge expressed by critical point theory is, therefore, epistemologically, a "knowing what" rather than a "knowing how": it simply indicates that *there is* a critical point, or threshold, but without making it possible to know exactly *where it lies or when it will be reached*'.

Again, Heritier (2012a: 311) notices the striking analogy between Einaudi's theory of critical point and Hayek's (1967) negative knowledge related to complex phenomena:

'the existence of a critical point in development beyond which the society moves towards decadence appears to be an open theoretical analysis. The existence of a historical point that defines a threshold is represented, but it cannot be predicted or programmed, nor even knowingly produced. In Hayekian epistemological terms, the doctrine of the Einaudian critical point is negative knowledge, which attests to the existence of a limit and at the same time to the need to limit the importance of *predictive* knowledge regarding the limit: hence the need to limit the anthropological importance of knowledge itself to the real and to the intersubjective relationships in all historic periods. I know that there is a limit, a threshold, but I don't know where this limit lies: this is the structure of the doctrine of the critical point, which, however, Einaudi develops, in contrast to Hayek, not in an epistemological but in a historic-descriptive sense: an element that integrates and enriches the Hayekian-Popperian formulation, but which in its turn, precisely because it is primarily historical, is much more limited than that'.

Last but not least, Heritier parallels Einaudi's theory of critical point to Jean Pierre Dupuy's theory of 'indigenous fixed point' and complex methodological individualism (ivi: 300–301). For a recent overview on complex methodological individualism see Di Iorio (2016).

In some respects, Einaudi's theory of the "critical point" can also be paralleled to Schelling's (1978) 'critical mass models' or to Granovetter's (1978) 'threshold models of collective behaviour'.

13 For an anthropological perspective on virtuous and vicious circles and the relevance of "thirdness" to break up vicious circle see Anspach (2002 [2007]).

14 For specific re-interpretations and applications of Puviani's theory of fiscal illusions, see, at least, Buchanan (1967), Da Empoli (2002), Fedeli, Forte (2013), Oates (1985).

15 In conformity with the centrality of the role of public opinion for a liberal society, Einaudi always emphasized that it was important for the budget to be in the public domain and that criticism should be open to the public: 'Bourbon finance excluded, and Cavourrian finance invoked, the possibility of public discussion. Good honest management of public expenditure, of which the Bourbons boasted, is not sufficient; what is important is that honesty and good intentions can be subjected to public criticism' (Einaudi 1959: 254). On this point, see Paradiso (2004).

16 See the following note.

17 I transcribe here, in full, the old § 10, which was later eliminated in the rewriting.

'Did Fasiani succeed, with his magnificent recent attempt [his book *Principii di scienza delle finanze* (1941)], in demonstrating that the models of the monopolistic, cooperative and modern state have their own theoretical virtue? I am skeptical with regard to the essential part of F.'s [Fasiani] investigation, i.e. the part that rightly takes up half of the pages of his treatise and which deals with the problems of tax shifting and the effects of taxation. If he had so wished, the A. [Author] could have written those pages, which are among the most memorable achievements of Italian economic science, without resorting to the tools of the three types of state. Had he opted for such an approach, those pages would certainly have lost none of their perspicuity and logical elegance. But an adequate demonstration of my negative attitude would require a lengthy analysis that would be beyond the scope of the present essay'.

At this point, Einaudi inserted the following long *note* that referred to his earlier review and to the exchange of correspondence that followed from it:

'See, in this regard, a brief mention in § 3 of my book review in the March 1942 issue of the *Rivista di Storia Economica* [E. 1942a]. My mention of the lack of logical connection between a certain definition of general taxation and the presence of the monopolistic type of state gave rise to a correspondence, the conclusion of which can be summarized as follows: 1) the present writer denies any such connection because he believes that if a tax is defined as general when, instead of inciding on 'a restricted sector of the economy', it weighs on 'vast sectors, or conceivably all the sectors' of the economy (F., I, 258), affecting them either as a single tax, or in conjunction with other taxes, then the hypothesis of the existence of a general tax is not *necessarily* linked to the hypothesis of the existence of a monopolistic state. Furthermore, the existence of the monopolistic state is not, in itself, necessarily linked to the hypothesis of the existence of general taxation even if one were to make the additional assumption that the revenue would utilized to increase the incomes of the dominant classes. In other words, there can be no demonstration that only the monopolistic state can set in place 'a general tax the revenue of which will be utilized to increase the income of a certain part of the population, i.e. of only some of those who have actually paid the tax' – this assertion being the generic manner of formulating the particular concept that the revenue is designed to increase the income of certain persons termed 'dominant'. A tax of this kind could be postulated even in the case of the cooperative state or of any other type of state: one need only think of cases where the revenue from taxes is obtained from all or many of the citizens but is utilized in favor of others, or of only certain groups of the population. Examples include interest on the public debt, old-age pensions and the like (the so-called *transfer expenditures*, which do not in their own right imply the consumption of goods and services, and which are to be distinguished from *exhaustive expenditures*, as the latter imply that another service is to be performed by the beneficiary in exchange for the expenditure: salaries to public officials, payment of supplies required by the state, etc., in other words consumption of goods and services which thus cannot be put to other uses. (Cf. Pigou [1928], *A Study in Public Finance*, pp. 19–20). Therefore, since the concept of a general tax yielding a revenue that is destined to increase the revenue of certain persons at the expense of others cannot be connected logically and necessarily to the concept of the monopolistic state, the hypothesis of the concept of the monopolistic state is superfluous and adds nothing to the analysis that can be made on the effects of the general tax, with or without the above-stated presumption. 2) But Fasiani contends that the 'demonstration that *transfer expenditures* are a characteristic belonging *exclusively* to the monopolistic state' is 'an arbitrary and excessive claim'; he is similarly dismissive of the 'demonstration that effects of this kind *cannot* be studied if one starts out from the hypothesis of the cooperative or modern state. In this problem, as in all others, *much less is needed*. It is sufficient to introduce the concept of *tendency* and a *general rule* . . . I do not deny that there exist taxes which transfer income in a cooperative state as well: for instance, from those who do not possess public debt bonds to those who do possess them. In other words, I do not deny that one *can* study the effects of a tax of this kind even in the hypothesis of a cooperative state. But I would argue that the tendency, in the cooperative state, is for taxation not to be of this nature, whereas it does have this nature in the monopolistic state. Accordingly, the most appropriate framework for studying its effects is that of the hypothesis of a monopolistic state rather than a cooperative state. If these propositions are exact, the following consequences hold: with my approach to a problem I know that taxation in the monopolistic state *tends* to have the effects of an income-transferring tribute, whereas taxation in the cooperative state *tends* to have the effects of a tribute whose revenue is employed in exhaustive expenditures' . . . And this, 'in my view is a *more general* truth than is obtained by studying the effects of taxation independently of the type of state in which it is applied'.

At this point the discussion could come to an end, since the wranglers are now in agreement in believing that the two hypotheses – general taxation with simple income transfer and the monopolistic state – are not linked by a logically necessary connection, but by another kind of connection, which Fasiani terms tendency or something occurring as a 'general rule' (frequency). Should we call such a connection abstract or empirical? Are the truths that can be derived therefrom logical uniformities or empirical uniformities? What is meant by a *more general* truth when it is applied to a hypothesis which, as an empirical or historical fact, has manifestations in the cooperative or modern state (interest on the public debt, old-age pensions, disability pensions, accident insurance compensation, unemployment benefits, etc., free education, social expenditure for public gardens, theatres, entertainment, etc.) that are perhaps considerably more substantial – indeed, looking at the absolute mass and the mass relatively to national income, one might well be inclined to say far more substantial – than the manifestations (the privy purse, court expenses, expenses for pomp and circumstance, maintenance of the various species of praetorians, oligarchs and their satellites etc. etc.) which can be observed, with due consideration of the national income of the era, in the so-called monopolistic states? Admittedly, an attempt to give a comparative assessment of the relative weight of all those items of expenditure in the two types of state is a rather challenging and probably vain enterprise. Nevertheless, it seems legitimate to wonder whether it might not be more appropriate to orient the discussion so that it would focus on the mere didactic expediency of following the one method or the other of presenting the arguments, instead of devoting time to discussions on the greater or lesser generality of self-evident truths. Personally, I prefer the first approach, which would involve studying the effects of taxation independently of the type of state in which they may – with greater or lesser frequency – be applied: such a method, it should be noted, is a theoretical or abstract investigation conducted *sub specie aeternitatis*, with the proviso that a theoretical-historical investigation will be carried out at a later date to determine where, i.e. in what type of state, the different types of taxes and their genuinely most frequent effects can be observed. The other method, which is the one preferred by F., seeks to investigate first and foremost what kind of taxes tend to be characteristic of the one or the other type of state, in order to assess, separately for each type of state, the kind of tax that would be best suited to the given state. However, in reflecting on this method, the present writer is unable to free himself from the disquieting realization that the method fails to clarify whether it deals with abstract or empirical-historical laws. This notwithstanding, the present writer's unease is dispelled by the crystal-clear brilliance of the demonstrations that F., no longer mindful of the type of state, immediately gives in the context of the abstract theory of tax shifting'. (E. 1942–43 [2014a]: 299–301).

18 As is known, the question of the realism of hypotheses or of economic science in general has never ceased to prompt epistemological reflection and has been given further impetus by Friedman's (1953) essay. On the new "critical" realism in economics, see Lawson (1994, 1997, 2003) and the articles collected in Fleetwood (1999) and Fullbrook (2009). For a different perspective on realism, anti-realism and "realisticness" see Mäki (1998, 2000, 2012).
19 On the notion of 'communicative-normative systems', see Heritier (2007). In many respects, the issue is similar to what is today called performativity. See MacKenzie, Muniesa, Siu (2007).
20 In this section, I take up a few considerations put forward in Silvestri (2008a, 2012a, 2012b).
21 These three declinations of good government were held together by the nineteenth-century conception of the public sphere and the role played therein by the middle class. In the Einaudian perspective, the circle of an ideal model of public space is completed by developing it into the nexus between the three spheres of the press, the parliament and the ruling class. Public opinion (the press and parliament), acting through struggle and critical debate involving ideas, values and visions of the world, not only fulfils the function of becoming a principle of selection of the "truth" – for the purposes of institution of the "law" and recognition of its legitimacy – but it also becomes a mechanism for choosing and controlling (and, if necessary, overthrowing) the ruling class and thus for recognizing its (legitimate) "authority". According to this model, the best ruling class is expected to emerge through the electoral competition for votes under the eyes of an illuminated and critical public opinion. It should be noted, though, that confidence in the possibility of this type of mediation accomplished by the public sphere depends to a large extent on the presupposition that good rulers would be expected to emerge from the middle class. This middle class, conceived as the fulcrum of the public sphere, would play an equally ideal role of mediety-mediation in the social equilibrium (Silvestri 2012a). From this perspective, Einaudi's middle class has a key role both in the "good government" as "mixed constitution" (see the conclusions of E. 1949a) and in the (good) society, constituting its founding ethos and main civic virtues in the same sense used by Adam Smith in the third book of *The Wealth of Nations* (Smith 1976: 405, 412), which has properly been recognised as the '*locus classicus* of the theme of commerce and liberty' (Forbes 1975: 193). See also Winch (1978: 70), and Silvestri (2012d). On the Smithian background of Einaudi's economic thought, see Meacci (1998). For a recent reappraisal of the so-called bourgeois virtues, see McCloskey (2006, 2010).

22 The significance of this essay has been highlighted by Mario Einaudi (1988: 11–12): 'a key text to fully understand Luigi Einaudi's thought'.

23 In many respects Einaudi's conundrum can be likened to the so-called Böckenförde (1967 [1991]: 60) dictum: 'The liberal secular state lives on premises that it cannot itself guarantee. On the one hand, it can subsist only if the freedom it consents to its citizens is regulated from within, inside the moral substance of individuals and of a homogeneous society. On the other hand, it is not able to guarantee these forces of inner regulation by itself without renouncing its liberalism.'

On the other hand, Einaudi's insistence on civic virtues may not only be traced back to the Italian literature on *oikonomia*, or to the Italian tradition of 'civil economy'(Porta 2010). It can also be paralleled to the notion of social capital (see Putnam 2001, Putnam, Leonardi, Nanetti 1993).

24 According to Bobbio (1974), the theme of struggle in Einaudi's thought had an illustrious antecedent in the celebrated Kantian concept of 'unsocial sociability' (Kant 1794 [1991]). For a different perspective, see Heritier (2012a: 298), who parallels Einaudi's anthropological assumptions of the theory of critical point – the dignity and freedom of man, and the always possible human elevation or degradation – to Pico della Mirandola's *De dignitate homini*.

25 Here Einaudi (1920b [1963]) contrasts two conceptions of man and, consequently, of society – namely, the perfectist vision of 'reasoning reason' which seeks to 'create the state and society by starting out from the premise of naturally good mankind perverted by political institutions' versus the 'Roman, Christian, British view of the real man, a mixture of virtues and vices, reason and passion, of historical man as he has evolved over the millennia, as he is molded by the land, the institutions of the past, of previous generations'.

26 This counterfactual line of reasoning also seems to evoke the celebrated maxim of James Madison: 'If men were angels, no government would be necessary'. Effectively, the *Federalist Papers* inspired Einaudi's reflection on the European federation.

27 On this point, see Dupuy (2002) and Heritier (2012a).

28 Here, Einaudi's critique of the welfarist approach seems almost to anticipate Sen's reflections. On this see at least Sen 1970, 1987, 1997.

29 Einaudi's concern about the deontology of the economist is far from over. In fact, the professional economic ethics has regained new attention, especially after the financial and economic crisis of 2008. See DeMartino (2011) and the many essays collected in DeMartino, McCloskey (2014a), in particular: DeMartino (2014), DeMartino, McCloskey (2014b), Dow (2014), Offutt (2014), Stiglitz (2014).

30 On this, see Machlup (1969) and, more recently, Hausman, McPherson (2006: 293–294).

31 As Einaudi wrote (COP: 2), 'here it is important to insist, when engaging in an exchange of ideas with philosophers, that there is one particular requirement of economic science which cannot be forfeited. Economic science, in my view, would cease to exist if it were to forsake reasoning with its own methods. As far as I have been able to see since the time when I started to write on this topic, the only philosopher who has perceived the need for this requirement is Croce. I lack the time to check this in further depth, but I imagine that Vailati was also of this opinion. The fact is that Croce and Vailati are probably the only Italian philosophers who studied economic science with genuine affection and have mastered its spirit. One can see, when reading Croce, that he made a very serious study of the classical economists and of the major thinkers who succeeded them, and that he was immediately aware of what they studied and how they studied the material'.

32 Although this reference to the two philosophers is not new in absolute terms – for they are already considered jointly precisely in the essay *In Remembrance of Giovanni Vailati* (E. 1971) – perhaps not enough attention has dwelt on the very fact of their being considered in unison: for one may well wonder what, in Einaudi's mind, two so strikingly different – if not indeed quite contrary – philosophers had in common. We know from the correspondence and from Einaudi's own statements that Einaudi

himself held both thinkers in very high regard (Croce, Einaudi 1988, E. 1971). While the relationship between Einaudi and Croce has been widely analyzed, the extent of the intellectual relationship between Einaudi and Vailati has only recently begun to be outlined (Baffigi 2010, Bruni 2003–2004). Vailati was a "pragmatist", although he himself had some doubts about this label, as he specified that his pragmatism had sprung from a blend of elements he had found to arise in common from his teacher (the mathematician Peano) and from his readings of Pierce. Croce, on the other hand, had sought to found idealism anew as immanentism or "absolute historicism".

Now, with regard to the rewriting of the present essay (at least), two possible reasons can be perceived that may have led Einaudi to consider Croce and Vailati as his joint reference points. a) Both scholars probably exerted some influence over the process whereby, as Einaudi's thought matured, he began to distance himself critically from Pareto, above all from Pareto's sociology (see Bruni 2003–2004). b) Both scholars, although starting out from different premises and a different focus of speculation, had argued in favour of a conventionalist and instrumentalist conception of science, and the thought of Mach was a reference framework shared by the two scholars. Naturally, we cannot exclude that Einaudi's interest, shared with Vailati, in the issue of language of science (see also Introduction, par. 3.2), may also be behind the rewriting of the conclusions against Croce.

33 The synthesis of the Croce–Pareto debate provided in the text is mainly drawn by Silvestri (2012c: 55–96, 2016). On the Croce–Pareto debate, see also Bruni (2002, Ch. 3), Busino (1973) [1975] and Faucci (2014: 130–151). For a recent reappraisal of Croce's economic thought, see Bodei (2003), Faucci (2003) and Montesano (2003).

34 The distinction between philosophy and economic science would eventually be fixed by Croce in a negative perspective that criticized the 'confusions between economic science and the philosophy of economics' and the 'mistakes deriving therefrom'. The three most common errors springing from this confusions are as follows:

1) Ending up by 'denying philosophy for economics'. This was the approach adopted by economists who 'mock' philosophy as 'empty prattle' and who even seek to 'destroy [philosophy] and replace [it with] the methods of empirical observation and of mathematical construction, and who, as they attempt to carry out this deed, go so far as to parade (however much they may protest the contrary) a particular and poorly self-aware empiricist and mathematical philosophy of theirs'.

   Croce famously demolished these economists with the verdict or *injunction* (which sounded like an *excommunication*), 'save yourselves the trouble of philosophizing. Calculate and don't bother to think!' At the same time, he admonished philosophers with an equal and opposite injunction (Croce 1909 [1945]: 262–263).

2) Awarding 'universal value to empirical concepts', such as the conceptions of 'liberism' that elevate the latter to a 'law of nature', or those that hypostatize 'historical and contingent facts' (ivi: 263–264).

3) Transforming 'the fictions of calculation into reality' (ivi: 265).

Now, it is precisely the aforementioned (1) injunction or excommunication by Croce that is conventionally held, in Italy, to mark the breakdown of the communication routes between philosophy on the one hand and economics (and social sciences) on the other and, at the same time, between philosophers and economists.

35 See also the debate that followed Putnam's works: Colander, Su (2013), Dasgupta (2005) and Putnam, Walsh (2012).

36 Though in a completely different context and for different purposes, this argument has been recently put forward by Murphy and Nagel (2002: 4): 'fiscal policy involves large empirical uncertainties about the economic consequences of different choices, and it is hard to disentangle the disagreements about justice from the disagreements about what will happen. A theory of justice cannot by itself approve or condemn a tax cut, for example; it requires some estimate of the effects of such a change on investment, employment, government revenue, and the distribution of after-tax income'.

Bibliography

Albert G. (2004). Pareto's Sociological Positivism. *Journal of Classical Sociology*, 4, 1: 59–86.

Allingham M.G., Sandmo A. (1972). Income Tax Evasion: A Theoretical Analysis. *Journal of Public Economics*, 1: 323–338.

Alm J. (2014). Expanding the Theory of Tax Compliance from Individual to Group Motivations. In F. Forte, R. Mudambi, P.M. Navarra (eds.), *A Handbook of Alternative Theories in Public Economics*. Chelthenam, UK: Edward Elgar, 260–277.

Alm J., McClelland G.H., Schulze W.D. (1992). Why Do People Pay Taxes? *Journal of Public Economics*, 48, 1: 21–38.

Andreoni J. (1988). Why Free Ride? Strategies and Learning in Public Good Experiments. *Journal of Public Economics*, 37: 291–304.

Andreoni J. (1990). Impure Altruism and Donation to Public Goods: A Theory of Warm-Glow Giving. *The Economic Journal*, 100: 464–447.

Anspach M. (2002 [2007]). *A charge de revanche: Figures élémentaires de la réciprocité*. Paris: Edition du Seuil. It. transl.: *A buon rendere. La reciprocità nella vendetta nel dono e nel mercato*. Torino: Bollati Boringhieri.

Backhaus J.G. (ed.) (2013). *Essentials of Fiscal Sociology: Conceptions of an Encyclopedia*, Series: Finanzsoziologie – Vol. 5. Frankfurt am Main: Peter Lang.

Backhaus J.G., Wagner R.E. (2005a). From Continental Public Finance to Public Choice: Mapping Continuity. *History of Political Economy*, Annual Supplement, 37: 314–332.

Backhaus J.G., Wagner R.E. (2005b). Continental Public Finance: Mapping and Recovering a Tradition. *Journal of Public Finance and Public Choice*, 23: 43–67.

Backhouse R.E., Dudley-Evans A., Henderson W. (1993). Exploring the Language and Rhetoric of Economics. In W. Henderson, A. Dudley-Evans, R. Backhouse (eds.), *Economics and Language*. London & New York: Routledge, 1–20.

Baffigi A. (2010). Teoria economica e legislazione sociale nel testo delle "Lezioni". In Gigliobianco (2010), 48–89.

Baranzini R., Bridel P. (1997). On Pareto's First Lectures on Pure Economics at Lausanne. *History of Economics Ideas*, 5, 3: 65–87.

Barucci P. (1974). Luigi Einaudi e la storia del 'dogma' economico. *Note economiche*, VII, 4: 39–68.

Baujard A. (2013). Value Judgments and Economics Expertise. *Working Paper GATE 2013–14*.

Becker G. (1968). Crime and Punishment: An Economic Approach. *Journal of Political Economy*, 76: 169–217.

Bellanca N. (1993). *La teoria della finanza pubblica in Italia, 1883–1946. Saggio storico sulla scuola italiana di economia pubblica*. Firenze: Leo Olschki.

Benda J. (1927). *La trahison des clercs*. Paris: Grasset.

Besley T. (2006). *Principal Agent? The Political Economy of Good Government*. Oxford: Oxford University Press.

Binder C., Heilmann C., Vromen J. (2015). The Future of the Philosophy of Economics: Papers from the XI. INEM Conference at Erasmus University Rotterdam. *Journal of Economic Methodology*, 22, 3: 261–263.

Blaug M. (1980 [1992]). *The Methodology of Economics: Or How Economists Explain*. Cambridge: Cambridge University Press.

Blaug M. (1998). The Positive-Normative Distinction. In J.B. Davis, D. Wade Hands, U. Mäki (eds.), *The Handbook of Economic Methodology*. Cheltenham, UK: Edward Elgar Publishing, 370–374.

Bobbio N. (1964). Introduzione. In Pareto (1964), XII–XXXVMI.

Bobbio N. (ed.) (1973). *Pareto e il sistema sociale*. Firenze: Sansoni.

Bobbio N. (1974). Il pensiero politico di Luigi Einaudi. *Annali della Fondazione Luigi Einaudi*, VIII: 183–215.

Bobbio N. (1983). Il Buongoverno. In *Atti della Accademia Nazionale dei Lincei*. Roma: Accademia Nazionale dei Lincei, 235–244.

Bobbio N. (2012). Comandi e consigli. In *Studi per una teoria generale del diritto*. Torino: Giappichelli.

Boccaccio M., De Bonis V. (2003). The Political Sociological Theories in the Italian Tradition of Public Finance. *Il pensiero economico italiano*, 11, 1: 75–97.

Böckenförde E.-W. (ed.) (1967 [1991]). Die Entstehung des Staates als Vorgang der Säkularisation. Engl. transl.: The Emergence of the State as a Process of Secularization. In *State, Society, and Liberty: Studies in Political Theory and Constitutional Law*. New York: Berg, 26–46.

Bodei R. (2003). Il ruolo dell'economia in Croce. *Economia politica*, XX, 2: 159–165.

Boland L. (1989). *The Methodology of Economic Model Building: Methodology After Samuelson*. London: Routledge.

Borgatta G. (1920). Lo studio scientifico dei fenomeni finanziari. *Giornale degli Economisti e Rivista di Statistica*, 31, 60: 1–24 and 81–116. Engl. transl.: The Scientific Study of Fiscal Phenomena. In McLure (2007), 203–248.

Bowles S., Gintis H. (2000). Reciprocity, Self-Interest, and the Welfare State. *Nordic Journal of Political Economy*, 26: 33–53.

Brennan G., Buchanan J.M. (1980 [2000]). *The Power to Tax: Analytical Foundations of a Fiscal Constitution*. Indianapolis, IN: Liberty Fund, Inc.

Bresciani Turroni C. (1942). *Introduzione alla politica economica*. Einaudi: Torino.

Bruguier Pacini G. (1936). Economia ed etica. *Civiltà fascista*, III, 11: 697–708.

Bruguier Pacini G. (1937). Recensione a L. Einaudi, "Nuovi Saggi". *Leonardo*. Firenze: Febbraio, 69–70.

Bruguier Pacini G. (1943). *Scienza economica, metodo storico e storicismo*. Padova: Cedam.

Bruguier Pacini G. (1950). *Luigi Einaudi moralista*. Nistri-Lischi: Pisa.

Bruni L. (2002). *Vilfredo Pareto and the Birth of Modern Microeconomics*. Cheltenham, UK: Edward Elgar.

Bruni L. (2003–2004). Che cos'è l'economia? Vailati, Pareto e Einaudi in dialogo. In Marchionatti, Becchio (2003–2004), 149–164.

Bruni L. (2015). Critical Point. In *A Lexicon of Social Well-Being*. Houndsmill, UK: Palgrave Macmillan, 33–36.

Bruni L., Montesano A. (2009). Introduction. In L. Bruni, A. Montesano (eds.), *New Essay on Pareto's Economic Theory*. London & New York: Routledge.

Buchanan J.M. (1960). "La scienza delle Finanze": The Italian Tradition in Fiscal Theory. In *Fiscal Theory and Political Economy: Selected Essays*. Chapel Hill: The University of North Carolina Press, 24–74.

Buchanan J.M. (1967 [1999]). *Public Finance in Democratic Process: Fiscal Institutions and Individual Choice*. Indianapolis, IN: Liberty Fund.

Buchanan J.M. (2000 [2005]). The Soul of Classical Liberalism. In *Why I, Too, Am Not a Conservative: The Normative Vision of Classical Liberalism*. Cheltenham, UK: Edward Elgar, 52–61.

Buchanan J.M., Musgrave R.A. (1999). *Public Finance and Public Choice: Two Contrasting Visions of the State*. Cambridge, MA & London, UK: MIT Press.

Busino G. (1973 [1975]). I fondamenti dell'economia e della sociologia nelle polemiche tra il Pareto e il Croce. *Rassegna Economica*, XXXVII, 1095–1135. In Id. *Sociologia e storia*. Guida: Napoli, 331–369.

Busino G. (2000). The Signification of Vilfredo Pareto's Sociology. *Revue européenne des sciences sociales*, 38, 117: 217–228.

Cabiati A. (1940). Intorno ad alcune recenti indagini sulla teoria pura del collettivismo. *Rivista di Storia Economica*, 5, 2: 73–110.

Caldwell B. (1982). *Beyond Positivism: Economic Methodology in the Twentieth Century*. London: Allen & Unwin.

Castro Caldas J., Neves V. (2012). The Meaning of Objectivity: What Can We Learn from Robbins and Myrdal? In José Castro Caldas and Vítor Neves (eds.), *Facts, Values and Objectivity in Economics*. Abingdon, Oxon: Routledge, 67–84.

Cavalieri D. (1994). Il corporativismo nella storia del pensiero economico italiano: una rilettura critica. *Il pensiero economico italiano*, II, 2: 7–49. Engl. transl.: Corporatism in Italian Economic Thought: A Reinterpretation. MPRA Paper No. 43839, posted January 25, 2013, http://mpra.ub.uni-muenchen.de/43839

Colander D., Su H.C. (2013). A Failure to Communicate: The Fact-Value Divide and the Putnam-Dasgupta Debate. *Erasmus Journal for Philosophy and Economics*, 6, 2: 1–23.

Colander D., Su H.C. (2015). Making Sense of Economists' Positive-Normative Distinction. *Journal of Economic Methodology*, 22, 2: 157–170.

Cowell F., Witzum A. (eds.) (2009). *Lionel Robbins's Essay on the Nature and Significance of Economic Science. 75th Anniversary Conference Proceedings*. London: Sunctory and Toyota International Centres for Economic Research and Development.

Cox J.C. (2012). Private Goods, Public Goods, and Common Pools with *Homo Reciprocans. Southern Economic Journal*, 79, 1: 1–14.

Croce B. (1900 [1953]). Sul principio economico. Lettera al professore Vilfredo Pareto. *Giornale degli Economisti*. July 15–26. Engl. transl.: On the Economic Principle. A Letter to Professor V. Pareto. *International Economic Papers*, 3: 172–190.

Croce B. (1901 [1953]). Replica all'articolo del prof. Pareto. *Giornale degli Economisti*, February, 121–130. Engl. transl.: On the Economic Principle. A Reply to Professor V. Pareto. *International Economic Papers*, 3: 197–202.

Croce B. (ed.) (1906 [1961]). Economia filosofica ed economia naturalistica. In *Materialismo storico ed economia marxistica*. Bari: Laterza, 265–275.

Croce B. (1907 [1964]). *Logica come scienza del concetto puro*. Bari: Laterza.

Croce B. (1909 [1945]). *Filosofia della pratica. Economia ed etica*. Bari: Laterza.

Croce B., Einaudi L. (1957). *Liberismo e liberalismo*. ed. by P. Solari. Milano-Napoli: Ricciardi.

Croce B., Einaudi L. (1988). *Carteggio (1902–1953)*. a cura di L. Firpo & Torino: Fondazione L. Einaudi.

Cullis J.G., Lewis A. (1997). Why People Pay Taxes: From a Conventional Economic Model to a Model of Social Convention. *Journal of Economic Psychology*, 18: 305–321.

Da Empoli D. (2002). The Theory of Fiscal Illusion in a Constitutional Perspective. *Public Finance Review*, 30, 5: 377–384.

Da Empoli D. (2010). Lo stato e il progresso economico e sociale. In Gigliobianco (2010), 90–104.

Dasgupta P. (2005). What Do Economists Analyze and Why: Values or Facts? *Economics and Philosophy*, 21: 221–278.

D'Auria M. (2012). Junius and the 'President Professor': Luigi Einaudi's European Federalism. In M. D'Auria, M. Hewitson (eds.), *Europe in Crisis: Intellectuals and the European Idea, 1917–1957*. New York: Berghahn Books, 289–304.

Davis J.B. (2014). Economists' Odd Stand on the Positive-Normative Distinction: A Behavioral Economics View. In G. DeMartino, D. McCloskey (eds.), *Handbook on Professional Economic Ethics: Views from the Economics Profession and Beyond*. Oxford: Oxford University Press. doi: 10.1093/oxfordhb/9780199766635.013.011

Davis J.B., Marciano A., Runde J. (eds.) (2004). *The Elgar Companion of Economics and Philosophy*. Aldershot: Edward Elgar.

Della Valle V. (2010). La lingua di Luigi Einaudi fra classicismo e pathos. In Gigliobianco (2010), 138–154.

Del Vecchio G. (1935 [1954]). Droit et économie. *Revue d'Économie Politique*, XLIX: 1457–1494, tr. it. *Diritto ed economia*, n. ed. riv. con una postilla. Roma: Studium.

de Marchi N. (ed.) (1988). *The Popperian Legacy in Economics*. Cambridge: Cambridge University Press.

de Marchi N. (ed.) (1992). *Post-Popperian Methodology of Economics: Recovering Practice*. Boston: Kluwer.

DeMartino G. (2011). *The Economist's Oath: On the Need for and Content of Professional Economic Ethics*. New York: Oxford University Press.

DeMartino G. (2014). "Econogenic Harm": On the Nature of and Responsibility for the Harm Economists Do as They Try to Do Good. In G. DeMartino, D. McCloskey (eds.), *Conducting Ethical Economic Research: Complications from the Field*. doi: 10.1093/oxfordhb/9780199766635.013.005

DeMartino G., McCloskey D. (eds.) (2014a). *Handbook on Professional Economic Ethics: Views from the Economics Profession and Beyond*. Oxford: Oxford University Press.

DeMartino G., McCloskey D. (2014b). Introduction, or Why This Handbook? In G. DeMartino, D. McCloskey (eds.), *Conducting Ethical Economic Research: Complications from the Field*. doi: 10.1093/oxfordhb/9780199766635.013.001

De Viti de Marco A. (1936). *First Principles of Public Finance*, with an Introduction by L. Einaudi, transl. by E. Pavlo Marget. London, Jonathan Cape & New York: Harcourt Brace & Co.

Di Iorio F. (2016). Introduction: Methodological Individualism, Structural Constraints, and Social Complexity. *Comos + Taxis. Studies in Emergent Order and Organization*, 3/2, 3: 1–8.

Dow S.C. (2014). Codes of Ethics for Economists, Pluralism, and the Nature of Economic Knowledge. In G. DeMartino, D. McCloskey (eds.), *Conducting Ethical Economic Research: Complications from the Field*. doi: 10.1093/oxfordhb/9780199766635.013.041

Dupuy J.-P. (2002). *Avions-nous oublié le mal? Penser la politique après l'11 septembre*. Paris: Bayard.

Einaudi L. (1907). *Le entrate pubbliche dello Stato sabaudo nei bilanci e nei conti dei tesorieri durante la guerra di successione spagnuola*. Torino: F.lli Bocca.

Einaudi L. (1908). *La finanza Sabauda all'aprirsi del secolo XVIII e durante la guerra di successione spagnuola*. Torino: STEN.

Einaudi L. (1914). *La finanza della guerra e delle opere pubbliche*. Torino: Tip. E. Bono.

Einaudi L. (1917). Le confessioni di un economista. *La riforma sociale*, XXIV, XXVIII, 10: 563–568.

Einaudi L. (ed.) (1918 [1920]). Il dogma della sovranità e l'idea della società delle nazioni. In *Lettere politiche di Junius*. Bari: Laterza, 143–156.

Einaudi L. (1920a). *Prediche*. Bari: Laterza.

Einaudi L. (ed.) (1920b [1963]). Perché la guerra continua. In *Cronache economiche e politiche di un trentennio (1893–1925)*. Vol. V. Torino: Einaudi, 967–977.

Einaudi L. (1920c). *Lettere politiche di Junius*. Bari: Laterza.

Einaudi L. (1921). La scienza economica ha fatto bancarotta? *Corriere della sera*, 1.

Einaudi L. (1922 [1988]). Avvertenza del compilatore. In F. Fracchia, *Appunti per la storia politica ed amministrativa di Dogliani*, raccolti e ordinati da L. Einaudi. Torino: Tip. San Giuseppe degli artigianelli, V–XII. Reprint in *Pagine doglianesi, 1893–1943*. Dogliani: Municipality and the "Luigi Einaudi" Civic Library, 32–34.

Einaudi L. (1923 [2006]). The Beauty of the Struggle. In Einaudi (2006), 66–72.

Einaudi L. (1925). Prefazione. In J.S. Mill, *La libertà*. Torino: Piero Gobetti editore, 3–6.

Einaudi L. (1926a). La fine del laissez-faire? *La Riforma Sociale*, XXXVII, 11–12: 570–573 Engli. transl.: The end of laissez faire?. In Einaudi (2006), 80–84.

Einaudi L. (1926b). Piero Gobetti nelle memorie e nelle impressioni dei suoi maestri. *Il Baretti*, III, 3, 16 Marzo (1926), 80.

Einaudi L. (1928a). Dei concetti di liberismo economico e di borghesia e sulle origini materialistiche della guerra. *La Riforma sociale*, XXXV, XXXIX, 9–10: 501–516.

Einaudi L. (1928b [1933]). Recensione a A.C. Pigou, "A Study in Public Finance". *La riforma sociale*, XXXV, XXXIX, 3–4: 159–187. Reprint with the title: Di alcuni importanti problemi di finanza. A proposito dell'ultima opera del Pigou, in Einaudi L. (1933). *Saggi*, parte II. Torino: Edizioni de "La riforma sociale", 93–123.

Einaudi L. (1930). Se esista storicamente la pretesa ripugnanza degli economisti verso il concetto dello stato produttore. *Nuovi studi di diritto, economia e politica*, IV, V: 302–314.

Einaudi L. (1932a). Del modo di scrivere la storia del dogma economico. *La Riforma Sociale*, XXXIX, XLIII, 2: 207–219.

Einaudi L. (1932b). Ancora intorno al modo di scrivere la storia del dogma economico. *La Riforma Sociale*, XXXIX, XLIII, 3: 308–313.

Einaudi L. (1933). *La condotta economica e gli effetti sociali della guerra italiana*. Bari: Laterza.

Einaudi L. (1936a [1953] [1960]). Il peccato originale e la teoria della classe eletta in Federico le Play. *Rivista di storia economica*, I, 2: 85–118. Reprint in L. Einaudi (1953), 307–344. Engl. transl.: "The doctrine of original sin and the theory of the elite in the writings of Frédéric Le Play", in Louis Sommers (ed. and transl.) (1960), *Essays in European Economic Thought*. Princeton, NJ: D. Van Nostrand Company Inc., 162–217.

Einaudi L. (1936b). *Introduction*. In De Viti de Marco (1936), 19–30.

Einaudi L. (1936c). Morale et économique. *Revue d'économie politique*, XLX: 289–311.

Einaudi L. (1936d). Lo strumento economico nell'interpretazione della storia. *Rivista di Storia Economica*, I, 1: 149–158.

Einaudi L. (1936e). Teoria della moneta immaginaria nel tempo da Carlomagno alla Rivoluzione francese. *Rivista di storia economica*, I, 1: 1–35. Engl. transl.: The Theory of Imaginary Money from Charlemagne to the French Revolution. In Einaudi (2006), 153–181.

Einaudi L. (1937). Tema per gli storici dell'economia: dell'anacoretismo economico. *Rivista di Storia Economica*, II, 2: 186–195.

Einaudi L. (1938a). Di una prima stesura della "Ricchezza delle nazioni" e di alcune tesi di Adamo Smith intorno alla attribuzione dei frutti del lavoro. *Rivista di Storia Economica*, III, 1: 50–60.

Einaudi L. (1938b). *Miti e paradossi della giustizia tributaria.* Torino: Einaudi.

Einaudi L. (1939). Del metodo nella storia delle dottrine. *Rivista di Storia Economica*, IV, 3: 234–237.

Einaudi L. (1940a [2014]). *Miti e paradossi della giustizia tributaria*, II ed. Torino: Einaudi. Partial transl.: *Myths and Paradoxes of Justice in Taxation*. In Einaudi (2014a), 67–147.

Einaudi L. (1940b [1945]). *Principii di scienza delle finanze*, III ed. Torino: Einaudi.

Einaudi L. (1940c). Le premesse del ragionamento economico e la realtà storica. *Rivista di Storia Economica*, V, 3: 179–199.

Einaudi L. (1941a). Ancora sulle premesse del ragionamento economico. *Rivista di Storia Economica*, VI, 1: 43–50.

Einaudi L. (1941b). Intorno al contenuto dei concetti di liberismo, comunismo, interventismo e simili. *Argomenti*, 9: 18–34.

Einaudi L. (1941c). Sismondi, economista appassionato. *Rivista di Storia Economica*, VI, 2: 127–134.

Einaudi L. (1941d). Mercantilismo, Calmieri, Tempora e Mores. *Rivista di Storia Economica*, VI, 3: 153–176.

Einaudi L. (1941e). *Saggi sul risparmio e l'imposta.* Torino: Einaudi.

Einaudi L. (1942a). Scienza e storia, o dello stacco dello studioso dalla cosa studiata. *Rivista di Storia economica*, VII, 1: 30–37.

Einaudi L. (1942b). Economia di concorrenza e capitalismo storico. La terza via fra i secoli XVIII e XIX. *Rivista di Storia Economica*, VII, 2: 49–72.

Einaudi L. (1942c). Dell'uomo, fine o mezzo, e dei beni d'ozio (book review of L. Bandini (1942). *Uomo e valore*, Torino: Einaudi). *Rivista di Storia Economica*, VII, 3–4: 117–130.

Einaudi L. (1942d). Del concetto dello 'stato fattore di produzione' e delle sue relazioni col teorema della esclusione del risparmio dall'imposta. *Giornale degli economisti e annali di economia*, July/August: 301–331.

Einaudi L. (1942e). Di alcuni connotati dello stato elencati dai trattatisti finanziari. *Rivista di Diritto finanziario e Scienza delle Finanze*, VI, 4: 191–200.

Einaudi L. (1942f). Postilla critica. *Giornale degli Economisti e annali di economia*, IV, 11/12: 512–517.

Einaudi L. (1942g [2014]). Introduzione. In Bresciani Turroni (1942). Engl. transl.: Introduction. In L. Einaudi (2014), 193–196.

Einaudi L. (1942–43 [2014a]). Ipotesi astratte e ipotesi storiche e dei giudizi di valore nelle scienze economiche. *Atti della R. Accademia delle Scienze di Torino*, 78, II: 57–119. Engl. transl.: Abstract Hypotheses and Historical Hypotheses and on Value Judgments in Economic Science. In R. Faucci, R. Marchionatti (eds.), *Selected Economic Essays. Vol. II*. New York: Palgrave Macmillan, 21–66.

Einaudi L. (1943a). Discutendo con Fasiani e Griziotti di connotati dello Stato e di catasto e imposta fondiaria. *Rivista di Diritto finanziario e Scienza delle Finanze*, VII, 3/4: 178–190.

Einaudi L. (1943b [2006]). *Per una federazione economica europea.* Roma: Movimento liberale italiano. Engl. transl.: Why we need a European economic federation. In Einaudi (2006), 245–249.

Einaudi L. (1944a [2001]). Liberalismo. In Einaudi (2001), 65–66.

Einaudi L. (1944b). *I problemi economici della Federazione europea.* Lugano: Edizioni di Capolago.

Einaudi L. (1945a [2001]). Il mito dello stato sovrano. In Einaudi (2001), 96–100.

Einaudi L. (1945b). Prefazione. In Luigi Vittorio Berliri (ed.), *La giusta imposta. Appunti per un sistema giuridico della pubblica contribuzione. Lineamenti di una riforma organica della finanza ordinaria.* Edizioni dell'Istituto italiano di studi legislativi, V–VII. Roma.

Einaudi L. (1948). *Principii di scienza delle finanze,* IV ed. Torino: Einaudi.

Einaudi L. (1949a). *Lezioni di politica sociale.* Torino: Einaudi.

Einaudi L. (1949b). Stato monopolistico e stato cooperativo in De Viti De Marco. *Rivista di diritto finanziario e scienza delle finanze,* VIII, 1: 5–7.

Einaudi L. (1949c). Prefazione. In G. Solari (ed.), *Studi storici di filosofia del diritto.* Torino: Giappichelli, V–XVII.

Einaudi L. (1950a [1955]). La scienza economica. Reminiscenze. 1896–1946. In C. Antoni, R. Mattioli (eds.), *Cinquant'anni di vita intellettuale italiana. 1896–1946.* Scritti in onore di Benedetto Croce per il suo ottantesimo anniversario. Napoli: Edizioni Scientifiche Italiane, 293–316. Engl. transl.: Fifty Years of Italian Economic Thought: 1896–1946: Reminiscences. *International Economic Papers.* London: Macmillan, 5: 7–25.

Einaudi L. (1950b). Mauro Fasiani. *Rivista di diritto finanziario e scienza delle finanze,* I: 199–201.

Einaudi L. (1950c). Scienza economica ed economisti nel momento presente. *Annuario dell'Università degli studi di Torino,* anno accademico 1949–50. Torino: Tip. Artigianelli, 27–63. Engl. transl: Economic Science and Economists at the Present Day. In Einaudi (2014a), 284–298.

Einaudi L. (1953). *Saggi bibliografici e storici intorno alle dottrine economiche.* Roma: Edizioni di storia e letteratura.

Einaudi L. (1954). *Il buongoverno. Saggi di economia e politica (1897–1954).* Ed. by E. Rossi. Bari: Laterza.

Einaudi L. (ed.) (1956). Conoscere per deliberare. In *Prediche inutili.* Torino: Einaudi, 1–12. Engl. transl.: Know before legislating. In Einaudi (2006), 27–35.

Einaudi L. (1959). *Miti e paradossi della giustizia tributaria.* Torino: Einaudi.

Einaudi L. (1959–65). *Cronache economiche e politiche di un trentennio,* 8 volumes. Torino: Einaudi.

Einaudi L. (1961). I consigli del buon senso di Luigi Einaudi. *Il Mondo,* novembre 28, 1961: 11–12.

Einaudi L. (1962). Politici ed economisti. *Il Politico,* Università di Pavia, XXVI, 2: 239–251. Engl. transl.: Politicians and Economists. *Il Politico,* Università di Pavia, XXVI, 2: 253–263.

Einaudi L. (1971). Ricordo di Giovanni Vailati. G. Vailati, Epistolario *(1891–1909),* a cura di G. Lanaro, con una introduzione di M. Dal Pra. Torino: Einaudi, XIX–XXVI.

Einaudi L. (1973). *Scritti economici, storici e civili.* Milano: Mondadori.

Einaudi L. (1994). *Memorandum.* Ed. by G. Berta. Marsilio: Venezia.

Einaudi L. (2000). *'From Our Italian Correspondent': Luigi Einaudi's Articles in* The Economist, *1908–1946,* R. Marchionatti (ed.), two volumes. Firenze: Leo Olschki.

Einaudi L. (2001). *Riflessioni di un liberale sulla democrazia. 1943–1947,* ed. by P. Soddu, Firenze: Leo Olschki.

Einaudi L. (2006). *Selected Economic Essays.* Vol. 1. Ed. by Luca Einaudi, R. Faucci, R. Machionatti. New York: Palgrave Macmillan.

Einaudi L. (2014a). *Selected Economic Essays.* Vol. 2. Ed. by R. Faucci, R. Machionatti. New York: Palgrave Macmillan.

Einaudi L. (2014b). *Selected Political Essay*. Vol. 3. Ed. by D. Da Empoli, C. Malandrino, V. Zanone. New York: Palgrave McMillan.

Einaudi Luca, Faucci R., Marchionatti R. (2006). Introduction. In Einaudi (2006), 1–25.

Einaudi Luigi R. (2010). Le molteplici eredità. Un ricordo personale di Luigi Einaudi. In Marchionatti, Soddu (2010), 309–335.

Einaudi M. (1988). Presentazione. In L. Einaudi (ed.), *Pagine doglianesi, 1893–1943*, a cura del Comune e della biblioteca civica "Luigi Einaudi". Dogliani, 11–12.

Eusepi G., Wagner R.E. (2013). Tax Prices in a Democratic Polity: The Continuing Relevance of Antonio De Viti de Marco. *History of Political Economy*, Duke University Press, 45, 1: 99–121.

Farese G. (2012). *Luigi Einaudi*. Soveria Mannelli: Rubbettino.

Fasiani M. (1932). Contributo alla teoria dell'"uomo corporativo". *Studi sassaresi*, X, 4: 317–335.

Fasiani M. (1932–33). Der gegenwärtige Stand der reine Theorie der Finanzwissenschaft in Italien, parti I, II e III, in *Zeitschrift für Nationalökonomie*, Band III, Heft 5: 651–91; Band IV, Heft 1: 79–107; Band IV, Heft 3: 357–88 (1932–33). Traduzione italiana, con varianti del curatore: La teoria della finanza pubblica in Italia. In M. Finoia (eds.), *Il pensiero economico italiano (1850–1950)*. Bologna: Cappelli (1980), 117–202.

Fasiani M. (1937). Principii generali e politiche delle crisi. *Annali d'economia*, XII, 1–4: 25–108.

Fasiani M. (1941). *Principii di Scienza delle Finanze*, 2 volumes. Torino: Giappichelli.

Fasiani M. (1942). Della teoria della produttività dell'imposta, del concetto di "stato fattore della produzione", e del teorema della doppia tassazione del risparmio. *Giornale degli Economisti e annali di economia*, 11/12: 491–511.

Fasiani M. (1943a). Di alcuni connotati del gruppo pubblico e di una definizione dei bisogni pubblici. *Rivista di diritto finanziario e Scienza delle Finanze*, June: 62–83.

Fasiani M. (1943b). "Postilla" a: Luigi Einaudi, "Discutendo con Fasiani e Griziotti di connotati dello Stato e di catasto e imposta fondiaria." *Rivista di diritto finanziario e Scienza delle Finanze*, VII, 3–4, 190–191.

Fasiani M. (1949 [2007]). Contributi di Pareto alla scienza delle finanze. *Giornale degli Economisti e annali di economia*, VIII, 3–4, March–April: 129–173. Reprinted in *Vilfredo Pareto, l'economista e il sociologo: scritti nell'anniversario della nascita*, Milano, casa editrice Rodolfo Malfasi, 1949. Engl. transl.: Pareto's Contributions to the Science of Public Finance. In McLure (2007), 266–305.

Fasiani M. (1951). *Principii di scienza delle finanze*, seconda edizione riv. e ampl., 2 vol. Torino: Giappichelli.

Faucci R. (1982). *La scienza economica in Italia. Da Francesco Ferrara a Luigi Einaudi (1850–1943)*. Napoli: Guida.

Faucci R. (1986). *Einaudi*. Torino: Utet.

Faucci R. (1989). Einaudi, Croce, Rossi: il liberalismo fra scienza economica e filosofia. *Quaderni di Storia dell'Economia Politica*, VII, 1: 113–133.

Faucci R. (2003). Croce e la scienza economica: dal marxismo al purismo alla critica del liberismo. *Economia politica*, XX, 2, agosto, 167–184.

Faucci R. (2014). *A History of Italian Economic Thought*. London: Routledge.

Fausto D. (1998). The Role of the Coercive Element in Fiscal Choice in the Italian Tradition in Public Finance. *Rivista Italiana degli Economisti*, III, 1: 3–25.

Fausto D. (2003). An Outline of the Main Italian Contributions to the Theory of Public Finance. *Il pensiero economico italiano*, XI, 1: 11–41.

Fausto D., De Bonis V. (eds.) (2003). The Theory of Public Finance in Italy from the Origin to the 1940s. *Il pensiero economico italiano*, XI, 1.

Fedeli S., Forte F. (2013). The Sociological Theory of Fiscal Illusion and the Laffer Curve. Reflections on an Italian Case. In Backhaus (2013), 95–114.

Fehr E., Gächter S. (2000). Fairness and Retaliation. The Economics of Reciprocity. *Journal of Economic Perspectives*, 14: 159–181.

Feld L.P., Frey B.S. (2000). Trust Breeds Trust: How Taxpayers are Treated. *Economics of Governance*, 3, 2: 87–99.

Feld L.P., Frey B.S. (2007). Tax Compliance as the Result of a Psychological Tax Contract: The Role of Incentives and Responsive Regulation. *Law and Policy*, 29, 1: 102–120.

Fiori S. (2007). Attilio Cabati and the Debate on Market Socialism. *History of Economic Ideas*, XV, 2: 127–141.

Fleetwood S. (ed.) (1999). *Critical Realism in Economics: Development and Debate*. London & New York: Routledge.

Forbes D. (1975). *Sceptical Whiggism, Commerce and Liberty*. In A.S. Skinner, T. Wilson (eds.), *Essay on Adam Smith*. Clarendon: Oxford, 179–201.

Forte F. (1982). *Luigi Einaudi: il mercato e il buon governo*. Torino: Einaudi.

Forte F. (2009). *L'economia liberale di Luigi Einaudi. Saggi*. Firenze: Leo Olschki.

Forte F. (2012). The Architecture of Luigi Einaudi's Good Government. In Heritier, Silvestri (2012a), 13–32.

Forte F., Marchionatti R. (2012). Luigi Einaudi's Economics of Liberalism. *The European Journal of the History of Economic Thought*, 19, 4: 587–624.

Forte F., Silvestri P. (2013). Pareto's Sociological Maximum of Utility of the Community and the Theory of the Elites. In Backhaus (2013), 231–265.

Fossati A. (2011). The Italian Tradition in Public Finance: An Annotated Bibliography of Mauro Fasiani. *Studi Economici*, 3: 5–122.

Fossati A. (2012). Pareto's Influence on Scholars from the Italian Tradition in Public Finance. *Journal of the History of Economic Thought*, 34: 43–66.

Fossati A. (2013). Vilfredo Pareto's Influence on the Italian Tradition in Public Finance: A Critical Assessment of Mauro Fasiani's Appraisal. *The European Journal of the History of Economic Thought*, 20: 466–488.

Fossati A. (2014a). Luigi Einaudi e Mauro Fasiani: il dibattito epistemologico dal 1941 al 1943. *Il Pensiero Economico Italiano*, 22, 1: 91–153.

Fossati A. (2014b). The Luigi Einaudi vs. Mauro Fasiani Epistemological Debate (1938–1943): The End of the Italian Tradition in Public Finance. *Studi Economici*, 113: 5–33.

Fossati A. (2015). Notes in the Margin to a Recent Collection of Essays by Luigi Einaudi. *Studi Economici*, 115: 86–99.

Fossati A. (unpublished). The Fiscal Economics of Antonio De Viti de Marco Revisited.

Fossati A., Silvestri P. (2012). Un inedito dissidio epistemologico sui *Miti e paradossi della giustizia tributaria* di Einaudi: le lettere perdute di Mauro Fasiani. *Studi Economici*, 3: 5–80.

Frey B.S. (1997). A Constitution for Knaves Crowds Out Civic Virtues. *Economic Journal*, 107: 1043–1053.

Friedman M. (1953). *Essays in Positive Economics*. Chicago: University of Chicago Press.

Fullbrook E. (ed.) (2009). *Ontology and Economics: Tony Lawson and His Critics*. London: Routledge.

Fusco A.M. (2009). Luigi Einaudi e John Maynard Keynes. Prediche e profezie. In *Visite in soffitta. Saggi di Storia del pensiero economico*. Napoli: Editoriale scientifica, 185–218.

Garofalo G. (2012). Luigi Einaudi and Federico Caffè: Outlines of a Social Policy for Good Governance. In Heritier, Silvestri (2012a), 45–56.

Gellner E. (1990). La trahison de la trahison de clercs. In I. Mclean, A. Montefiore, P. Winch (eds.), *The Political Responsibility of Intellectuals*. Cambridge: Cambridge University Press, 17–27.

Gigliobianco A. (ed.) (2010). *Luigi Einaudi: Libertà economica e coesione sociale*. Bari: Laterza.

Gintis H. (2000). Beyond Homo Oeconomicus: Evidence from Experimental Economics. *Ecological Economics*, 35: 311–322.

Giolitti A. (1943). [Review of] "W. Röpke, *Die Gesellshaftskrisis der Gegenwart*". *Archivio della cultura italiana*, V, 1, gennaio-giugno: 98–102.

Giordano A. (2006). *Il pensiero politico di Luigi Einaudi*. Genova: Name.

Giurato L. (2009). Searching for Fairness in Taxation: Lessons from the Italian School of Public Finance. In G. Brennan, G. Eusepi (eds.), *The Economics of Ethics and the Ethics of Economics: Values, Markets and the State*. Cheltenham & Northampton, UK: Edward Elgar, 161–187.

Granovetter M. (1978). Threshold Models of Collective Behavior. *American Journal of Sociology*, 83, 6: 1420–1443.

Groenewegen P. (1996). Introduction. In P. Groenewegen (ed.), *Economics and Ethics?*. London: Routledge 1–14.

Hamlin A., Pettit P. (eds.) (1989). *The Good Polity. Normative Analysis of the State*. Oxford: Blackwell.

Hausman D.M. (1988). An Appraisal of Popperian Methodology. In de Marchi (1988), 65–85.

Hausman D.M. (2013). Philosophy of Economics. *The Stanford Encyclopedia of Philosophy* (Winter 2013 Edition), Edward N. Zalta (ed.), http://plato.stanford.edu/archives/win2013/entries/economics/

Hausman D.M., McPherson M.S. (2006). *Economic Analysis, Moral Philosophy and Public Policy*. Cambridge: Cambridge University Press.

Hayek F.A.v. (ed.) (1935). *Collectivist Economic Planning*. London: Routledge & Kegan Paul.

Hayek F.A.v. (1967). *Studies in Philosophy, Politics and Economics*. Chicago: University of Chicago Press.

Hayek F.A.v. (1970 [2014]). *The Market and Other Orders*. Ed. by B. Caldwell. Chicago: University of Chicago Press.

Hayek F.A.v. (1973). *Law, Legislation and Liberty, Vol I: Rules and Order*. Chicago: University of Chicago Press.

Hayek F.A.v. (1976). *Law, Legislation and Liberty, Vol II: The Mirage of Social Justice*. Chicago: University of Chicago Press.

Heritier P. (2007). *Società post-hitleriane? Materiali didattici di estetica giuridica 2.0*. Torino: Giappichelli.

Heritier P. (2012a). Useless Non-Preaching? The Critical Point and the Complex Anthropology of Freedom in Luigi Einaudi. In Heritier, Silvestri (2012a), 275–312.

Heritier P. (2012b). *Estetica Giuridica. A partire da Legendre: Il fondamento finzionale del diritto positivo*. Vol. II. Torino: Giappichelli.

Heritier P., Silvestri P. (eds.) (2012a). *Good Government, Governance and Human Complexity. Luigi Einaudi's Legacy and Contemporary Society*. Firenze: Leo Olschki.

Heritier P., Silvestri P. (2012b). Introduction. Luigi Einaudi: Poised Between Ideal and Real. In Heritier, Silvestri (2012a), VII–XVIII.

Jannacone P. (1912). Il "paretaio". *La riforma sociale*, XIX, XXIII, 5: 337–368.

Kant I. (1794 [1991]). Idea for a Universal History with a Cosmopolitan Purpose. In H.S. Reiss (ed.), *Kant. Political Writings*. Cambridge Texts in the History of Political Thought (2nd ed.). Cambridge: Cambridge University Press, 41–53.

Kayaalp O. (1985). Public Choice Elements in the Italian Theory of Public Goods. *Public Finance/Finances Publiques*, 3: 395–410.

Kayaalp O. (1989). Early Italian Contributions to the Theory of Public Finance: Pantaleoni, De Viti De Marco, and Mazzola. In D.A. Walker (ed.), *Perspectives on the History of Economic Thought*. Vol. I. Aldershot: Edward Elgar, 155–166.

Kayaalp O. (2004). *The National Element in the Development of Fiscal Theory*. New York: Palgrave Macmillan.

Keynes J.M. (1926). *The End of Laissez-Faire*. London: Hogarth Press.

Kimball R. (2009). The Treason of the Intellectuals and "The undoing of thought". In J. Benda (ed.), *The Treason of the Intellectuals*. New Brunswick & London: Transaction Publishers, IX–XXVIII.

Lawson T. (1994). A Realist Theory for Economics. In Roger E. Backhouse (ed.), *New Direction in Economics Methodology*. London: Routledge, 257–285.

Lawson T. (1997). *Economics and Reality*. London: Routledge.

Lawson T. (2003). *Reorienting Economics*. London: Routledge.

Leoni B. (1964). *Luigi Einaudi e la scienza del governo*. Torino: Einaudi.

Le Play F. (1877). *L'organisation du travail selon la coutume des ateliers et la loi du décalogue : avec un précis d'observations comparées sur la distinction du bien et du mal dans le régime du travail, les causes du mal actuel et les moyens de réforme, les objections et les réponses, les difficultés et les solutions* (4th ed.). Tours: A. Mame et fils.

Le Play F. (1878). *La réforme sociale en France déduite de l'observation comparée des peuples européens* (6th ed.). Tours: A. Mame et fils.

Le Play F. (1881). *La constitution essentielle de l'humanité: exposé des principes et des coutumes qui créent la prospérité ou la souffrance des nations*. Tours: A. Mame et fils.

Liberati P., Paradiso M. (2014). The Positive Theory of Benefit Taxation in the Italian School of Public Finance. *Working Papers* no. 190. Dipartimento di Economia Università degli studi Roma Tre. http://dipeco.uniroma3.it/db/docs/WP%20190.pdf

Machlup F. (1969). Positive and Normative Economics. In R. Heilbroner (ed.), *Economic Means and Political Ends. Essays in Political Economics*. Englewood Cliffs, NJ: Prentice-Hall, 99–124.

MacKenzie D., Muniesa F., Siu L. (eds.) (2007). *Do Economists Make Markets? On the Performativity of Economics*. Princeton: Princeton University Press.

Magnani I. (2005). Il paretaio. *Economia politica. Rivista di teoria e analisi*, XXII, 1: 69–100.

Mäki U. (1998). Realisticness. In U. Mäki, J.B. Davis, D.W. Hands (eds.), *The Handbook of Economic Methodology*, Cheltenham, UK: Edward Elgar, 409–413.

Mäki U. (2000). Reclaiming Relevant Realism. *Journal of Economic Methodology*, 7, 1: 109–125.

Mäki U. (2012). Realism and Antirealism About Economics. In U. Mäki (ed.), D.M. Gabbay, P. Thagard and J. Woods (series eds.), *Philosophy of Economics* (series *Handbook of the Philosophy of Science, Volume 13*). Amsterdam: Elsevier, 3–24.

Marchionatti R. (2000a). L'economia sperimentale di Vilfredo Pareto. In R. Marchionatti, C. Malandrino (eds.), *Economia, sociologia e politica nell'opera di Vilfredo Pareto*. Firenze: Leo Olschki, 97–122.

Marchionatti R. (2000b). La 'pericolosità del camminare dritti sui fili di rasoio'. Einaudi critico di Keynes. In C. Malandrino (ed.), *Una rivista all'avanguardia. La Riforma sociale 1894–1935*. Firenze: Leo Olschki, 379–415.

Marchionatti R., Becchio G. (eds.) (2003–2004). *La scuola di Torino. Da Cognetti de Martiis a Einaudi*. Torino: Quaderni dell'Università di Torino.

Marchionatti R., Cassata F., Becchio G., Mornati F. (2013). When Italian Economics "Was Second to None". Luigi Einaudi and the Turin School of Economics. *The European Journal of the History of Economic Thought*, 20, 5: 776–811.

Marchionatti R., Gambino E. (1997). Pareto and Political Economy as a Science: Methodological Revolution and Analytical Advances in Economic Theory in the 1890s. *Journal of Political Economy*, 105, 6: 1322–1348.

Marchionatti R., Mornati F. (2007). Introduction. In V. Pareto, R. Marchionatti, F. Mornati (eds.), *Considerations on the Fundamental Principles of Pure Political Economy*. London: Routledge, XI–XXIX.

Marchionatti R., Soddu P. (eds.) (2010). *Luigi Einaudi nella cultura, nella società e nella politica del Novecento*. Firenze: Leo Olschki.

Masini F. (2009). Economics and Political Economy in Lionel Robbins's Writing. *Journal of the History of Economic Thought*, 31, 4: 421–436.

Masini F. (2012). Luigi Einaudi and the Making of the Neoliberal Project. *History of Economic Thought and Policy*, 1, 1: 39–59.

Mauss M. (1990 [1923–24]). *The Gift: The Form and Reason for Exchange in Archaic Societies*. New York: W.W. Norton & Company.

McCloskey D. (1985). *The Rhetoric of Economics*. Wisconsin: The University of Wisconsin Press.

McCloskey D. (2006). *The Bourgeois Virtues: Ethics for an Age of Commerce*. Chicago: University of Chicago Press.

McCloskey D. (2010). *Bourgeois Dignity: Why Economics Can't Explain the Modern World*. Chicago: University of Chicago Press.

McLure M. (2007). *The Paretian School and the Italian Fiscal Sociology*. New York: Palgrave Macmillan.

Meacci F. (1998). Luigi Einaudi. In F. Meacci (ed.), *Italian Economists of the 20th Century*. Cheltenham, UK: Edward Elgar.

Medema S. (2005). 'Marginalizing' Government: From la scienza delle finanze to Wicksell. *History of Political Economy*, 37, 1: 1–25.

Medema S.G. (2009). *The Hesitant Hand: Taming Self-Interest in the History of Economic Ideas*. Princeton: Princeton University Press.

Michels R. (1932). Ancora intorno al modo di scrivere la storia del dogma economico. *La Riforma sociale*, XXXIX, XLIII: 303–308.

Mongin P. (2006). Value Judgments and Value Neutrality in Economics. *Economica*, 72: 257–286.

Montesano A. (2003). Croce e la scienza economica. *Economia politica*, XX, 2: 201–223.

Morelli U. (1990). *Contro il mito dello stato sovrano. Luigi Einaudi e l'unità europea*. Milano: Franco Angeli.

Mornati F. (2004). La riflessione epistemologica della Scuola di Torino: Pasquale Jannaccone critico di Pareto. *Il Pensiero Economico Italiano*, XII/2: 162–175.

Mornati F. (2006). An Analytical-Epistemological Reconstruction of the Genesis of Pareto's Manuale di Economia Politica. *Rivista Internazionale di Scienze Economiche e Commerciali*, LIII/4: 579–591.

Mosca G. (1982). *Teorica dei governi e governo parlamentare*. In G. Sola (ed.), *Scritti politici*. Vol. I. Torino: Utet.

Mosca M. (2005). De Viti De Marco. Historian of economic analysis. *The European Journal of the History of Economic Thought*, 2: 241–259.

Murphy L., Nagel T. (2002). *The Myth of the Owernship, Tax and Justice*. New York: Oxford University Press.

Musgrave R.A. (1939). The Voluntary Exchange Theory of Public Economy. *The Quarterly Journal of Economics*, 53, 2: 213–237.

Musgrave R.A., Peacock A. T. (1958a). *Classics in the Theory of Public Finance*. London: Macmillan.

Musgrave R.A., Peacock A.T. (1958b). Introduction. In Musgrave, Peacock (1958a), IX–XIX.

Myrdal K.G. (1953). *The Political Element in the Development of Economic Theory*. London: Routledge.

Myrdal K.G. (1958). *Value in Social Theory. A Selection of Essays on Methodology*. London: Routledge & Kegan Paul.

Oates W.E. (1985). *On the Nature and Measurement of Fiscal Illusion: A Survey*. Department of Economics, University of Maryland.

Oddenino A., Silvestri P. (2011). Autonomie locali e istituzioni sovranazionali. Il problema del buongoverno tra globalizzazione e localizzazione alla luce del pensiero einaudiano. In S. Sicardi (ed.), *Le autonomie territoriali e funzionali nella provincia di Cuneo in prospettiva transfrontaliera (alla luce del principio di sussidiarietà)*, Napoli: ESI, Quaderni del Dipartimento di Scienze Giuridiche dell'Università di Torino, 97–132.

Offutt S. (2014). Ethics and the Government Economist. In G. DeMartino, D. McCloskey (eds.), *Conducting Ethical Economic Research: Complications from the Field*. doi: 10.1093/oxfordhb/9780199766635.013.033

Pantaleoni M. (1883). Contributo alla teoria del riparto delle spese pubbliche. *Rassegna italiana*, 15: 25–70.

Paradiso M. (2004). Einaudi e il mito del pareggio di bilancio. *Il pensiero economico italiano*, XII, 2: 107–117.

Pareto V. (1900 [1953]). Sul fenomeno economico. Lettera a Benedetto Croce. *Giornale degli economisti*, agosto, 139–162. Engl. transl.: On the Economic Phenomenon. A Reply to Benedetto Croce. *International Economic Papers*, 3: 180–196.

Pareto V. (1901 [1953]). Ancora sul principio economico. *Giornale degli economisti*, febbraio, 131–138. Engl. transl.: On the Economic Principle. A Reply to Benedetto Croce. *International Economic Papers*, 3: 180–196.

Pareto V. (1906). *Manuale di economia politica, con una introduzione alla scienza sociale*. Milano: Società editrice libraria.

Pareto V. (1916 [1964]). *Trattato di sociologia generale*, Milano: Edizioni di Comunità.

Pareto V. (1917). Discorso per il Giubileo. In *Scritti sociologici*, ed. by G. Busino, Torino: Utet, (1966), 729–736.

Pascal B. (2003). *Pensées*. Trans. W.F. Trotter, introduction by T.S. Elliot. Mineola, NY: Dover Publications.

Passerin d'Entrèves A. (1937 [1992]). Morale, diritto ed economia. Libreria Internazionale F.lli Treves, Pavia, reprint in *Saggi di storia del pensiero politico. Dal medioevo alla società contemporanea*. Milano: F. Angeli, 341–357.

Passerin d'Entrèves A. (1940). *The Medieval Contribution to Political Thought. Thomas Aquinas, Marsilius of Padua, Richard Hooker*. Oxford: Oxford University Press.

Passerin d'Entrèves A. (1962). *La dottrina dello Stato: elementi di analisi e di interpretazione.* Torino: Giappichelli. Engl. transl.: *The Notion of the State. An Introduction to Political Theory.* Oxford: Clarendon Press, 1969.

Passerin d'Entrèves A. (1971). Luigi Einaudi e la "storia delle dottrine". *Il Pensiero politico,* IV: 450–456.

Peil J., van Staveren, I. (2009). *Handbook of Economics and Ethics.* Cheltenham, UK & Northampton: Edward Elgar.

Persson T., Tabellini G. (2003). *The Economic Effects of Constitutions.* Cambridge, MA: MIT Press.

Pigou A.C. (1928). *A Study in Public Finance.* London: Macmillan and Co.

Porta P.L. (2010). Libertà, mercato, giustizia sociale. In Gigliobianco (2010), 19–47.

Portinaro P.P. (1979). Luigi Einaudi, la sociologia e la questione dei giudizi di valore. *Annali della Fondazione Luigi Einaudi,* XIII: 247–272.

Prato G. (1907). *Il costo della guerra di successione spagnuola e le spese pubbliche in Piemonte dal 1700 al 1713.* Torino: F.lli Bocca.

Prato G. (1908). *La vita economica in Piemonte a mezzo il secolo XVIII.* Torino: STEN.

Putnam H. (2002). *The Collapse of the Fact/Value Dichotomy, and Other Essays.* Cambridge, MA: Harvard University Press.

Putnam H. (2012). For Ethics and Economics Without the Dichotomies. In Putnam, Walsh (2012), 111–129. First published in 2003 in the *Review of Political Economy,* 15: 305–412.

Putnam H., Walsh V. (2012). Introduction. In H. Putnam, V. Walsh (eds.), *The End of Value-Free Economics.* London: Routledge, 1–5.

Putnam R.D. (2001). *Bowling Alone: The Collapse and Revival of American Community.* New York: Simon and Schuster.

Putnam R.D., Leonardi R., Nanetti R.Y. (1993). *Making Democracy Work: Civic Traditions in Modern Italy.* Princeton, NJ: Princeton University Press.

Puviani A. (1903). *Teoria della illusione finanziaria.* Palermo: Sandron.

Quadrio Curzio A., Rotondi C. (2005). Luigi Einaudi: il disegno istituzionale ed economico per l'Europa. In *Luigi Einaudi: Istituzioni, mercato e riforma sociale.* Roma: Accademia nazionale dei Lincei, Bardi, 163–194.

Reviglio F. (2012). Government and Market Failures in Luigi Einaudi and To-day. In Heritier, Silvestri (2012a), 33–44.

Robbins L. (1932). *An Essay on the Nature and Significance of Economic Science.* London: Macmillan.

Romano R. (1973). Introduzione. In Einaudi (1973), XI–XLIII.

Romeo R. (1974). Luigi Einaudi e la storia delle dottrine e dei fatti economici. In Various Authors, *Commemorazione di Luigi Einaudi nel centenario della nascita (1874–1974).* Torino: Fondazione Luigi Einaudi, 93–114.

Röpke W. ([1942] 1946). *Die Gesellshaftskrisis der Gegenwart,* Ital. transl.: *La crisi sociale del nostro tempo.* Roma: Einaudi.

Ross D., Kincaid H. (2009). Introduction: The New Philosophy of Economics. In D. Ross, H. Kincaid (eds.), *The Oxford Handbook of Philosophy of Economics.* Oxford: Oxford University Press, 3–32.

Samuels W.J. (1990). Introduction. In W.J. Samuels (ed.), *Economics as Discourse: An Analysis of the Language of Economics.* Boston: Kluwer Academic Publishers, 1–14.

Scarantino A. (2009). On The Role of Values in Economics: Robbins and His Critics. *Journal of the History of Economic Thought,* 31: 449–473.

Schelling T.C. (1978). *Micromotives and Macrobehavior.* New York: Norton.

Schumpeter J.A. (1949). Science and Ideology. *American Economic Review*, XXXIX, 2: 345–359.

Schumpeter J.A. (1954). *History of Economic Analysis*. New York: Oxford University Press.

Seligman E. (1926). The Social Theory of Public Finance. *Political Science Quarterly* 41: 354.

Sen A. (1970). *Collective Choices and Social Welfare*. Edinburgh: Oliver & Boyd.

Sen A. (1987). *On Ethics and Economics*. Oxford: Basil Blackwell.

Sen A. (1997). *On Economic Inequality: Expanded Edition with a Substantial Annexe by James E. Foster and Amartya Sen*. Oxford: Clarendon Press.

Sensini G. (1912). *La teoria della "rendita"*. Roma: Loescher.

Silvestri P. (2006). Il buongoverno nel pensiero di Einaudi e Mosca: tra governo della legge e governo degli uomini. *Annali della Fondazione Luigi Einaudi*, XL: 157–196.

Silvestri P. (2007). Rileggendo Einaudi e Croce: spunti per un liberalismo fondato su un'antropologia della libertà. *Annali della Fondazione Luigi Einaudi*, XLI, 201–240.

Silvestri P. (2008a). *Il liberalismo di Luigi Einaudi o del Buongoverno*. Soveria Mannelli: Rubbettino.

Silvestri P. (2008b). Il normativo nell'homo œconomicus, il normativo dell'homo œconomicus. In E. Di Nuoscio, P. Heriter (eds.), *Le culture di Babele. Saggi di antropologia filosofico-giuridica*. Milano: Medusa, 173–192.

Silvestri P. (2009). Mosca, Ruffini ed Einaudi. Politica, diritto ed economia in difesa della libertà. In R. Marchionatti (ed.), *La Scuola di economia di Torino. Co-protagonisti ed epigoni*. Firenze: Leo Olschki, 41–64.

Silvestri P. (2010a). Veritas, Auctoritas, Lex. Scienza economica e sfera pubblica: sulla normatività del Terzo. *Il pensiero economico italiano*, 2: 37–65.

Silvestri P. (2010b). Liberalismo, legge, normatività. Per una rilettura epistemologica del dibattito Croce–Einaudi. In R. Marchionatti, P. Soddu (eds.), *Luigi Einaudi nella cultura, nella società e nella politica del Novecento*. Firenze: Leo Olschki, 211–239.

Silvestri P. (2011). Buon governo. In F. Grassi Orsini, G. Nicolosi (eds.), *Dizionario del liberalismo italiano*. Vol. I. Soveria Mannelli: Rubbettino, 152–162.

Silvestri P. (2012a). The Ideal of Good Government in Luigi Einaudi's Thought and Life: Between Law and Freedom. In Heritier, Silvestri (2012a), 55–95.

Silvestri P. (2012b). After-Word. Which (Good-Bad) Man? For Which (Good-Bad) Polity? In Heritier, Silvestri (2012a), 313–332.

Silvestri P. (2012c). *Economia, diritto e politica nella filosofia di Croce. Tra finzioni, istituzioni e libertà*. Torino: Giappichelli.

Silvestri P. (2012d). Il "good government" in Adam Smith: tra *Jurisprudence*, *Political Economy* e *Theory of Moral Sentiments*. *Teoria e critica della regolazione sociale*, Quaderno (2012), 1–30.

Silvestri P. (2015). Anthropology of Freedom and Tax Justice: Between Exchange and Gift. Thoughts for an Interdisciplinary Research Agenda. *Teoria e critica della regolazione sociale*, 2: 115–132.

Silvestri P. (2016). Disputed (Disciplinary) Boundaries. Philosophy, Economics and Value Judgments. *History of Economic Ideas*, 2/XXVI (forthcoming).

Smart W. (1916). *Second Thought of an Economist*, With a Biographical Sketch by Thomas Jones. London: Macmillan.

Smith A. (1776 [1976]). *An Enquiry Into the Nature and Causes of The Wealth of Nations*. Oxford: Clarendon Press.

Solari G. (2006). *Luigi Einaudi e il liberalismo democratico. Teoria politica*, 2: 77–105.

Starobinski J. (1994). *Largesse*. Paris: Edition de la Réunion des Musées nationaux.

Stiglitz J.E. (2014). Ethics, Economic Advice, and Economic Policy. In G. DeMartino, D. McCloskey (eds.), *Conducting Ethical Economic Research: Complications from the Field*. doi: 10.1093/oxfordhb/9780199766635.013.020

Tomatis F. (2011). *Verso la città divina. L'incantesimo della libertà in Luigi Einaudi*. Roma: Città Nuova.

Torgler B. (2007). *Tax Compliance and Tax Morale: A Theoretical and Empirical Analysis*, Cheltenham, UK & Northampton: Edward Elgar Publishing.

Vailati G. (1898 [1957]). Alcune osservazioni sulle questioni di parole nella storia della scienza e della cultura, Prolusione a un corso sulla storia della meccanica, letta il 12 dicembre 1898 all'Università di Torino. In Vailati (1957), 67–112.

Vailati G. (1906 [1957]). Pragmatismo e logica matematica. *Leonardo*, IV, febbraio: 16–25. In Vailati (1957), 196–207.

Vailati G. (1957). *Il metodo della filosofia. Saggi scelti*, ed. by Ferruccio Rossi-Landi. Bari: Laterza.

van de Laar E., Peil J. (2009). Positive Versus Normative Economics. In Peil, van Staveren (2009), 374–382.

Wagner R.E. (2003). Public Choice and the Diffusion of Classical Italian Public Finance. *Il pensiero economico italiano*, XI, 1: 271–282.

Walsh V. (2009). Fact/Value Dichotomy. In Peil, van Staveren (2009), 144–151.

Walzer M. (1988). *The Company of Critics. Social Criticism and Political Commitment in the Twentieth Century*. New York: Basic Books.

Weber M. (1949). *The Methodology of the Social Sciences*. Ed. and trans. E.A. Shils, H.A. Finch. New York: Free Press.

Weston S. (2009). Positive-Normative Distinction in British History of Economic Thought. In Peil, van Staveren (2009), 366–373.

Wicksell K. (1896 [1958]). *Finanztheoretische Untersuchungen*. Jena: Gustav Fischer. Engl. transl.: *A New Principle of Just Taxation*. In Musgrave, Peacock (1958a), 72–118.

Wicksteed P.H. (1910). *The Common Sense of Political Economy Including a Study of the Human Basis of Econonomic Law*. London: Macmillan and Co.

Winch D. (1978). *Adam Smith's Politics. An Essay in Historiographic Revision*. Cambridge: Cambridge University Press.

Yuengert A. (2000). The Positive-Normative Distinction Before the Fact-Value Distinction. *Pepperdine University*. http://216.236.251.131/ace/pdf/Yuengert_PosNorm.pdf

Index

For Product Safety Concerns and Information please contact our EU
representative GPSR@taylorandfrancis.com
Taylor & Francis Verlag GmbH, Kaufingerstraße 24, 80331 München, Germany